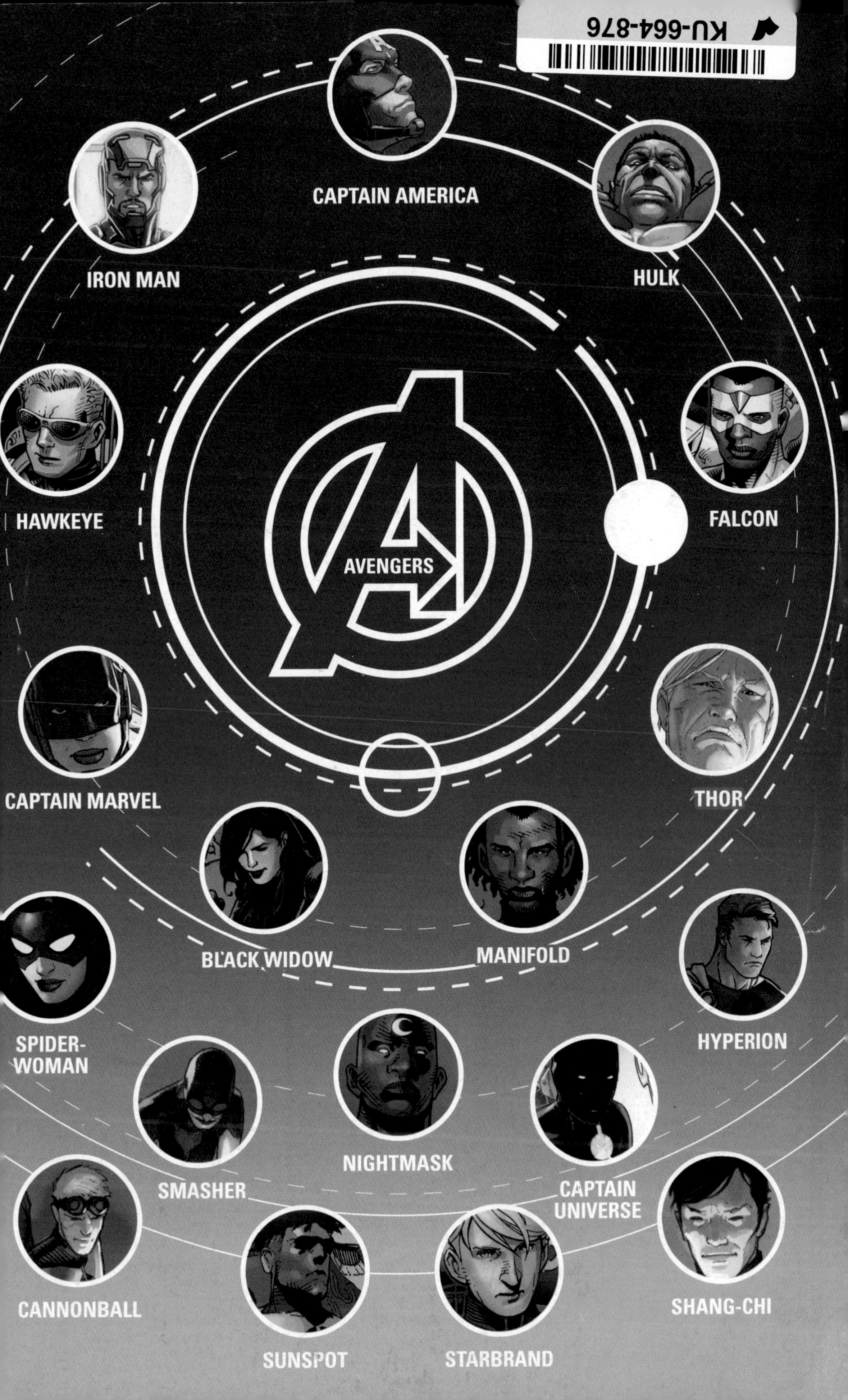
CAPTAIN AMERICA
IRON MAN
HULK
AVENGERS
HAWKEYE
FALCON
CAPTAIN MARVEL
THOR
BLACK WIDOW
MANIFOLD
SPIDER-WOMAN
HYPERION
NIGHTMASK
SMASHER
CAPTAIN UNIVERSE
CANNONBALL
SHANG-CHI
SUNSPOT
STARBRAND

"ROGUE PLANET"

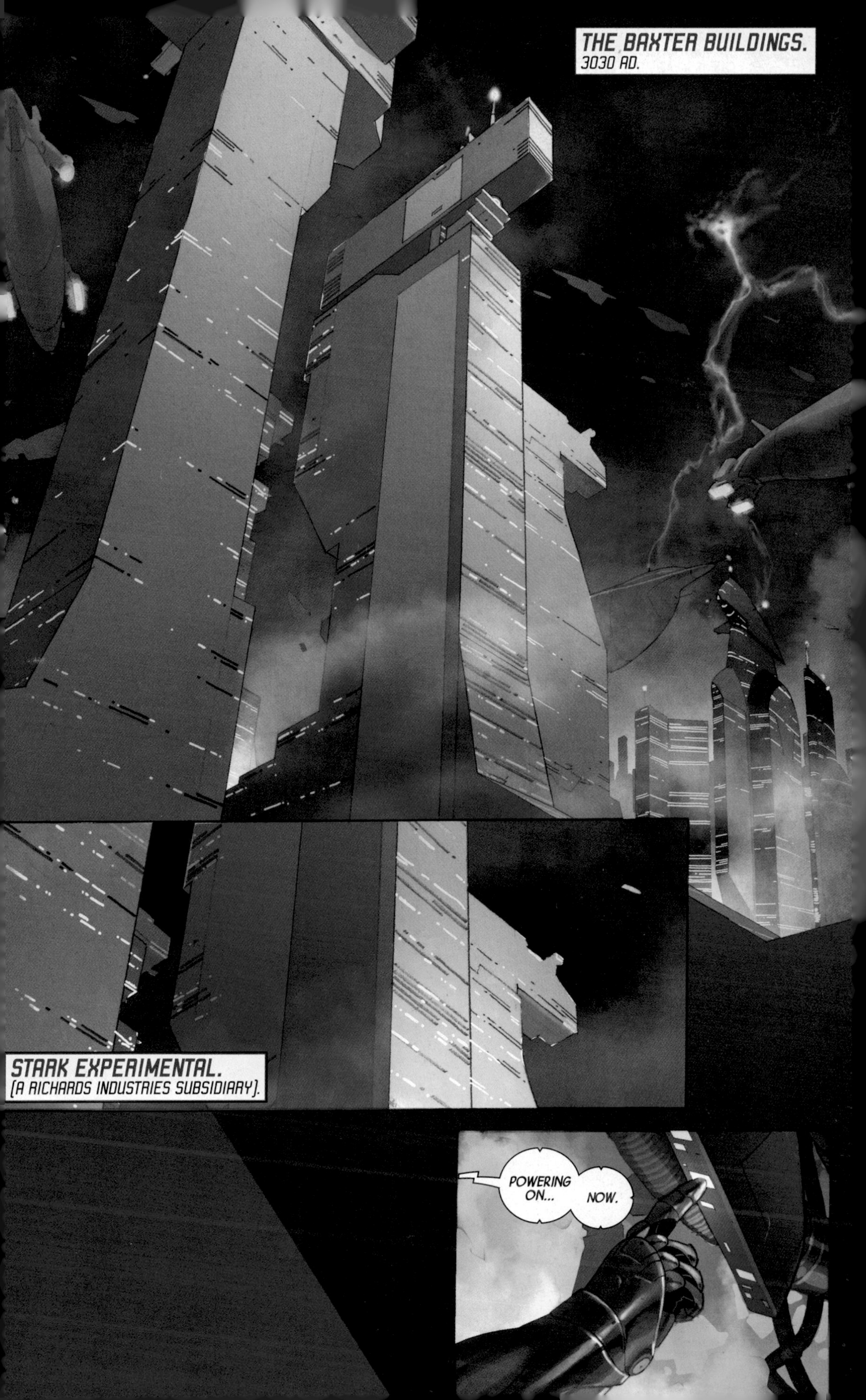
THE BAXTER BUILDINGS.
3030 AD.
STARK EXPERIMENTAL.
(A RICHARDS INDUSTRIES SUBSIDIARY).
POWERING ON...
NOW.

THEY SAY ONE IS MEASURED BY HOW THEY SPEND THEIR LAST DAYS, STARK...
HOW WILL YOU SIZE UP, I WONDER?
BZZZT
BZZZT
BZZZT
GONNA SIT THERE AND NATTER ALL DAY, OR ARE YOU GOING TO DO YOUR PART, OLD MAN?
FLIPPING THE SWITCH, CYCLING ON...
FULL CONTAINMENT ACHIEVED.
DO YOU KNOW HOW MANY IRON MEN I HAVE SEEN IN THEIR FINAL MOMENTS?
I DON'T CARE.
ACTIVATING THE SCATTER FIELD. ONE MINUTE TO LAUNCH.
BOOONNG! BOONGG!
AH, AND THAT WOULD BE THE SECURITY ALARM. HE IS COMING, STARK.
JUST AS YOU KNEW HE WOULD WHEN YOU TURNED THE MACHINE ON...
IT MIGHT AS WELL HAVE BEEN AN INVITATION. LAST CHANCE TO STAND DOWN. LAST CHANCE TO SAVE YOURSELF.
TELL ME SOMETHING, XHANG...
CAN YOU EVEN REMEMBER WHAT IT WAS LIKE TO DO THINGS INSTEAD OF JUST TALKING ALL. DAY. LONG?
BZZZ
WE CAN'T CUT THROUGH...
WE'RE NOT GOING TO GET IN.

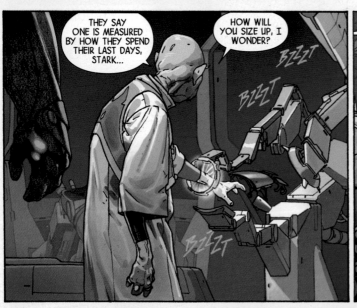

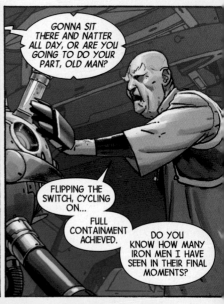

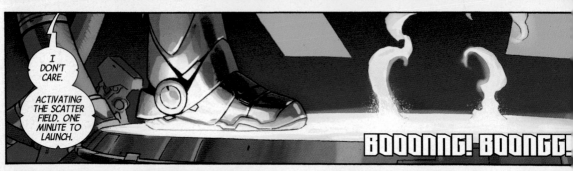

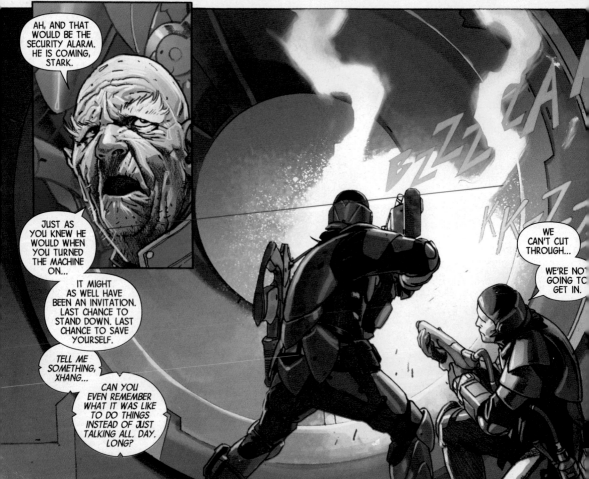

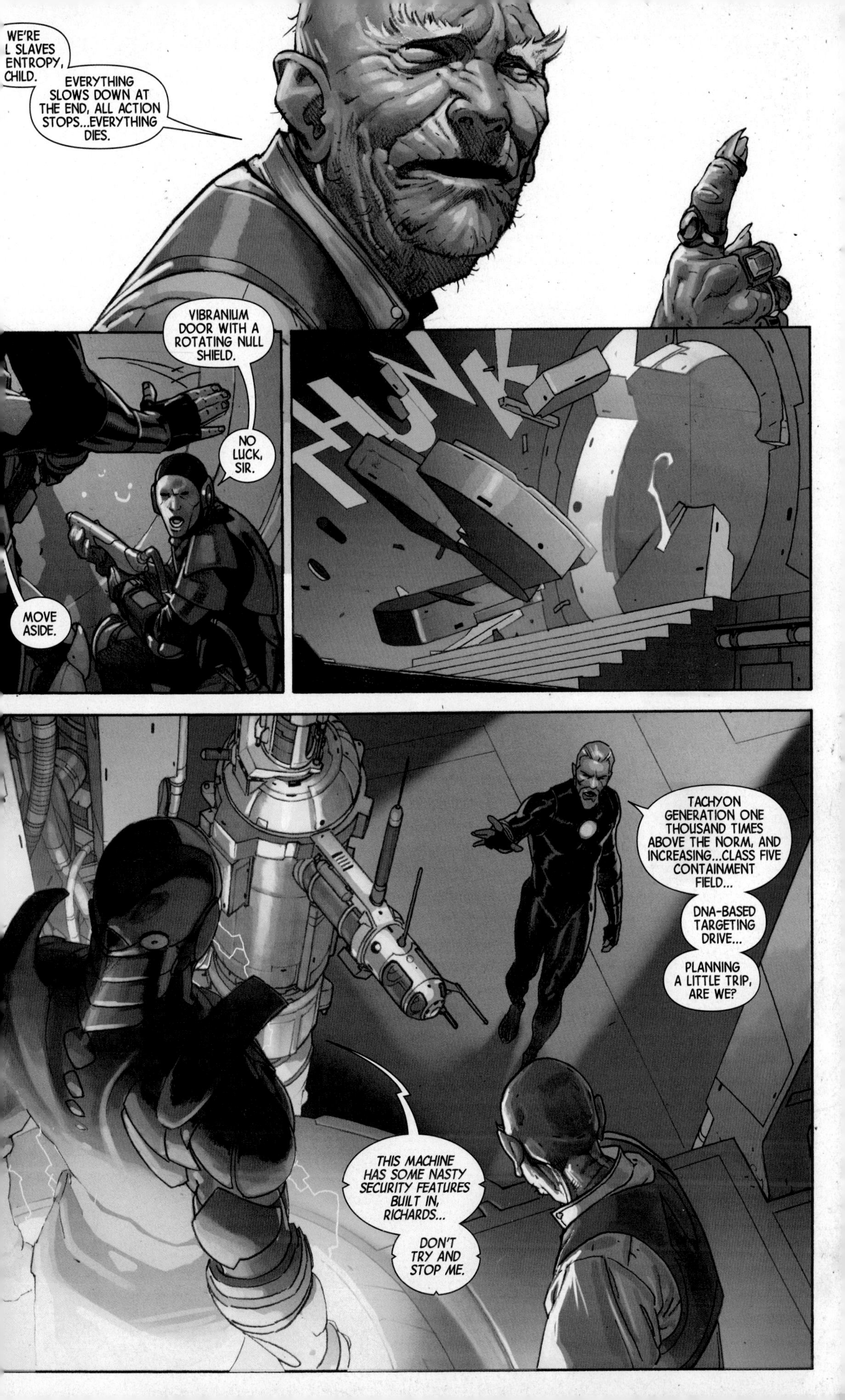
WE'RE
L SLAVES
ENTROPY,
CHILD.
EVERYTHING SLOWS DOWN AT THE END, ALL ACTION STOPS...EVERYTHING DIES.
VIBRANIUM DOOR WITH A ROTATING NULL SHIELD.
NO LUCK, SIR.
MOVE ASIDE.
TACHYON GENERATION ONE THOUSAND TIMES ABOVE THE NORM, AND INCREASING...CLASS FIVE CONTAINMENT FIELD...
DNA-BASED TARGETING DRIVE...
PLANNING A LITTLE TRIP, ARE WE?
THIS MACHINE HAS SOME NASTY SECURITY FEATURES BUILT IN, RICHARDS...
DON'T TRY AND STOP ME.

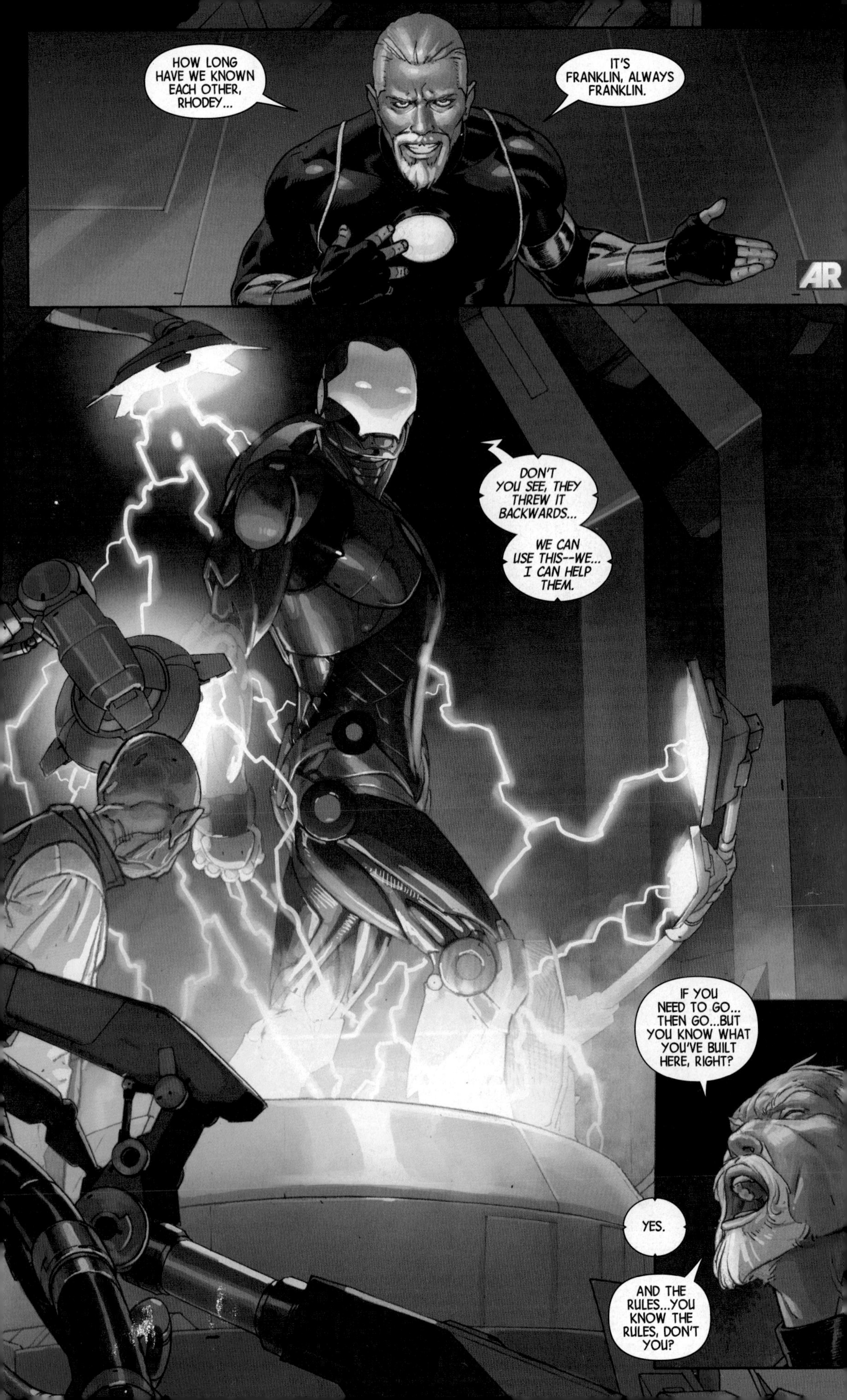
HOW LONG HAVE WE KNOWN EACH OTHER, RHODEY...
IT'S FRANKLIN, ALWAYS FRANKLIN.
DON'T YOU SEE, THEY THREW IT BACKWARDS...
WE CAN USE THIS--WE... I CAN HELP THEM.
IF YOU NEED TO GO... THEN GO...BUT YOU KNOW WHAT YOU'VE BUILT HERE, RIGHT?
YES.
AND THE RULES...YOU KNOW THE RULES, DON'T YOU?

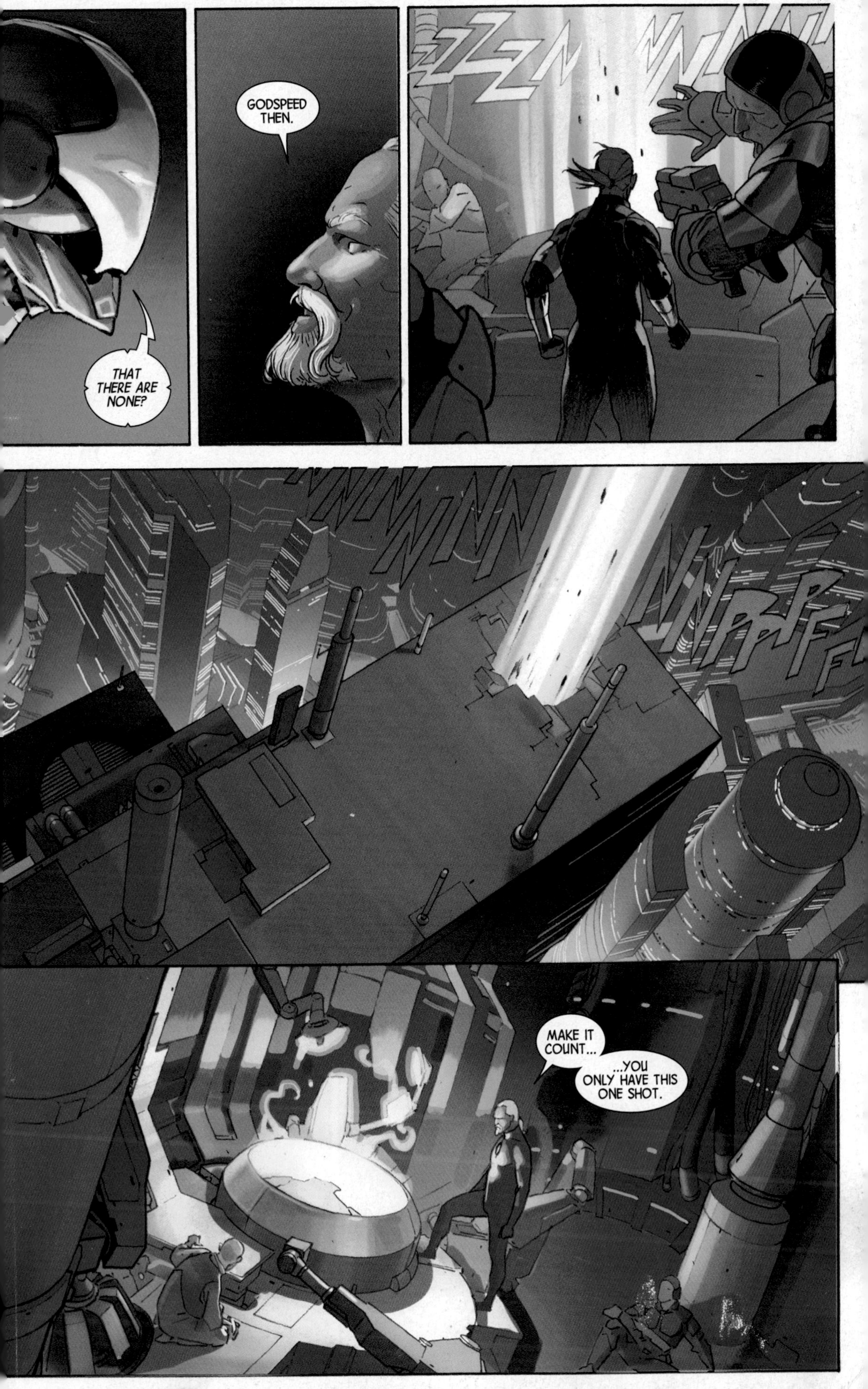

THAT THERE ARE NONE?
GODSPEED THEN.
ZZZZNNNNNN
NNNNNNNNNNNNNRPFF
MAKE IT COUNT...
...YOU ONLY HAVE THIS ONE SHOT.

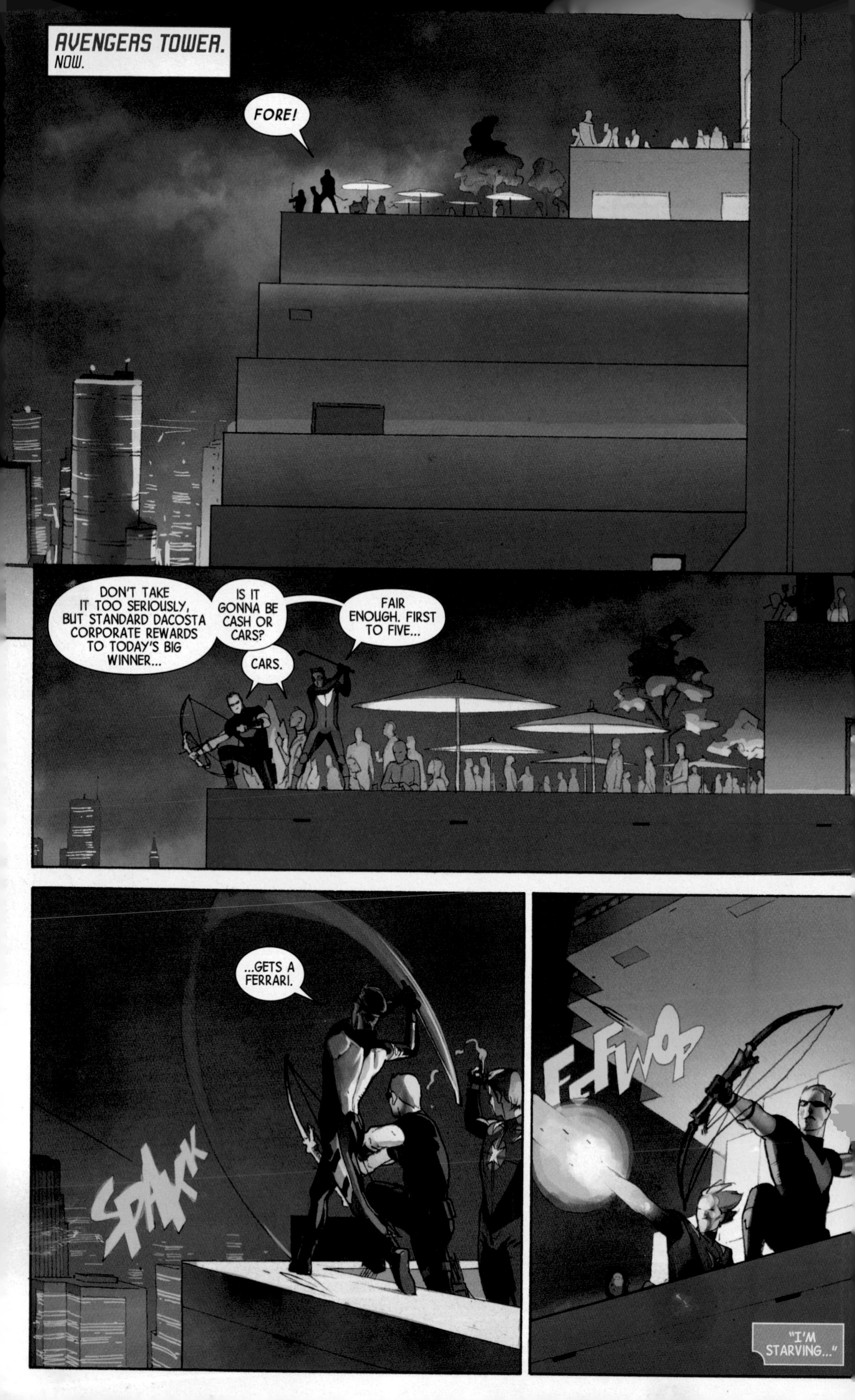
AVENGERS TOWER.
NOW.
FORE!
DON'T TAKE IT TOO SERIOUSLY, BUT STANDARD DACOSTA CORPORATE REWARDS TO TODAY'S BIG WINNER...
IS IT GONNA BE CASH OR CARS?
CARS.
FAIR ENOUGH. FIRST TO FIVE...
...GETS A FERRARI.
SPAK
"I'M STARVING..."

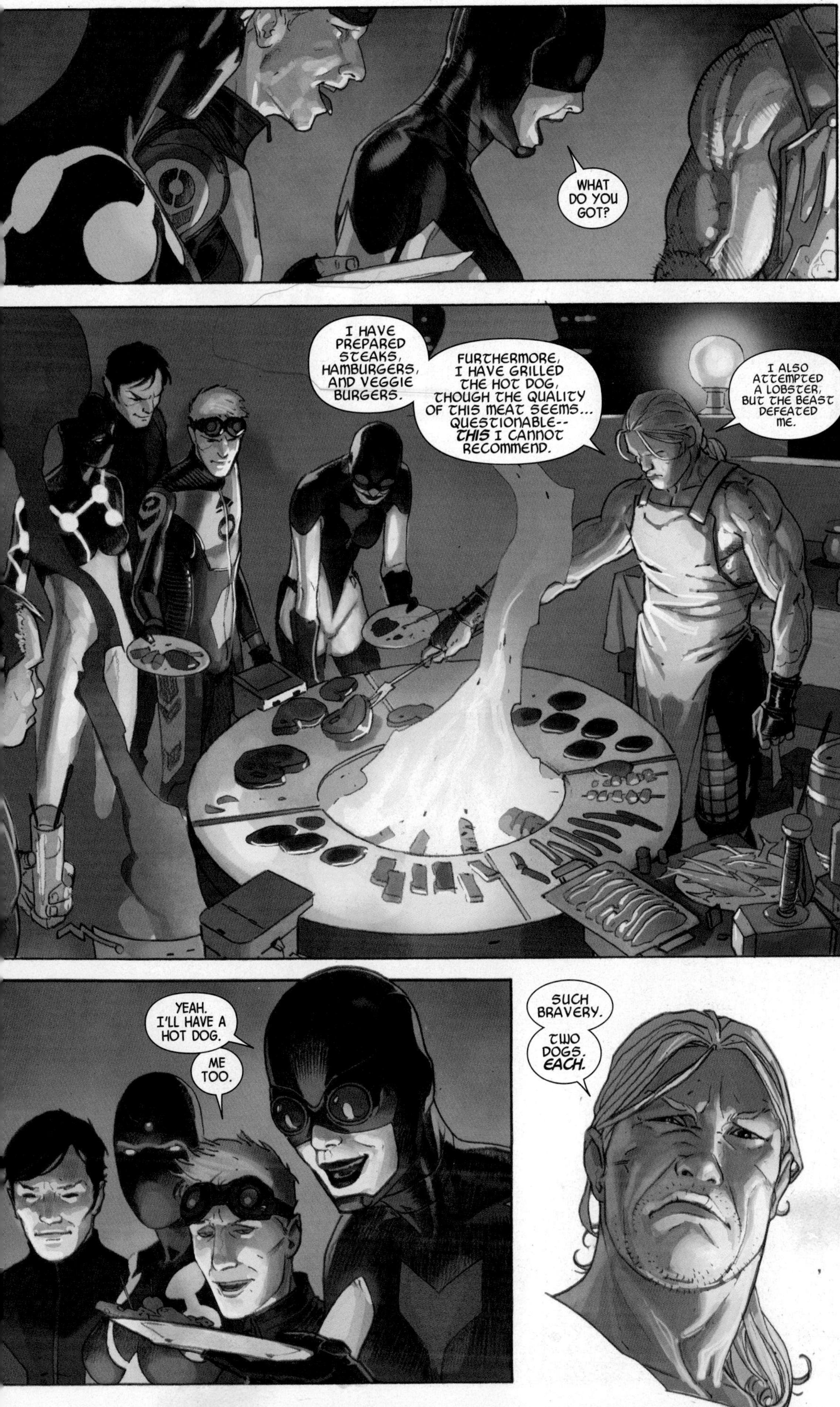
WHAT DO YOU GOT?
I HAVE PREPARED STEAKS, HAMBURGERS, AND VEGGIE BURGERS.
FURTHERMORE, I HAVE GRILLED THE HOT DOG, THOUGH THE QUALITY OF THIS MEAT SEEMS... QUESTIONABLE-- THIS I CANNOT RECOMMEND.
I ALSO ATTEMPTED A LOBSTER, BUT THE BEAST DEFEATED ME.
YEAH. I'LL HAVE A HOT DOG.
ME TOO.
SUCH BRAVERY.
TWO DOGS. EACH.

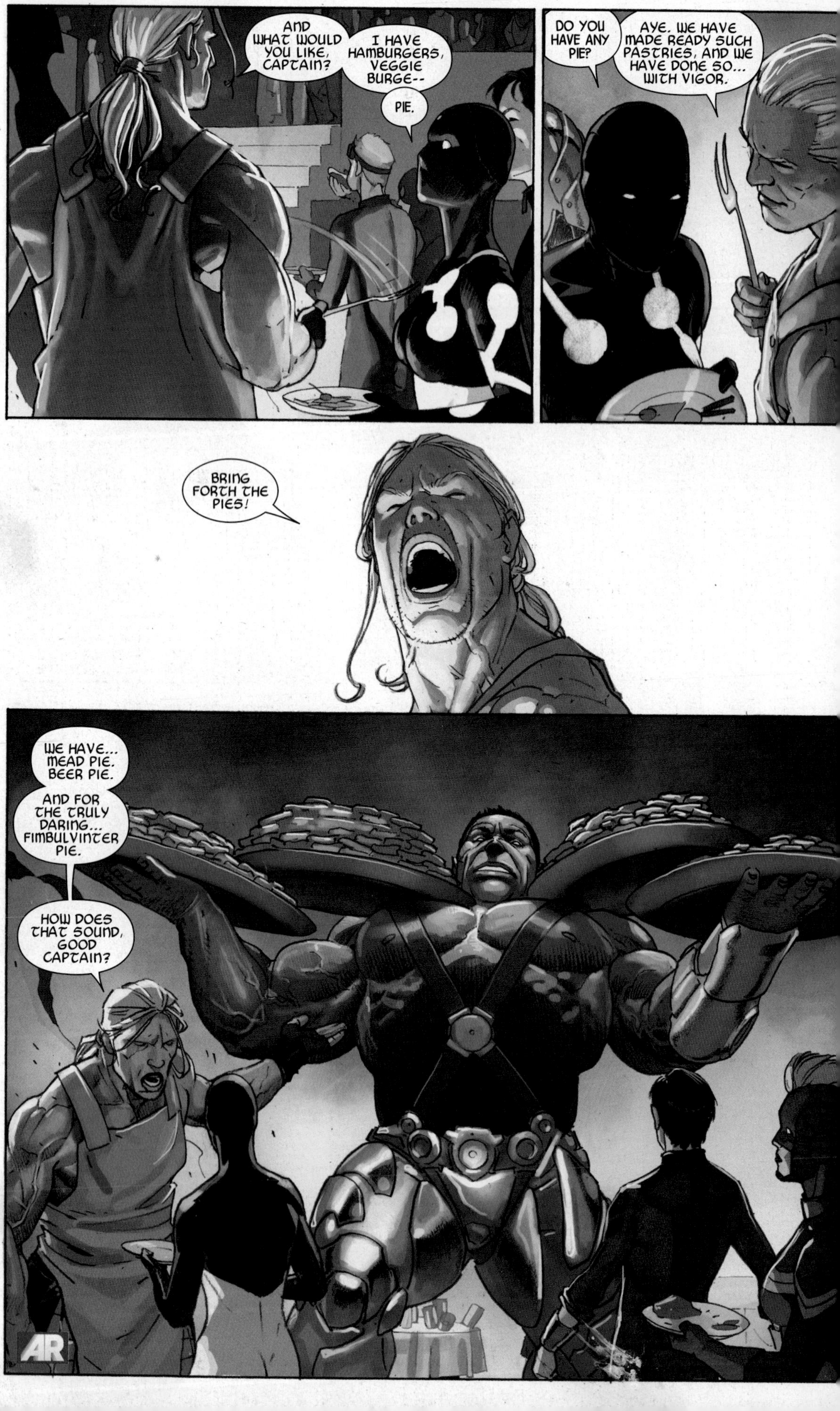
AND WHAT WOULD YOU LIKE, CAPTAIN?
I HAVE HAMBURGERS, VEGGIE BURGE--
PIE.
DO YOU HAVE ANY PIE?
AYE. WE HAVE MADE READY SUCH PASTRIES, AND WE HAVE DONE SO... WITH VIGOR.
BRING FORTH THE PIES!
WE HAVE... MEAD PIE. BEER PIE.
AND FOR THE TRULY DARING... FIMBULVINTER PIE.
HOW DOES THAT SOUND, GOOD CAPTAIN?

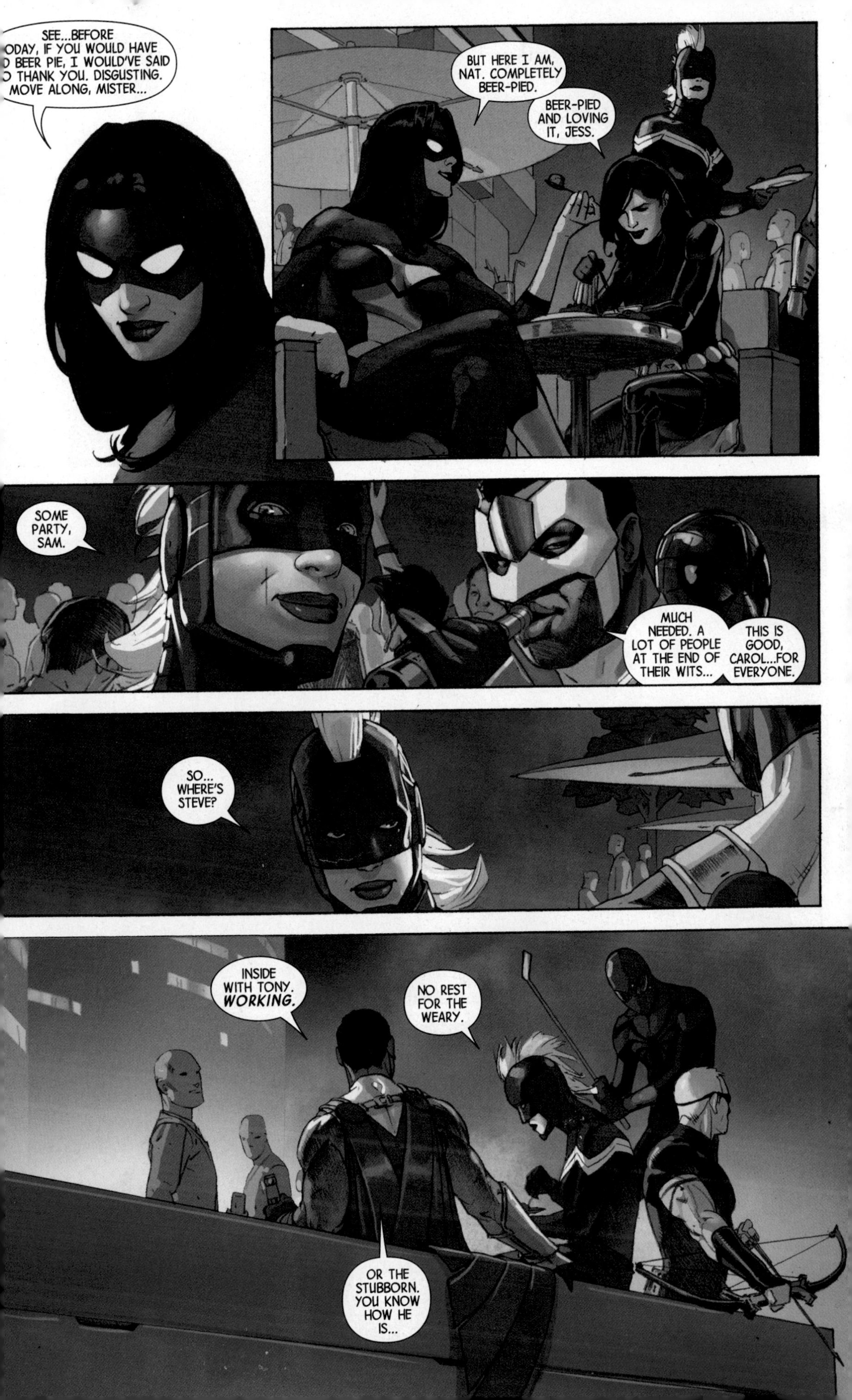
SEE...BEFORE ODAY, IF YOU WOULD HAVE D BEER PIE, I WOULD'VE SAID O THANK YOU. DISGUSTING. MOVE ALONG, MISTER...
BUT HERE I AM, NAT. COMPLETELY BEER-PIED.
BEER-PIED AND LOVING IT, JESS.
SOME PARTY, SAM.
MUCH NEEDED. A LOT OF PEOPLE AT THE END OF THEIR WITS...
THIS IS GOOD, CAROL...FOR EVERYONE.
SO... WHERE'S STEVE?
INSIDE WITH TONY. *WORKING.*
NO REST FOR THE WEARY.
OR THE STUBBORN. YOU KNOW HOW HE IS...

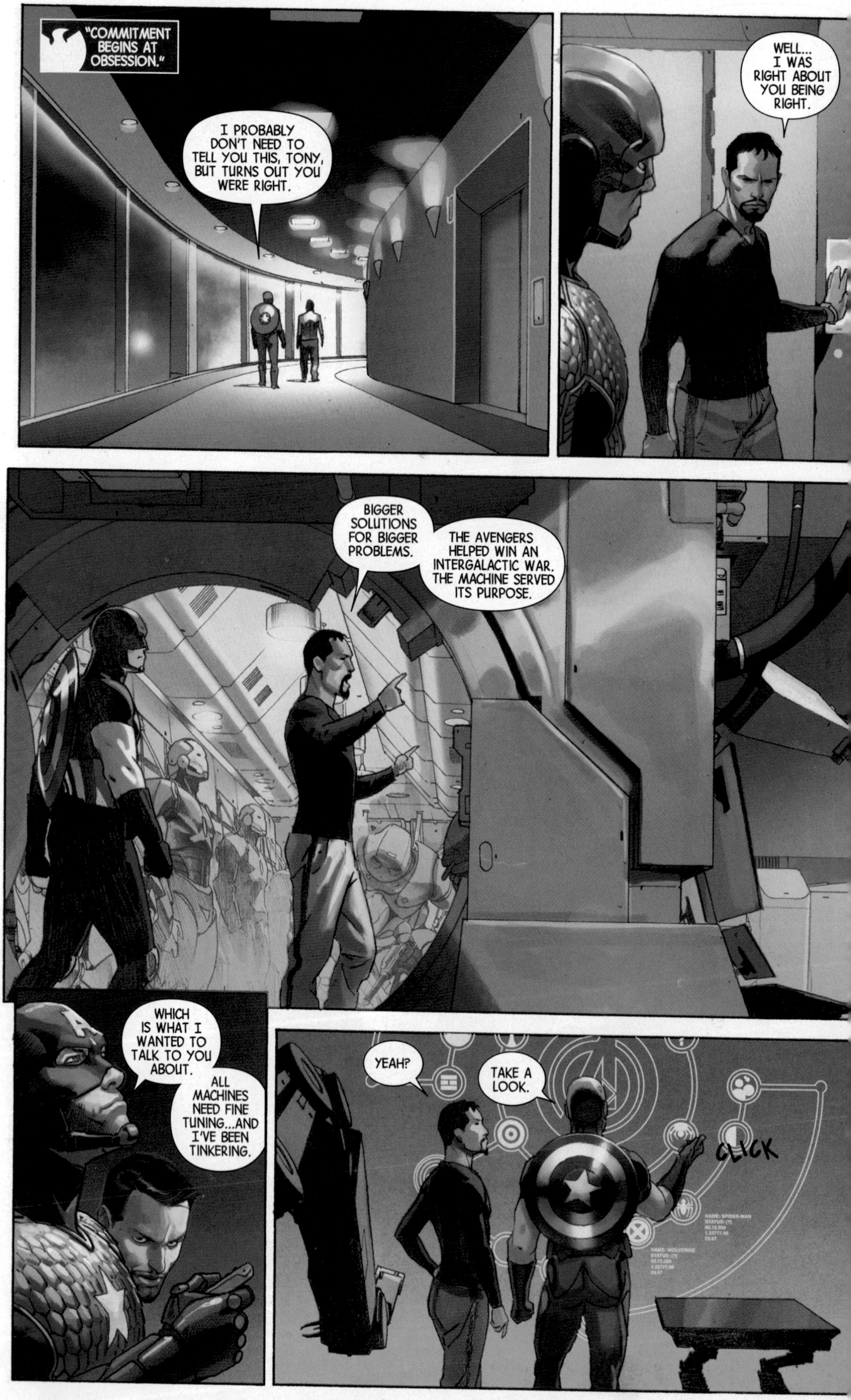
"COMMITMENT BEGINS AT OBSESSION."
I PROBABLY DON'T NEED TO TELL YOU THIS, TONY, BUT TURNS OUT YOU WERE RIGHT.
WELL... I WAS RIGHT ABOUT YOU BEING RIGHT.
BIGGER SOLUTIONS FOR BIGGER PROBLEMS.
THE AVENGERS HELPED WIN AN INTERGALACTIC WAR. THE MACHINE SERVED ITS PURPOSE.
WHICH IS WHAT I WANTED TO TALK TO YOU ABOUT.
ALL MACHINES NEED FINE TUNING...AND I'VE BEEN TINKERING.
YEAH?
TAKE A LOOK.
CLICK
NAME: SPIDER-MAN
STATUS: (?)
NAME: WOLVERINE
STATUS: (?)

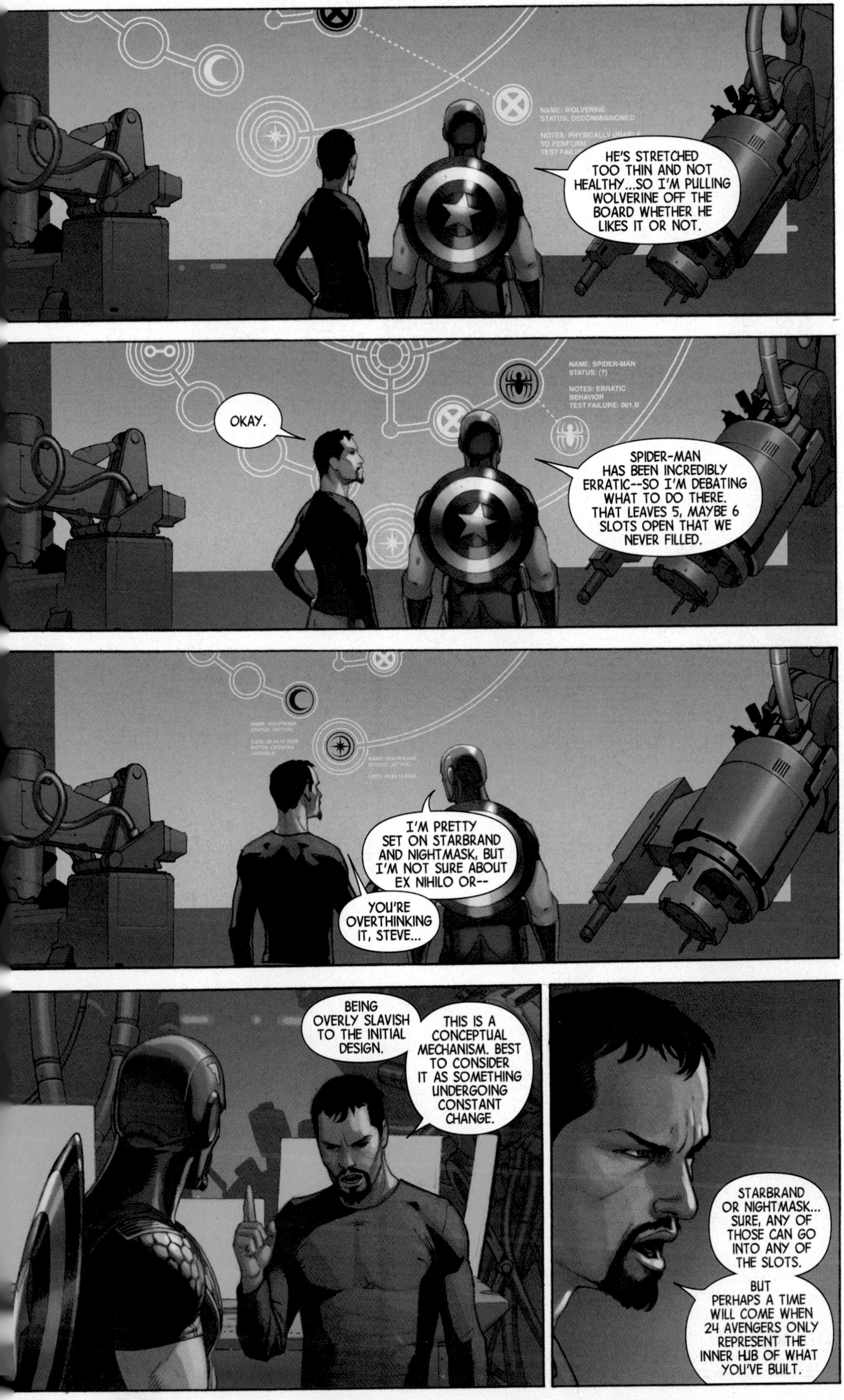
NAME: WOLVERINE
STATUS: DECOMMISSIONED
NOTES: PHYSICALLY UNABLE
TO PERFORM
HE'S STRETCHED TOO THIN AND NOT HEALTHY...SO I'M PULLING WOLVERINE OFF THE BOARD WHETHER HE LIKES IT OR NOT.
NAME: SPIDER-MAN
STATUS: (?)
NOTES: ERRATIC
BEHAVIOR
TEST FAILURE: 001.B
OKAY.
SPIDER-MAN HAS BEEN INCREDIBLY ERRATIC--SO I'M DEBATING WHAT TO DO THERE. THAT LEAVES 5, MAYBE 6 SLOTS OPEN THAT WE NEVER FILLED.
I'M PRETTY SET ON STARBRAND AND NIGHTMASK, BUT I'M NOT SURE ABOUT EX NIHILO OR--
YOU'RE OVERTHINKING IT, STEVE...
BEING OVERLY SLAVISH TO THE INITIAL DESIGN.
THIS IS A CONCEPTUAL MECHANISM. BEST TO CONSIDER IT AS SOMETHING UNDERGOING CONSTANT CHANGE.
STARBRAND OR NIGHTMASK... SURE, ANY OF THOSE CAN GO INTO ANY OF THE SLOTS.
BUT PERHAPS A TIME WILL COME WHEN 24 AVENGERS ONLY REPRESENT THE INNER HUB OF WHAT YOU'VE BUILT.

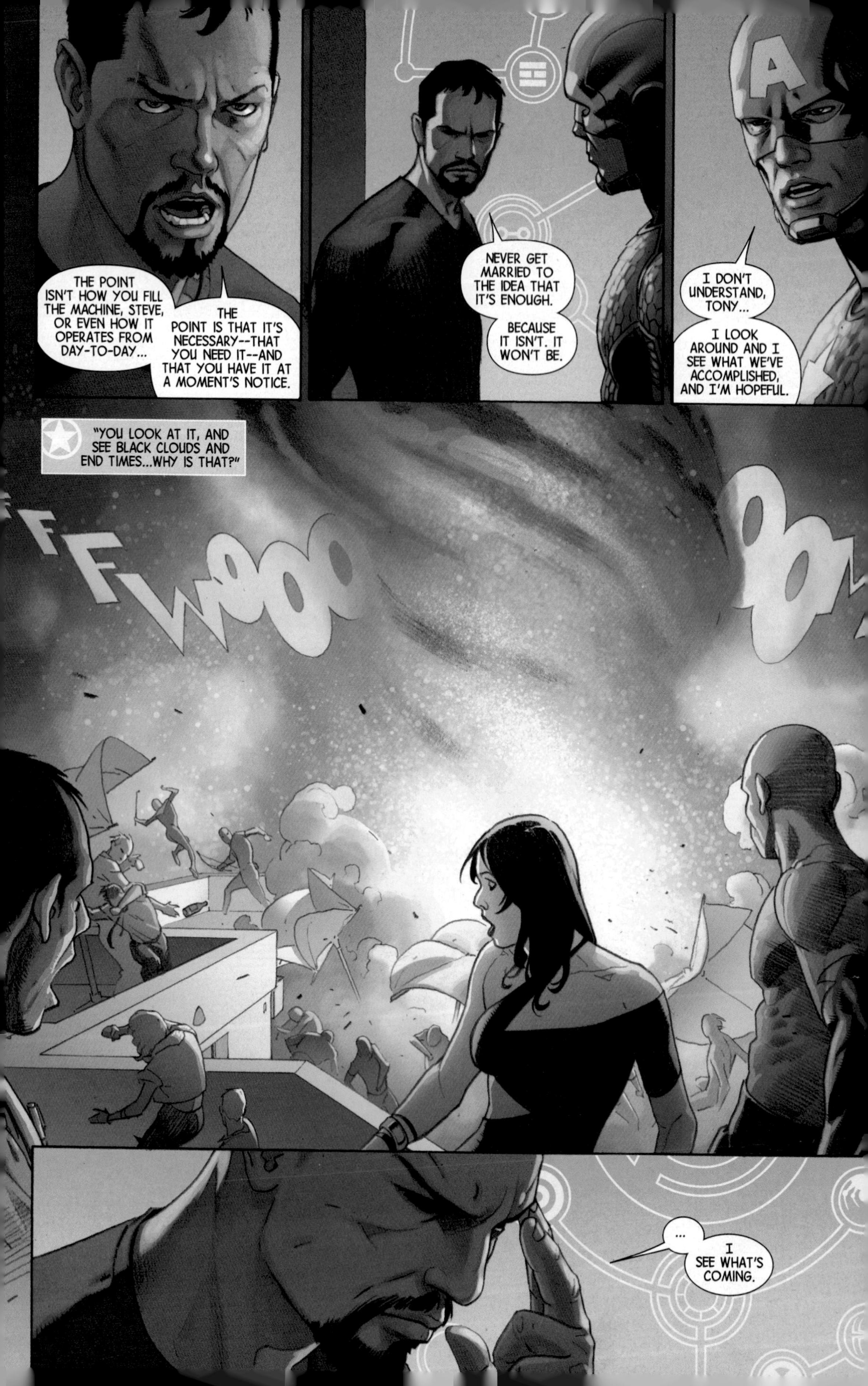
THE POINT ISN'T HOW YOU FILL THE MACHINE, STEVE, OR EVEN HOW IT OPERATES FROM DAY-TO-DAY...
THE POINT IS THAT IT'S NECESSARY--THAT YOU NEED IT--AND THAT YOU HAVE IT AT A MOMENT'S NOTICE.
NEVER GET MARRIED TO THE IDEA THAT IT'S ENOUGH.
BECAUSE IT ISN'T. IT WON'T BE.
I DON'T UNDERSTAND, TONY...
I LOOK AROUND AND I SEE WHAT WE'VE ACCOMPLISHED, AND I'M HOPEFUL.
"YOU LOOK AT IT, AND SEE BLACK CLOUDS AND END TIMES...WHY IS THAT?"
FFWOOOOOM
...
I SEE WHAT'S COMING.

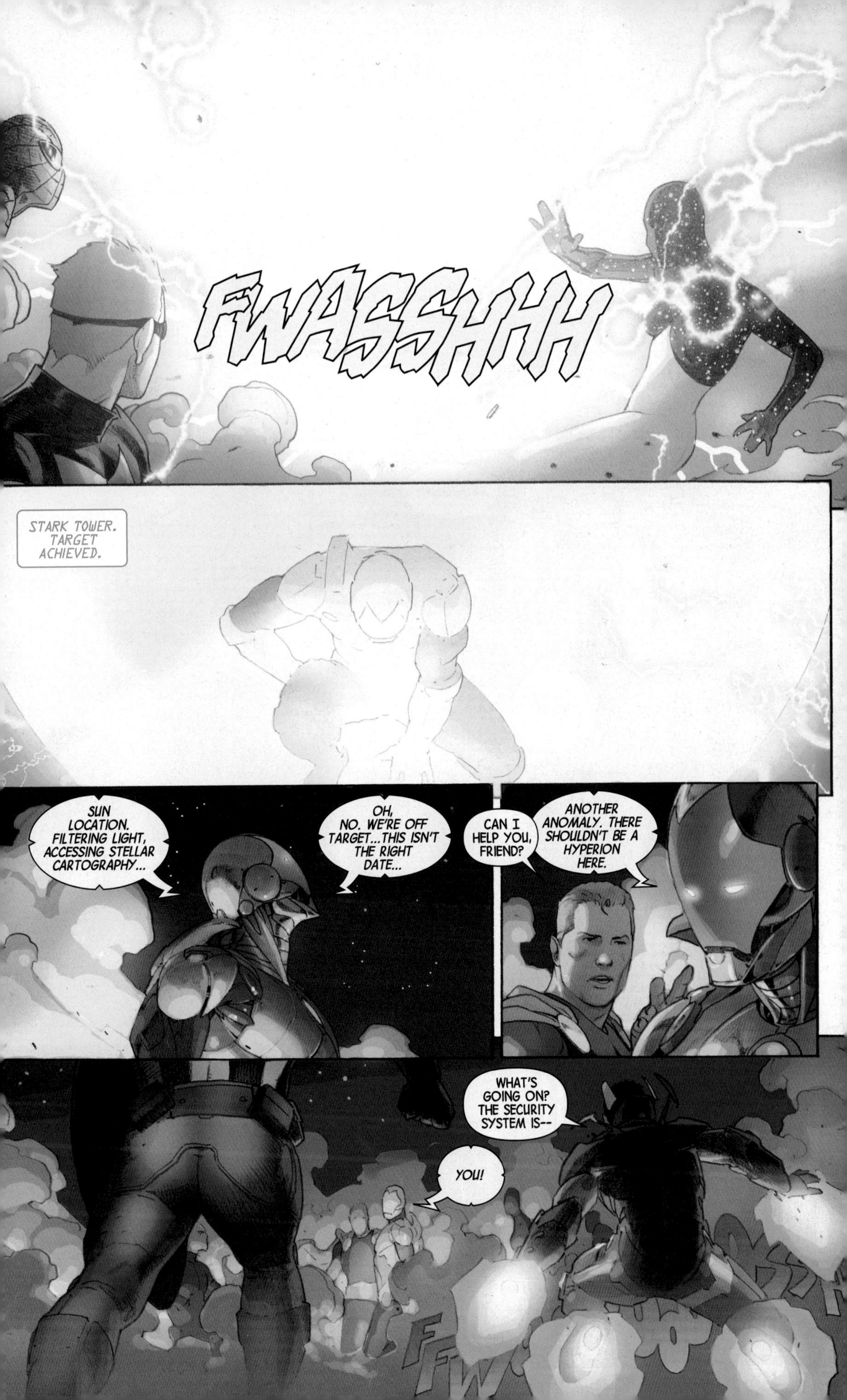
FWASSHHH
STARK TOWER. TARGET ACHIEVED.
SUN LOCATION. FILTERING LIGHT, ACCESSING STELLAR CARTOGRAPHY...
OH, NO. WE'RE OFF TARGET...THIS ISN'T THE RIGHT DATE...
CAN I HELP YOU, FRIEND?
ANOTHER ANOMALY. THERE SHOULDN'T BE A HYPERION HERE.
WHAT'S GOING ON? THE SECURITY SYSTEM IS--
YOU!

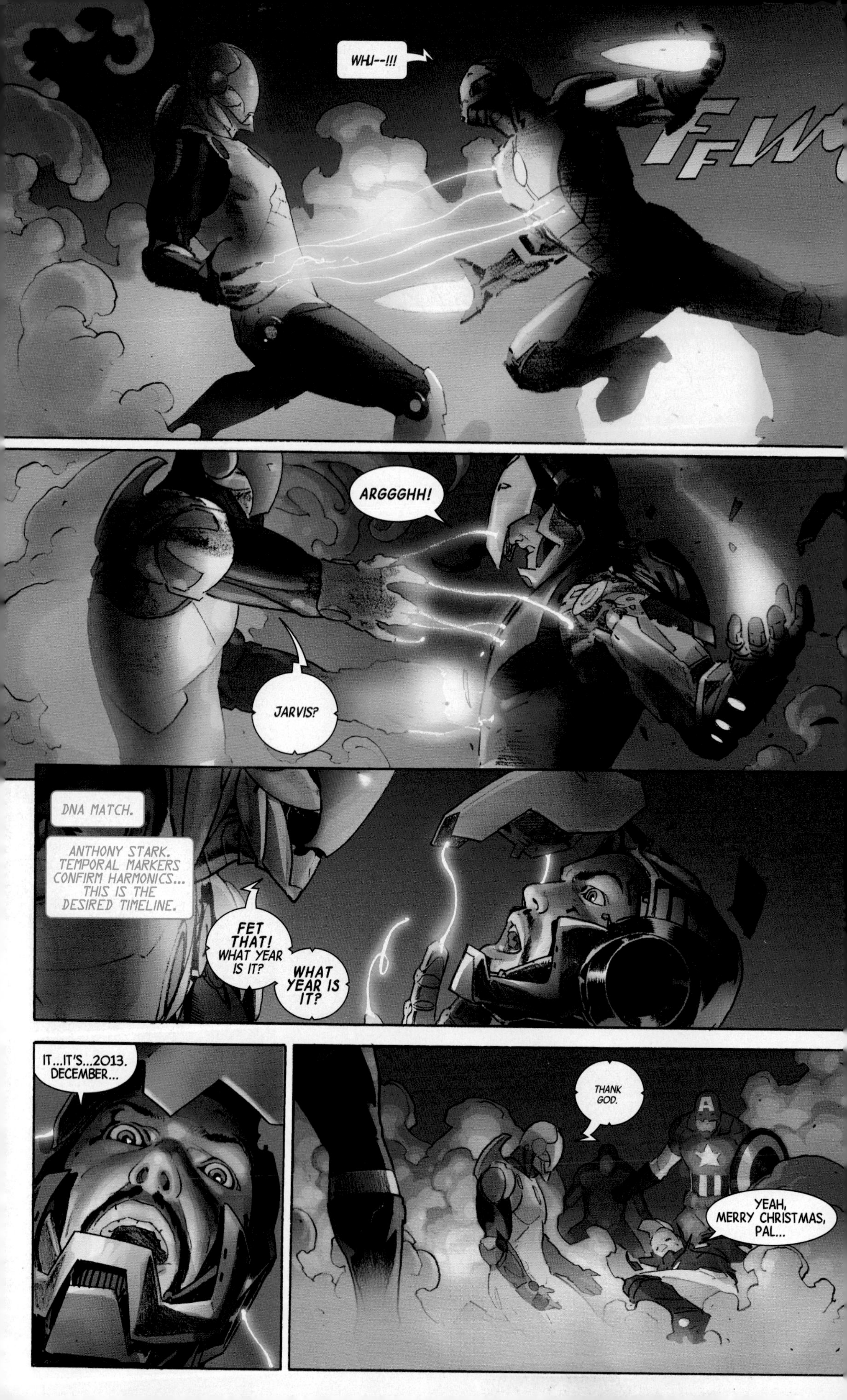
WHU--!!!
FFWM
ARGGGHH!
JARVIS?
DNA MATCH.
ANTHONY STARK. TEMPORAL MARKERS CONFIRM HARMONICS... THIS IS THE DESIRED TIMELINE.
FET THAT! WHAT YEAR IS IT?
WHAT YEAR IS IT?
IT...IT'S...2013. DECEMBER...
THANK GOD.
YEAH, MERRY CHRISTMAS, PAL...

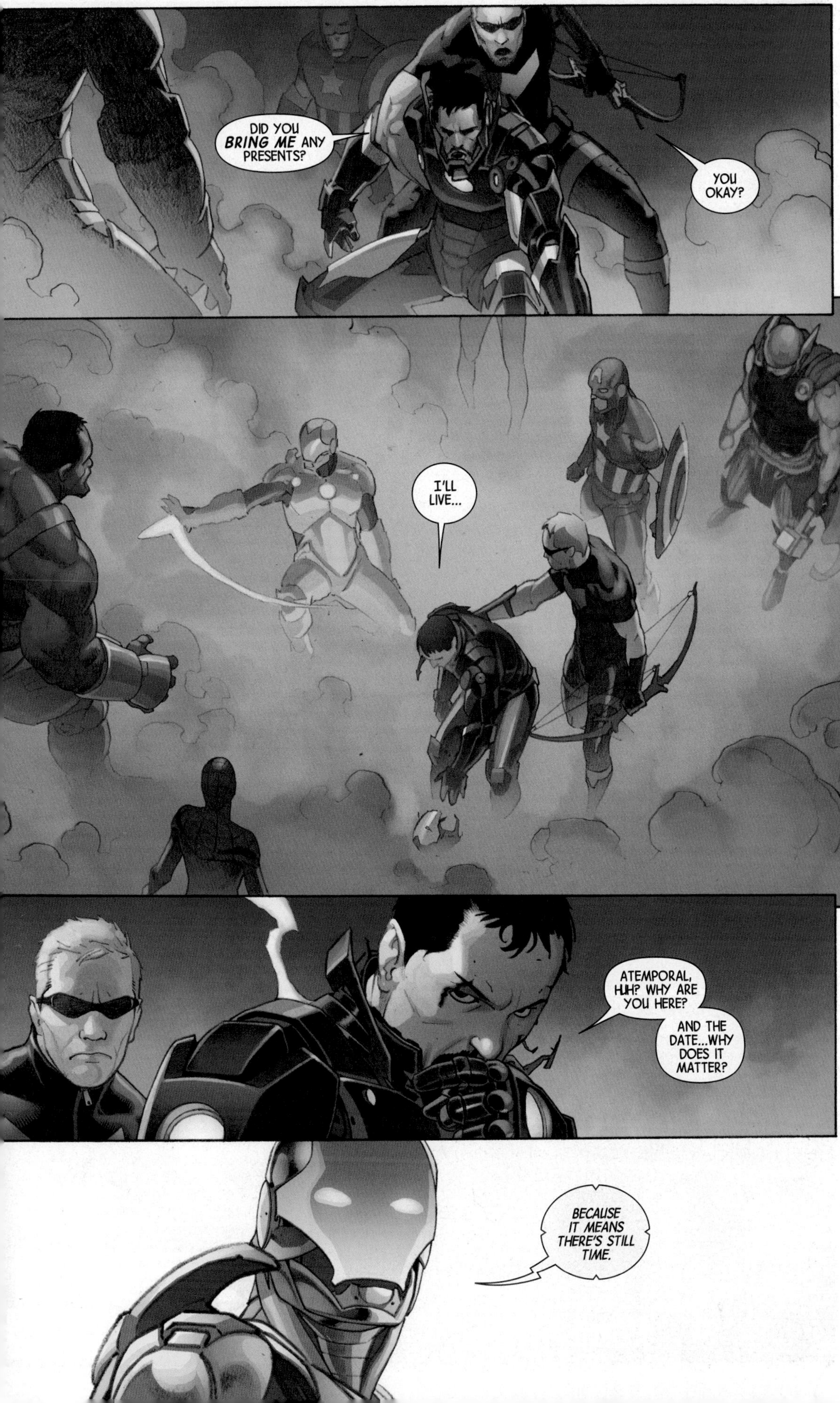

DID YOU *BRING ME* ANY PRESENTS?
YOU OKAY?
I'LL LIVE...
ATEMPORAL, HUH? WHY ARE YOU HERE?
AND THE DATE...WHY DOES IT MATTER?
BECAUSE IT MEANS THERE'S STILL TIME.

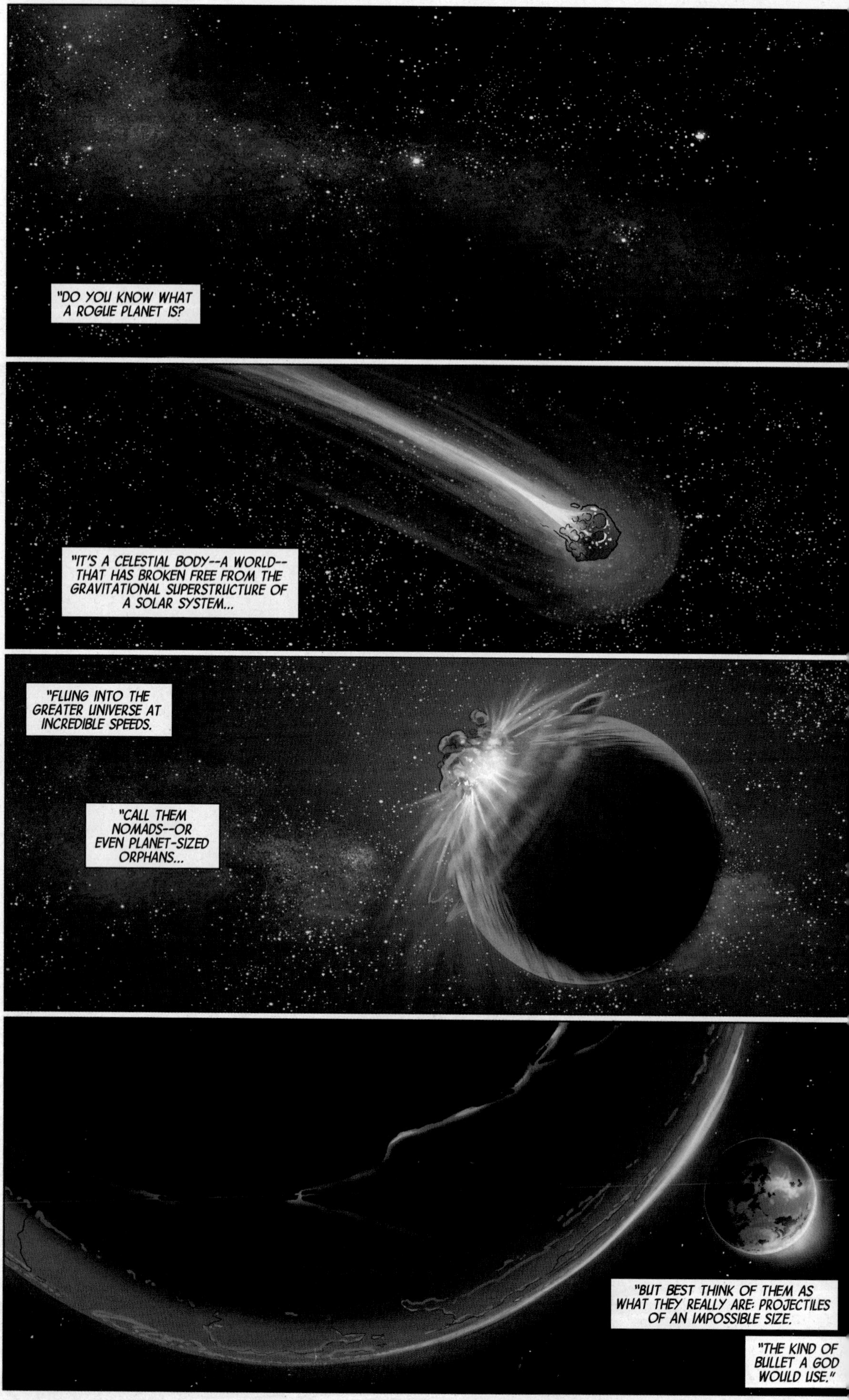
"DO YOU KNOW WHAT A ROGUE PLANET IS?
"IT'S A CELESTIAL BODY--A WORLD--THAT HAS BROKEN FREE FROM THE GRAVITATIONAL SUPERSTRUCTURE OF A SOLAR SYSTEM...
"FLUNG INTO THE GREATER UNIVERSE AT INCREDIBLE SPEEDS.
"CALL THEM NOMADS--OR EVEN PLANET-SIZED ORPHANS...
"BUT BEST THINK OF THEM AS WHAT THEY REALLY ARE: PROJECTILES OF AN IMPOSSIBLE SIZE.
"THE KIND OF BULLET A GOD WOULD USE."

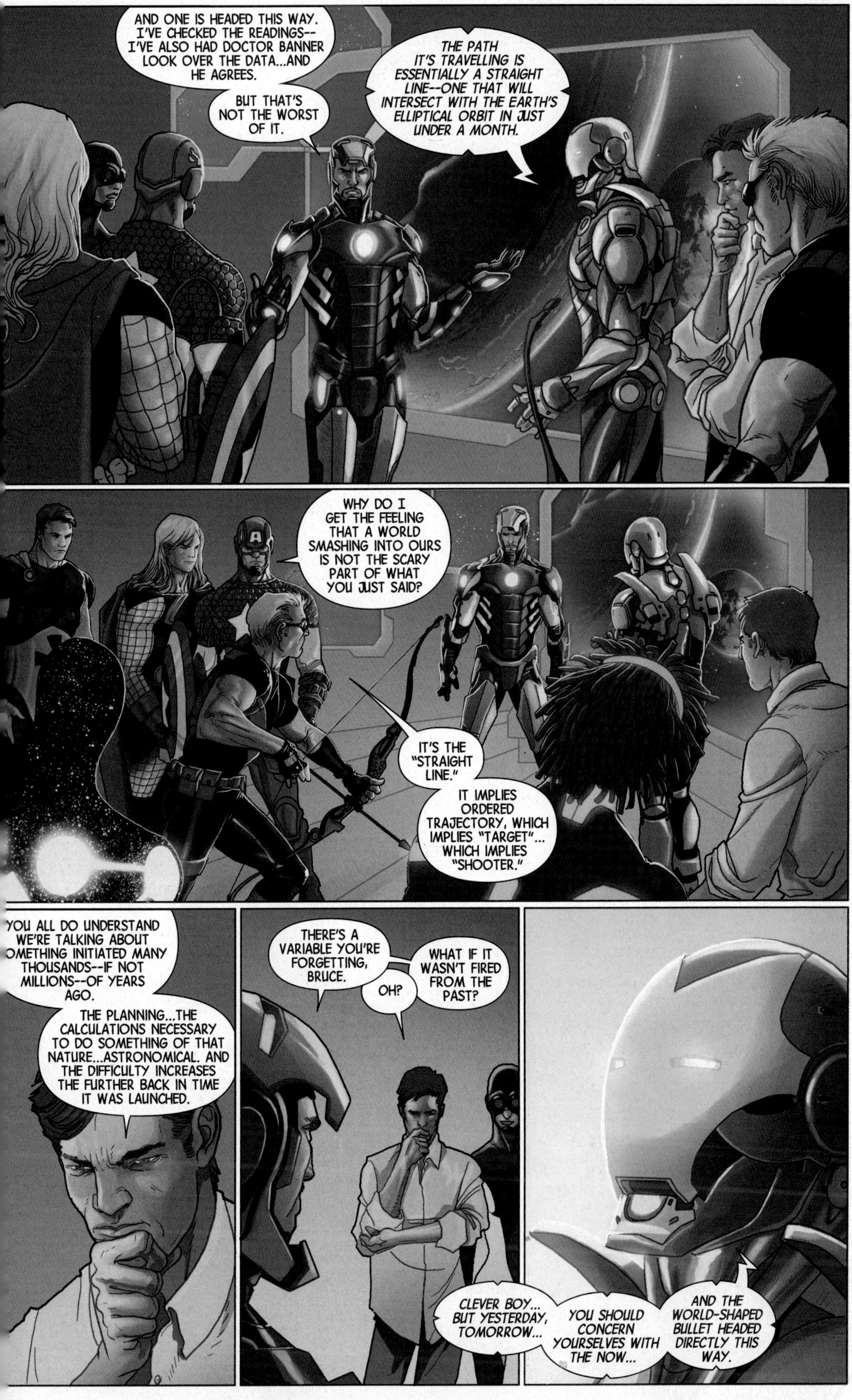
AND ONE IS HEADED THIS WAY. I'VE CHECKED THE READINGS-- I'VE ALSO HAD DOCTOR BANNER LOOK OVER THE DATA...AND HE AGREES.
BUT THAT'S NOT THE WORST OF IT.
THE PATH IT'S TRAVELLING IS ESSENTIALLY A STRAIGHT LINE--ONE THAT WILL INTERSECT WITH THE EARTH'S ELLIPTICAL ORBIT IN JUST UNDER A MONTH.
WHY DO I GET THE FEELING THAT A WORLD SMASHING INTO OURS IS NOT THE SCARY PART OF WHAT YOU JUST SAID?
IT'S THE "STRAIGHT LINE."
IT IMPLIES ORDERED TRAJECTORY, WHICH IMPLIES "TARGET"... WHICH IMPLIES "SHOOTER."
YOU ALL DO UNDERSTAND WE'RE TALKING ABOUT OMETHING INITIATED MANY THOUSANDS--IF NOT MILLIONS--OF YEARS AGO.
THE PLANNING...THE CALCULATIONS NECESSARY TO DO SOMETHING OF THAT NATURE...ASTRONOMICAL. AND THE DIFFICULTY INCREASES THE FURTHER BACK IN TIME IT WAS LAUNCHED.
THERE'S A VARIABLE YOU'RE FORGETTING, BRUCE.
OH?
WHAT IF IT WASN'T FIRED FROM THE PAST?
CLEVER BOY... BUT YESTERDAY, TOMORROW...
YOU SHOULD CONCERN YOURSELVES WITH THE NOW...
AND THE WORLD-SHAPED BULLET HEADED DIRECTLY THIS WAY.

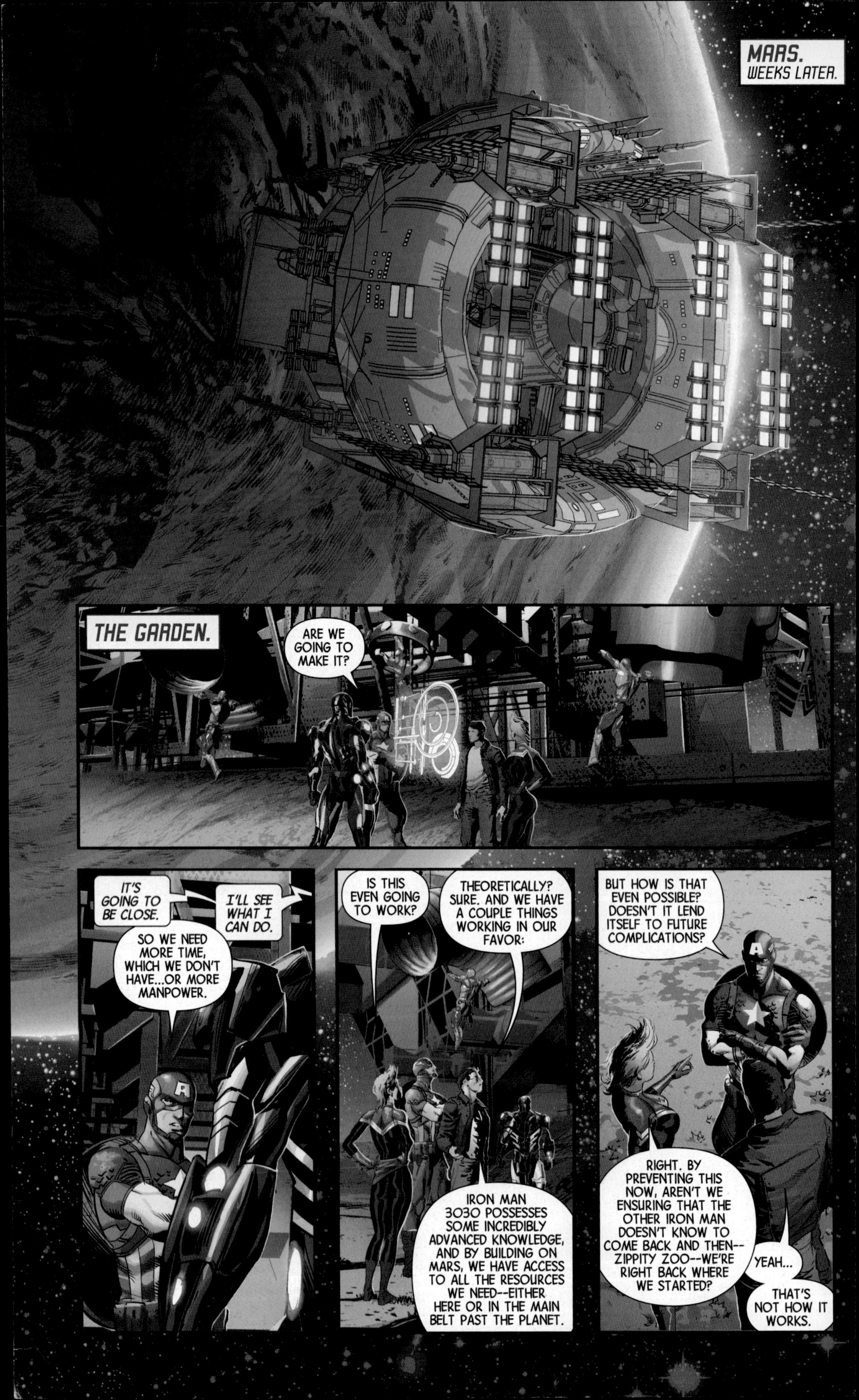
MARS.
WEEKS LATER.
THE GARDEN.
ARE WE GOING TO MAKE IT?
IT'S GOING TO BE CLOSE.
I'LL SEE WHAT I CAN DO.
SO WE NEED MORE TIME, WHICH WE DON'T HAVE...OR MORE MANPOWER.
IS THIS EVEN GOING TO WORK?
THEORETICALLY? SURE. AND WE HAVE A COUPLE THINGS WORKING IN OUR FAVOR:
IRON MAN 3030 POSSESSES SOME INCREDIBLY ADVANCED KNOWLEDGE, AND BY BUILDING ON MARS, WE HAVE ACCESS TO ALL THE RESOURCES WE NEED--EITHER HERE OR IN THE MAIN BELT PAST THE PLANET.
BUT HOW IS THAT EVEN POSSIBLE? DOESN'T IT LEND ITSELF TO FUTURE COMPLICATIONS?
RIGHT. BY PREVENTING THIS NOW, AREN'T WE ENSURING THAT THE OTHER IRON MAN DOESN'T KNOW TO COME BACK AND THEN-- ZIPPITY ZOO--WE'RE RIGHT BACK WHERE WE STARTED?
YEAH...
THAT'S NOT HOW IT WORKS.

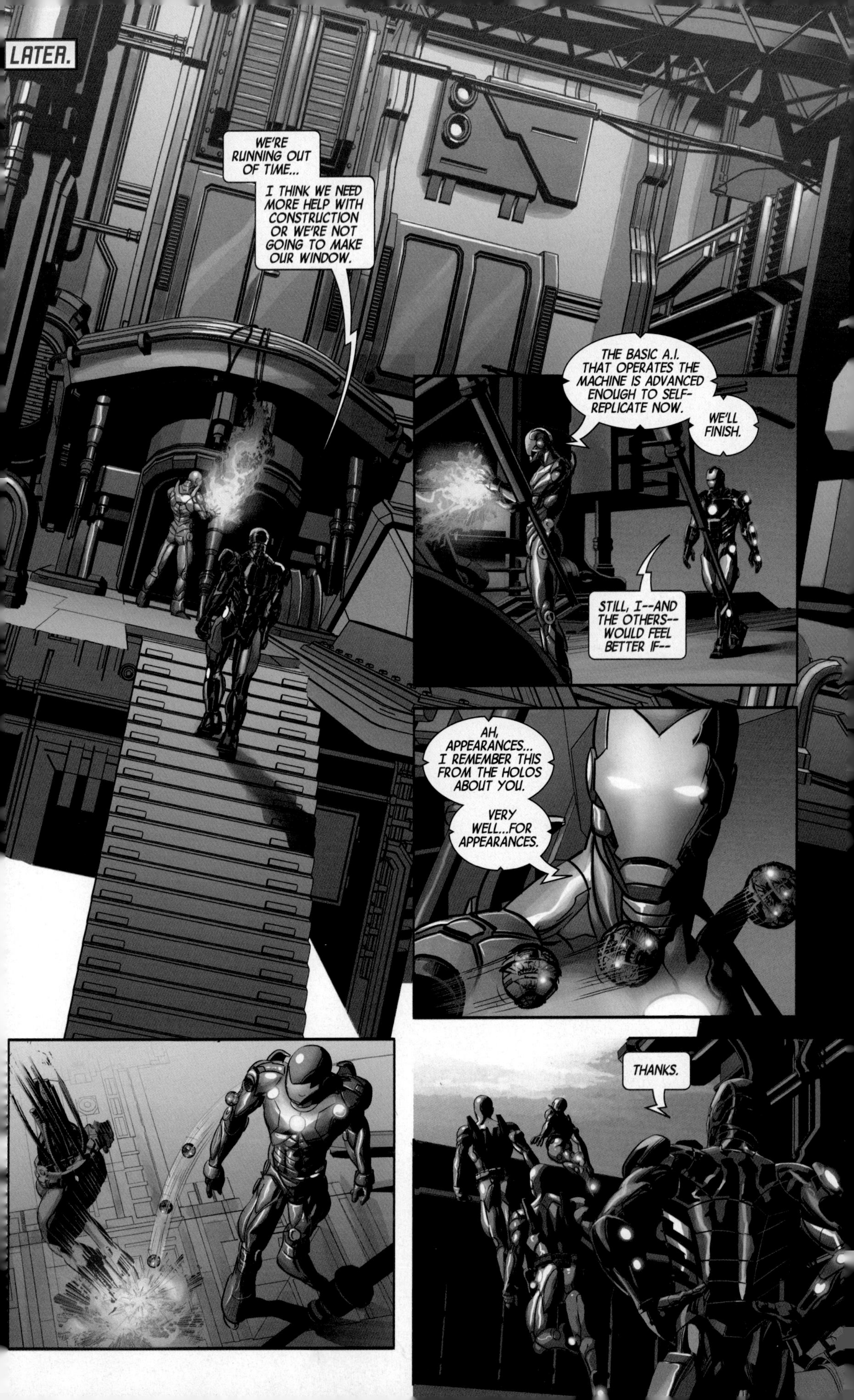
LATER.
WE'RE RUNNING OUT OF TIME...
I THINK WE NEED MORE HELP WITH CONSTRUCTION OR WE'RE NOT GOING TO MAKE OUR WINDOW.
THE BASIC A.I. THAT OPERATES THE MACHINE IS ADVANCED ENOUGH TO SELF-REPLICATE NOW.
WE'LL FINISH.
STILL, I--AND THE OTHERS--WOULD FEEL BETTER IF--
AH, APPEARANCES... I REMEMBER THIS FROM THE HOLOS ABOUT YOU.
VERY WELL...FOR APPEARANCES.
THANKS.

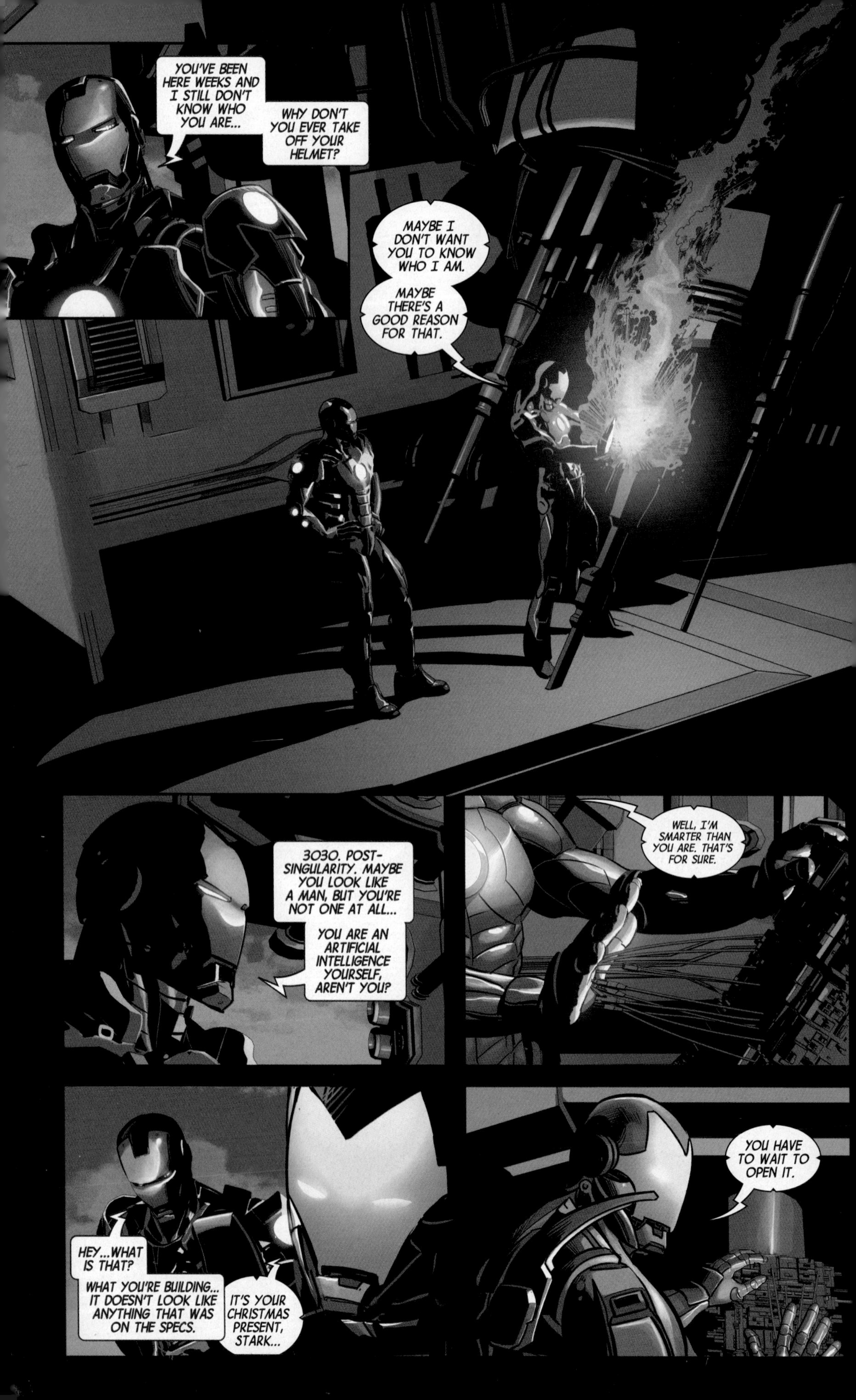
YOU'VE BEEN HERE WEEKS AND I STILL DON'T KNOW WHO YOU ARE...
WHY DON'T YOU EVER TAKE OFF YOUR HELMET?
MAYBE I DON'T WANT YOU TO KNOW WHO I AM.
MAYBE THERE'S A GOOD REASON FOR THAT.
3030. POST-SINGULARITY. MAYBE YOU LOOK LIKE A MAN, BUT YOU'RE NOT ONE AT ALL...
YOU ARE AN ARTIFICIAL INTELLIGENCE YOURSELF, AREN'T YOU?
WELL, I'M SMARTER THAN YOU ARE. THAT'S FOR SURE.
HEY...WHAT IS THAT?
WHAT YOU'RE BUILDING... IT DOESN'T LOOK LIKE ANYTHING THAT WAS ON THE SPECS.
IT'S YOUR CHRISTMAS PRESENT, STARK...
YOU HAVE TO WAIT TO OPEN IT.

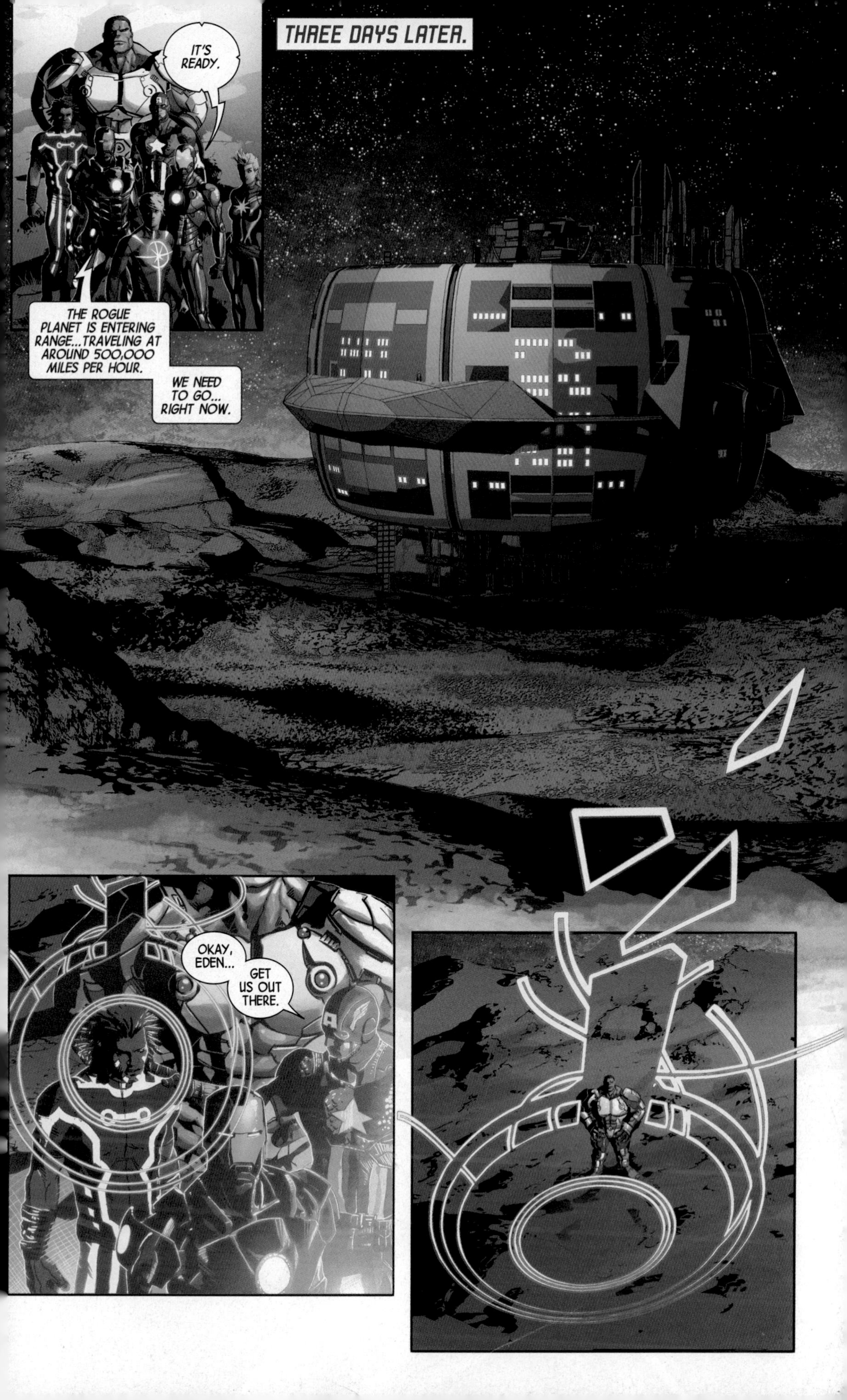
IT'S READY.
THREE DAYS LATER.
THE ROGUE PLANET IS ENTERING RANGE...TRAVELING AT AROUND 500,000 MILES PER HOUR.
WE NEED TO GO... RIGHT NOW.
OKAY, EDEN...
GET US OUT THERE.

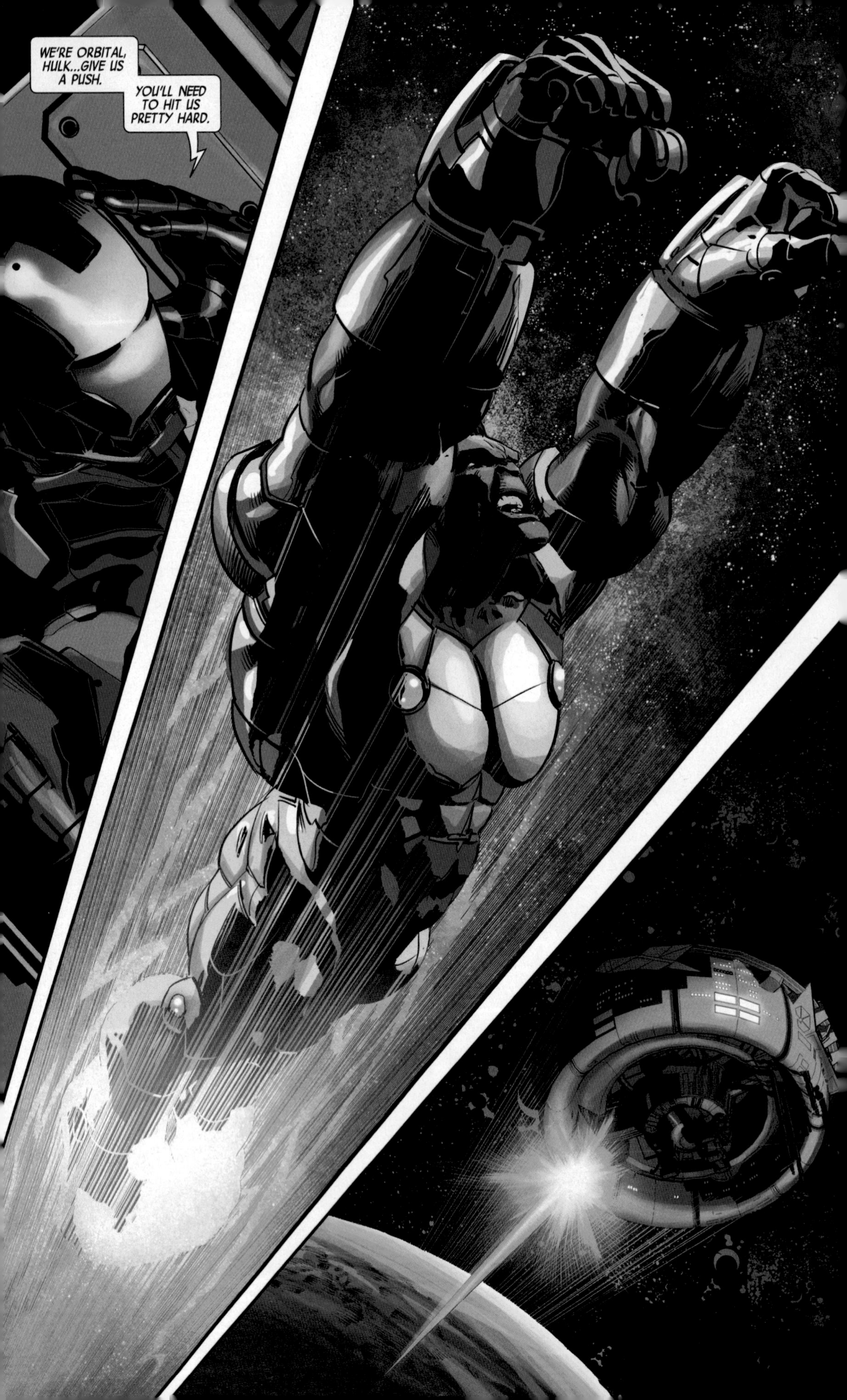
WE'RE ORBITAL, HULK...GIVE US A PUSH.
YOU'LL NEED TO HIT US PRETTY HARD.

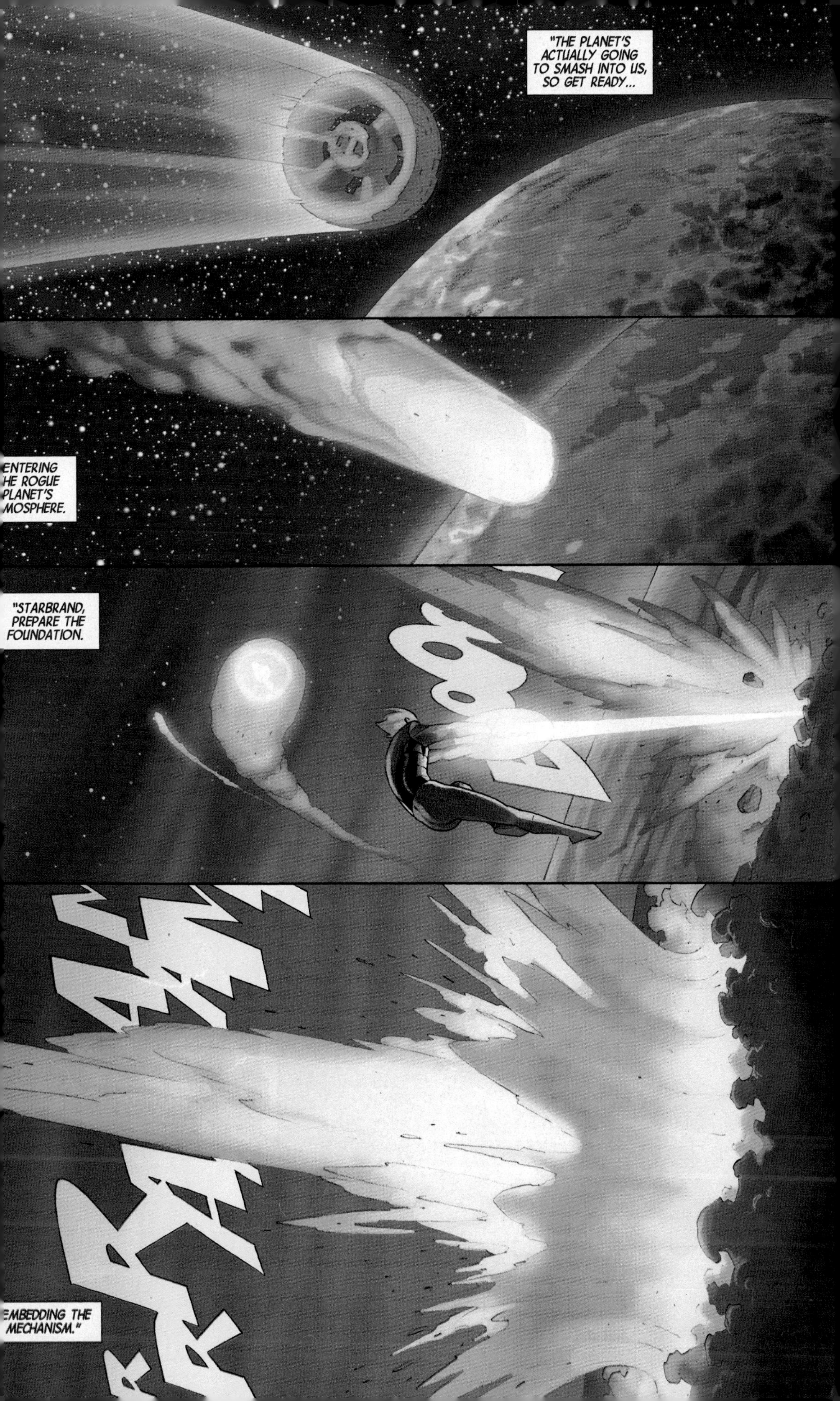
"THE PLANET'S ACTUALLY GOING TO SMASH INTO US, SO GET READY...
ENTERING HE ROGUE PLANET'S MOSPHERE.
"STARBRAND, PREPARE THE FOUNDATION.
EMBEDDING THE MECHANISM."

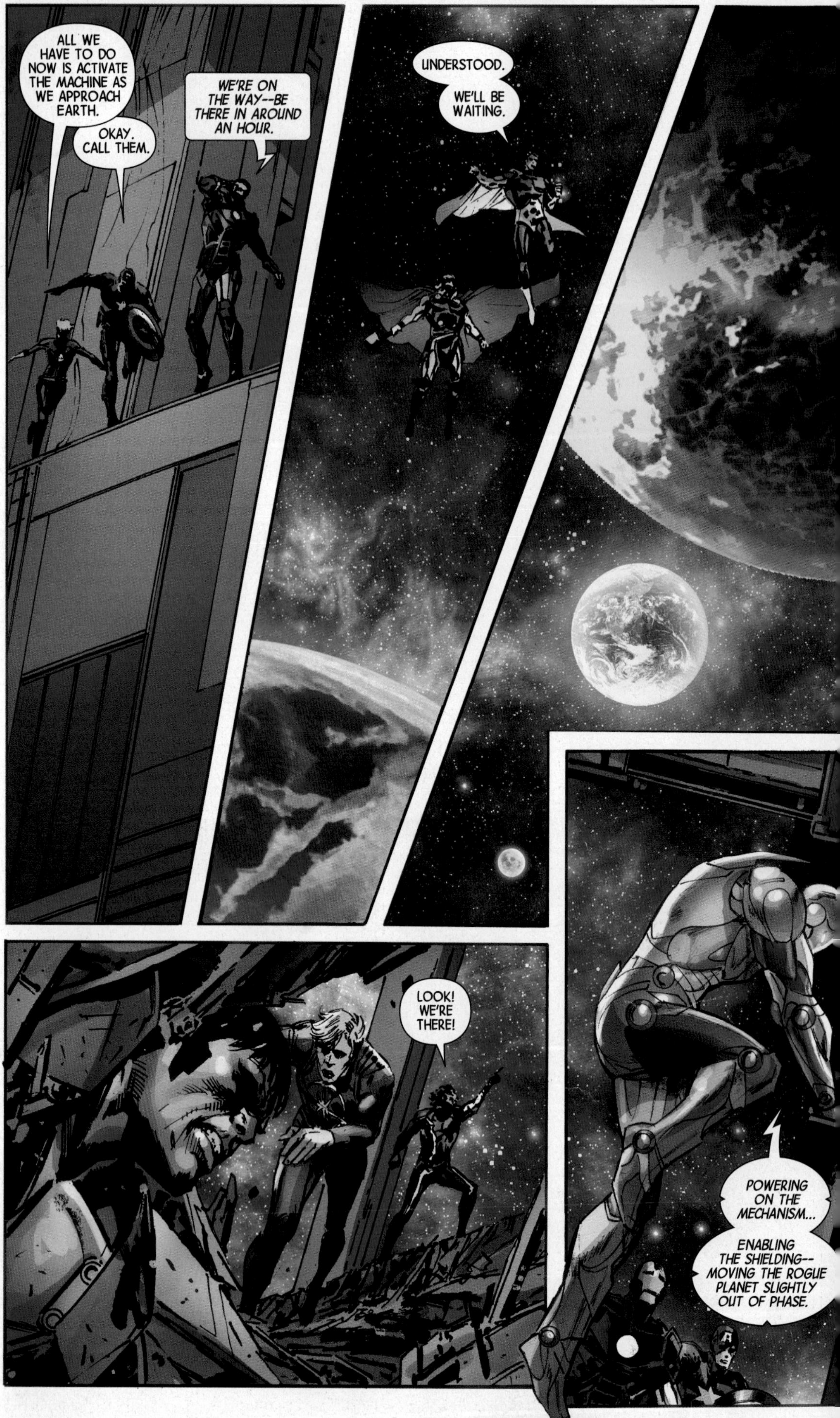

ALL WE HAVE TO DO NOW IS ACTIVATE THE MACHINE AS WE APPROACH EARTH.
OKAY. CALL THEM.
WE'RE ON THE WAY--BE THERE IN AROUND AN HOUR.
UNDERSTOOD.
WE'LL BE WAITING.
LOOK! WE'RE THERE!
POWERING ON THE MECHANISM...
ENABLING THE SHIELDING-- MOVING THE ROGUE PLANET SLIGHTLY OUT OF PHASE.

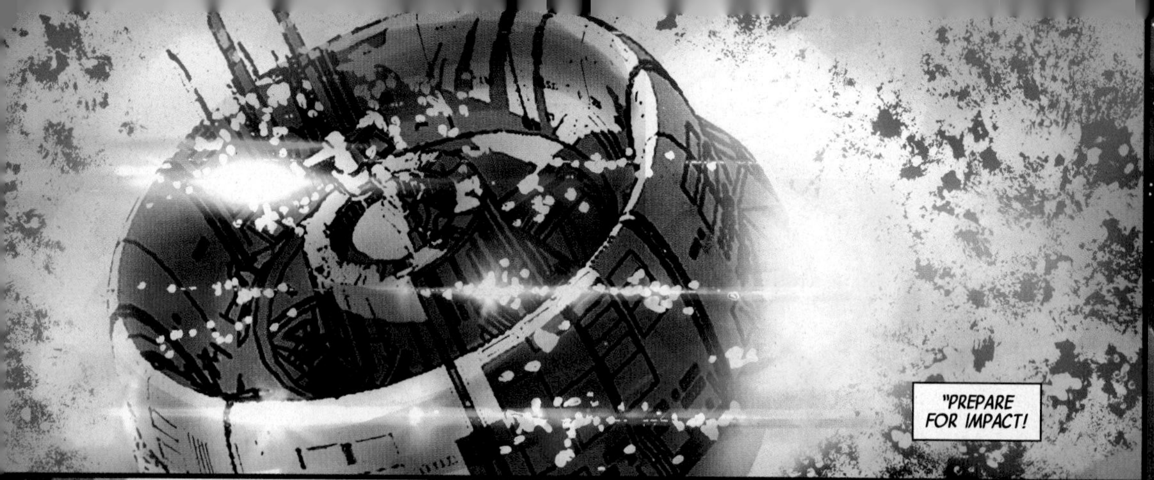
"PREPARE
FOR IMPACT!

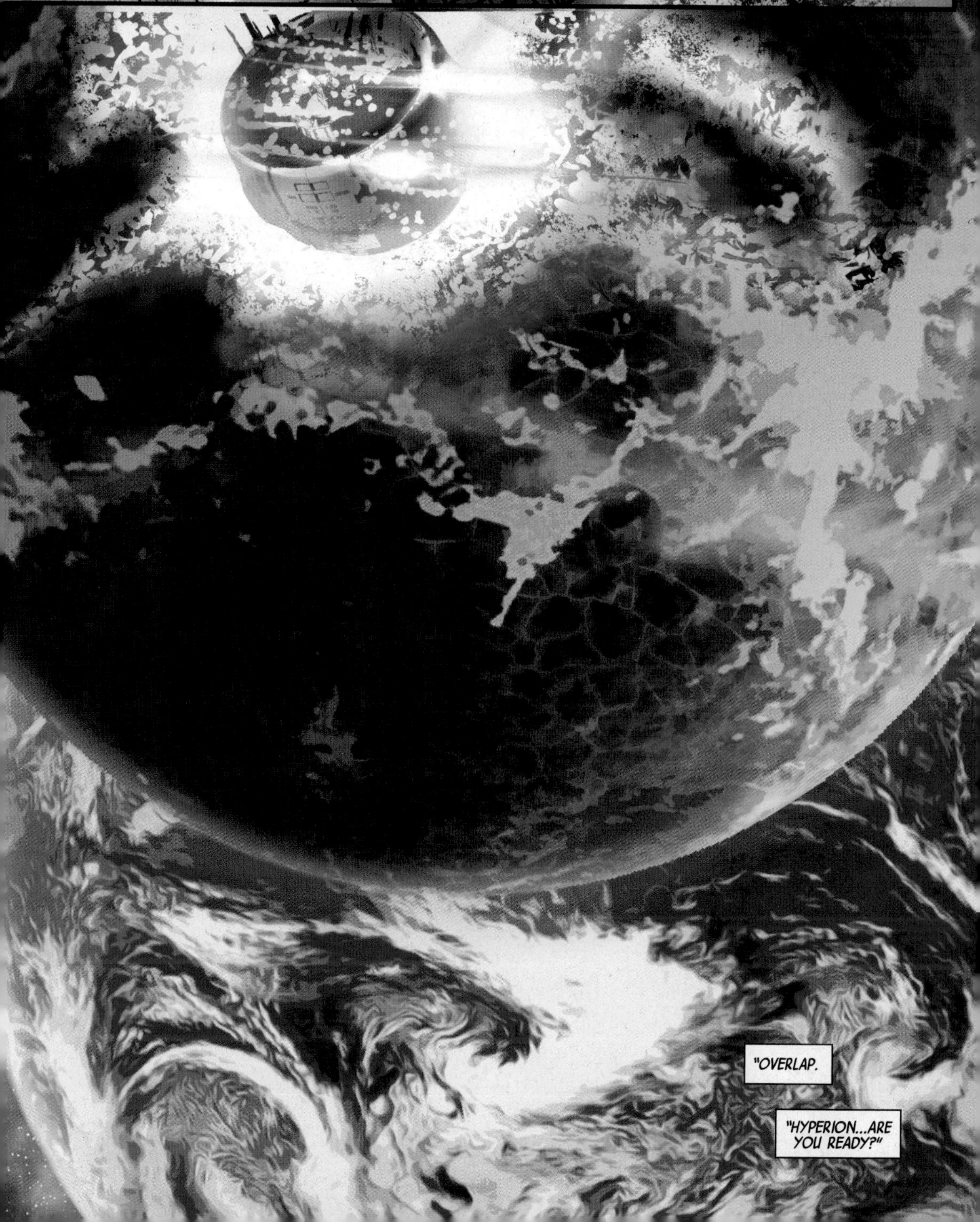
"OVERLAP.
"HYPERION...ARE
YOU READY?"

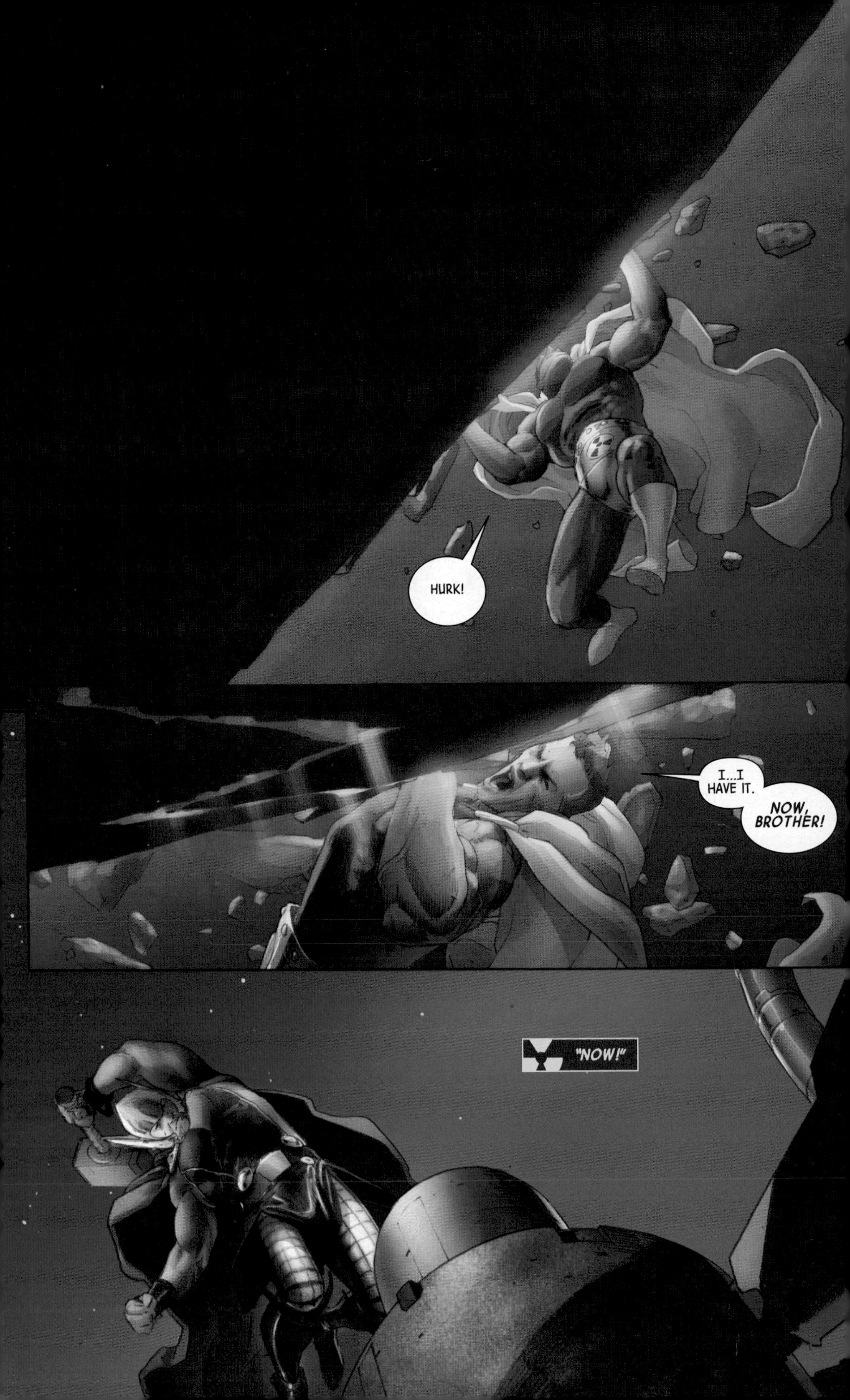
HURK!
I...I HAVE IT.
NOW, BROTHER!
"NOW!"

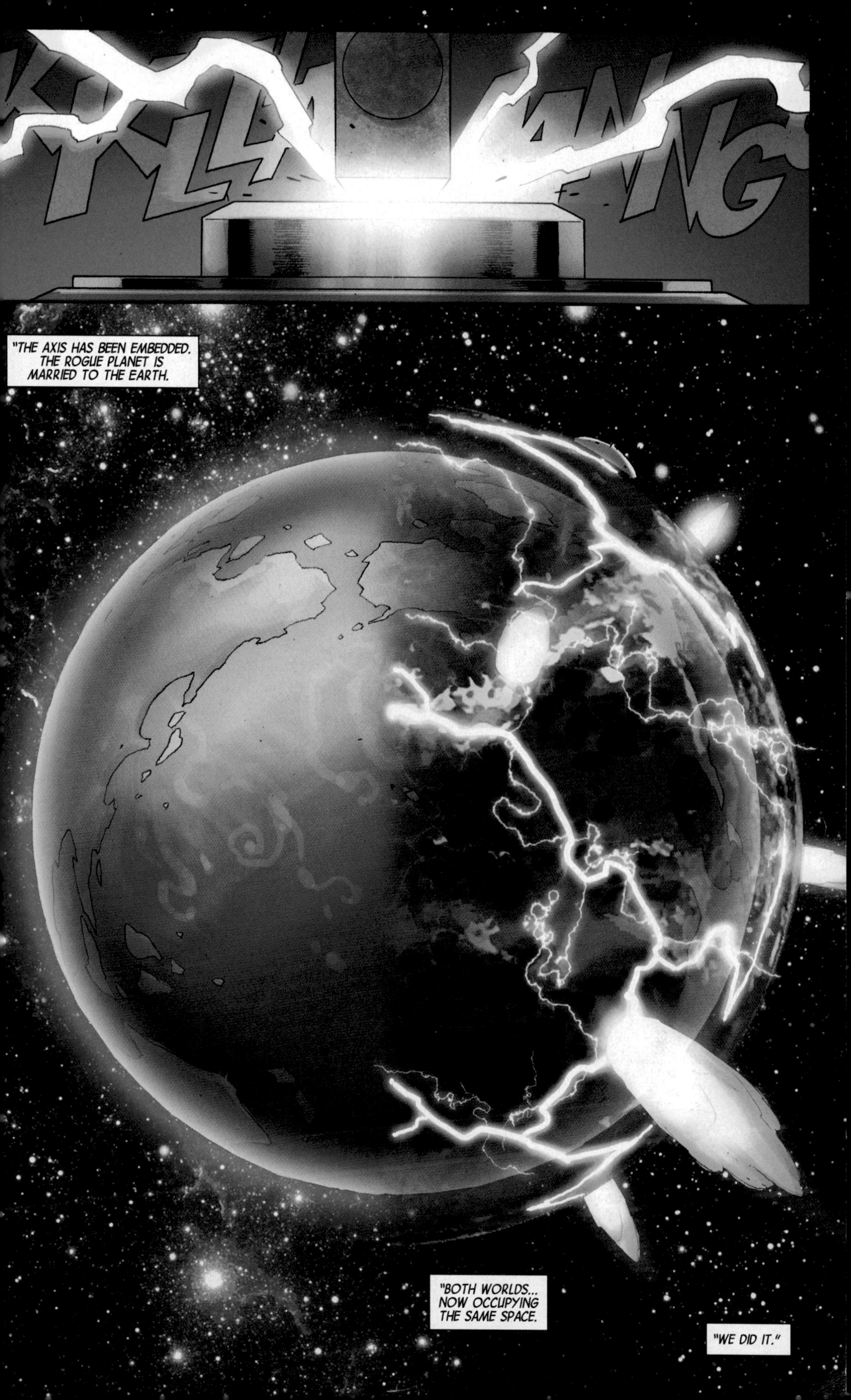
"THE AXIS HAS BEEN EMBEDDED. THE ROGUE PLANET IS MARRIED TO THE EARTH.
"BOTH WORLDS... NOW OCCUPYING THE SAME SPACE.
"WE DID IT."

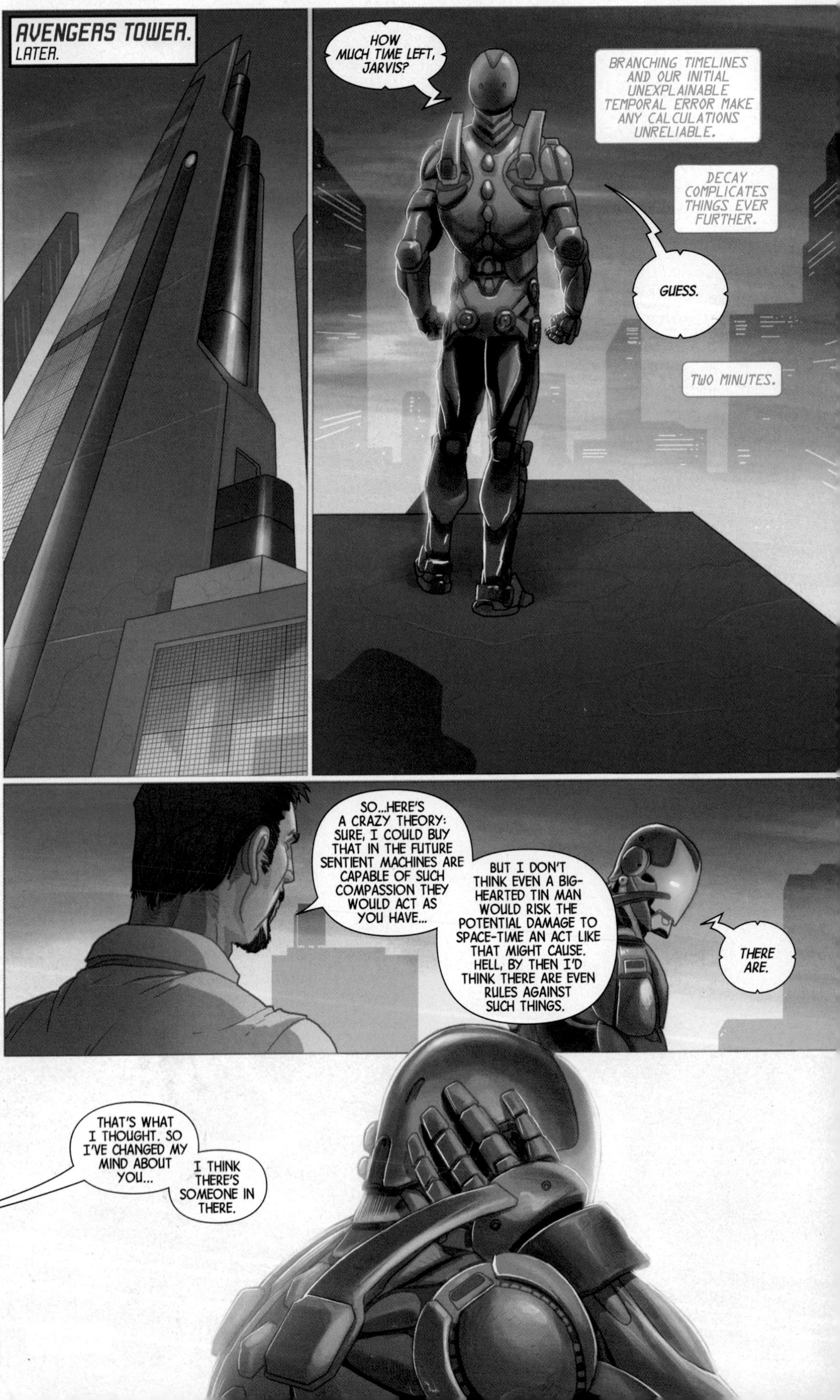
AVENGERS TOWER.
LATER.
HOW MUCH TIME LEFT, JARVIS?
BRANCHING TIMELINES AND OUR INITIAL UNEXPLAINABLE TEMPORAL ERROR MAKE ANY CALCULATIONS UNRELIABLE.
DECAY COMPLICATES THINGS EVER FURTHER.
GUESS.
TWO MINUTES.
SO...HERE'S A CRAZY THEORY: SURE, I COULD BUY THAT IN THE FUTURE SENTIENT MACHINES ARE CAPABLE OF SUCH COMPASSION THEY WOULD ACT AS YOU HAVE...
BUT I DON'T THINK EVEN A BIG-HEARTED TIN MAN WOULD RISK THE POTENTIAL DAMAGE TO SPACE-TIME AN ACT LIKE THAT MIGHT CAUSE. HELL, BY THEN I'D THINK THERE ARE EVEN RULES AGAINST SUCH THINGS.
THERE ARE.
THAT'S WHAT I THOUGHT. SO I'VE CHANGED MY MIND ABOUT YOU...
I THINK THERE'S SOMEONE IN THERE.

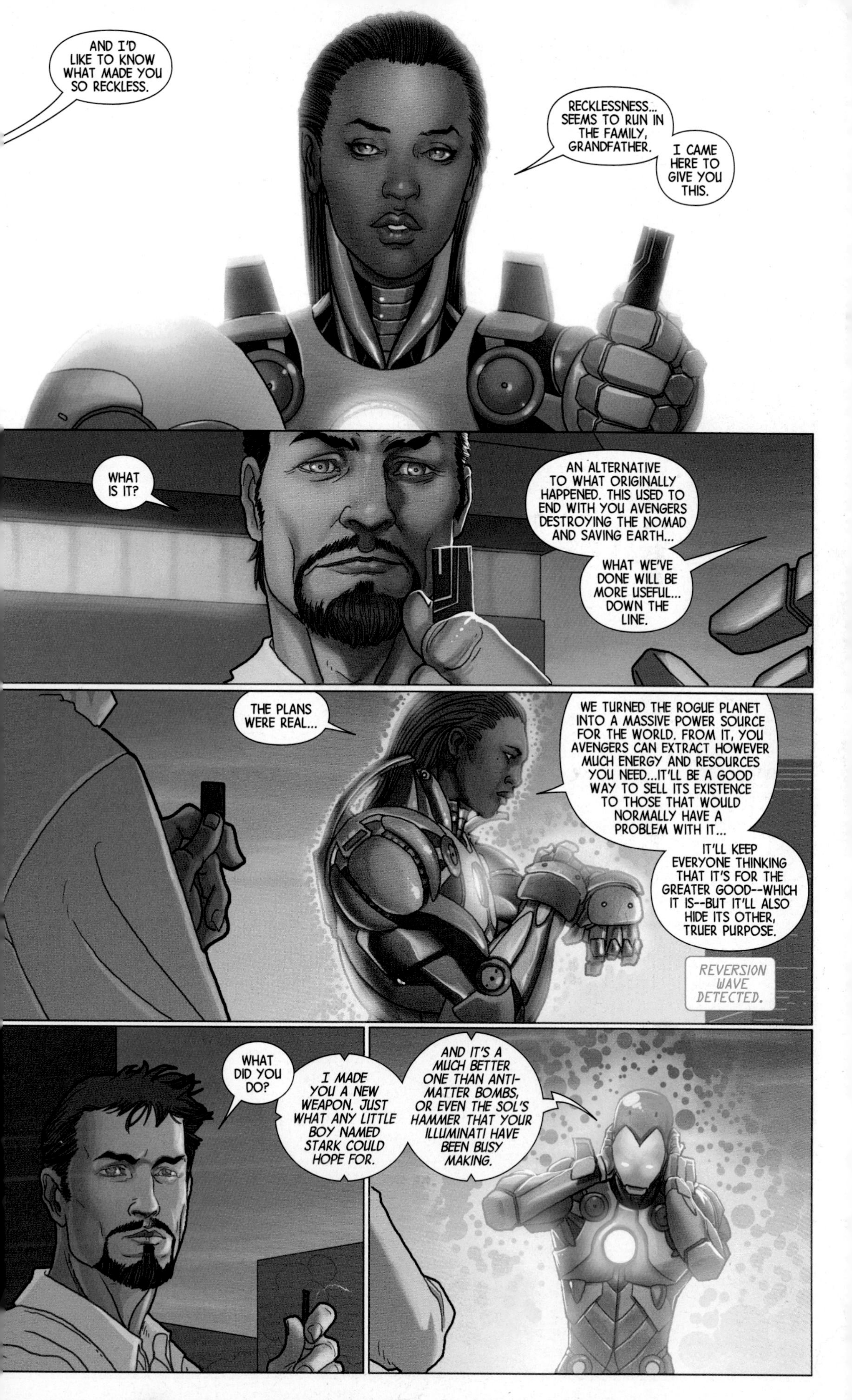
AND I'D LIKE TO KNOW WHAT MADE YOU SO RECKLESS.
RECKLESSNESS... SEEMS TO RUN IN THE FAMILY, GRANDFATHER.
I CAME HERE TO GIVE YOU THIS.
WHAT IS IT?
AN ALTERNATIVE TO WHAT ORIGINALLY HAPPENED. THIS USED TO END WITH YOU AVENGERS DESTROYING THE NOMAD AND SAVING EARTH...
WHAT WE'VE DONE WILL BE MORE USEFUL... DOWN THE LINE.
THE PLANS WERE REAL...
WE TURNED THE ROGUE PLANET INTO A MASSIVE POWER SOURCE FOR THE WORLD. FROM IT, YOU AVENGERS CAN EXTRACT HOWEVER MUCH ENERGY AND RESOURCES YOU NEED...IT'LL BE A GOOD WAY TO SELL ITS EXISTENCE TO THOSE THAT WOULD NORMALLY HAVE A PROBLEM WITH IT...
IT'LL KEEP EVERYONE THINKING THAT IT'S FOR THE GREATER GOOD--WHICH IT IS--BUT IT'LL ALSO HIDE ITS OTHER, TRUER PURPOSE.
REVERSION WAVE DETECTED.
WHAT DID YOU DO?
I MADE YOU A NEW WEAPON. JUST WHAT ANY LITTLE BOY NAMED STARK COULD HOPE FOR.
AND IT'S A MUCH BETTER ONE THAN ANTI-MATTER BOMBS, OR EVEN THE SOL'S HAMMER THAT YOUR ILLUMINATI HAVE BEEN BUSY MAKING.

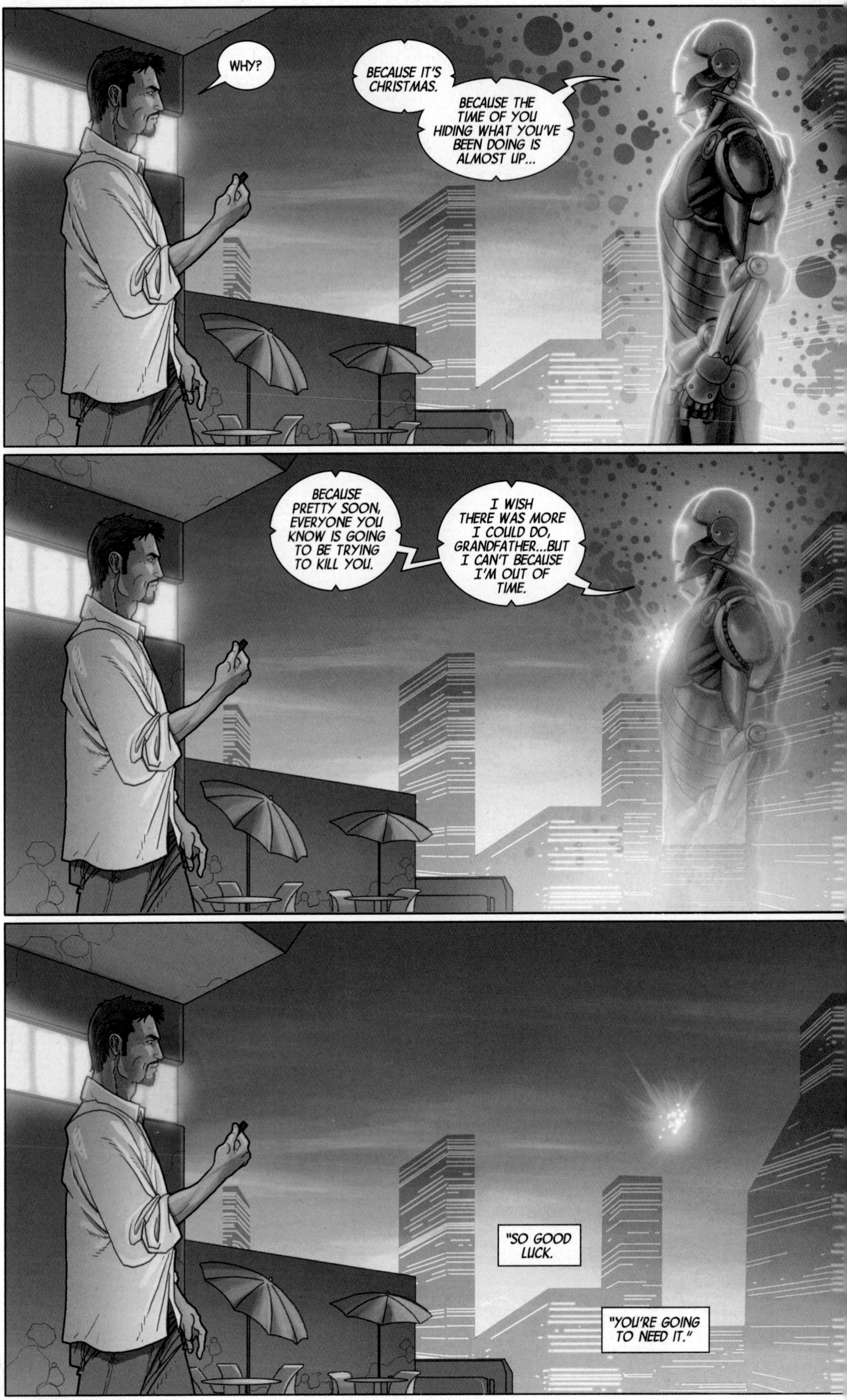
WHY?
BECAUSE IT'S CHRISTMAS.
BECAUSE THE TIME OF YOU HIDING WHAT YOU'VE BEEN DOING IS ALMOST UP...
BECAUSE PRETTY SOON, EVERYONE YOU KNOW IS GOING TO BE TRYING TO KILL YOU.
I WISH THERE WAS MORE I COULD DO, GRANDFATHER...BUT I CAN'T BECAUSE I'M OUT OF TIME.
"SO GOOD LUCK.
"YOU'RE GOING TO NEED IT."

"CARVE A HOLE...CLIMB INSIDE"

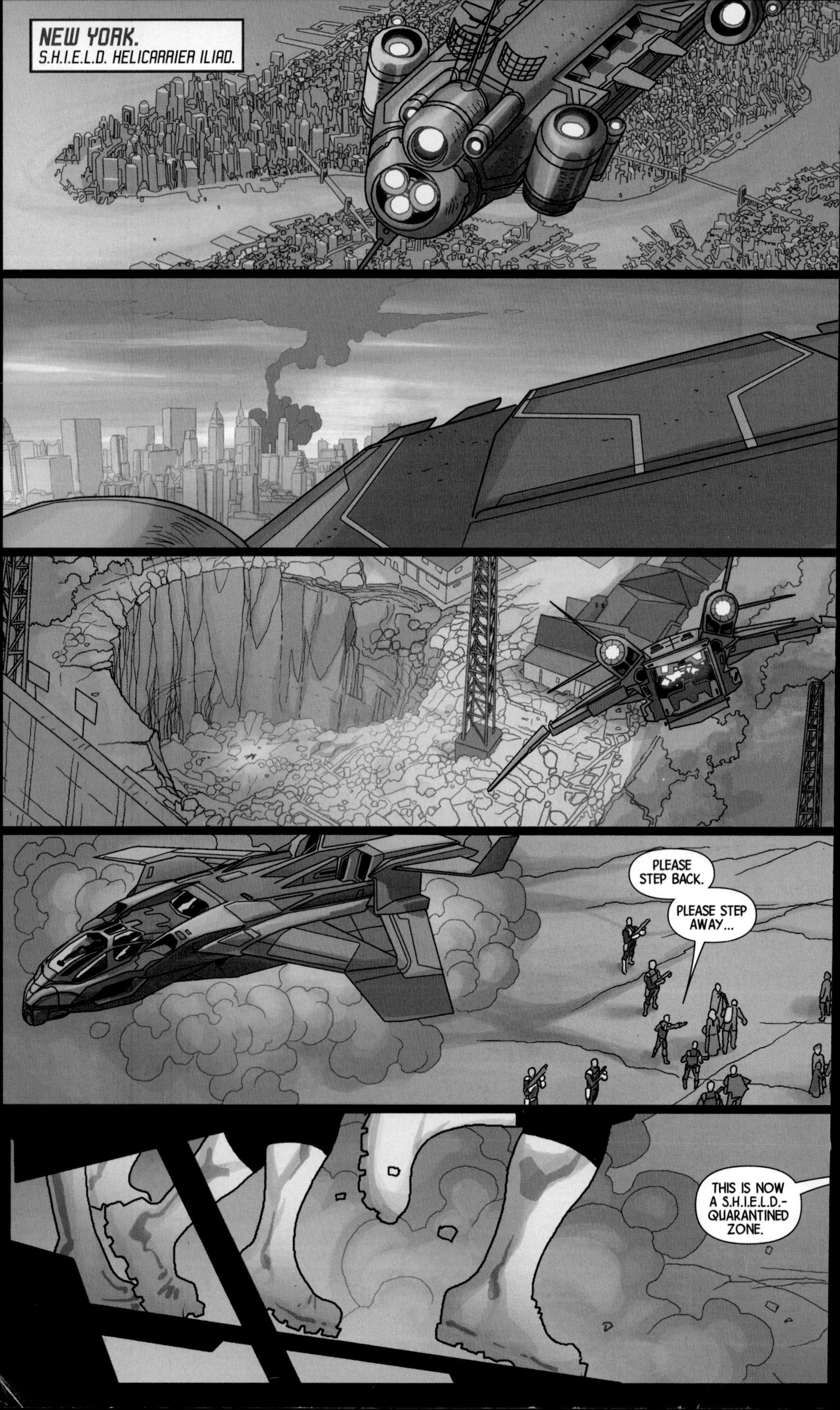
NEW YORK.
S.H.I.E.L.D. HELICARRIER ILIAD.
PLEASE STEP BACK.
PLEASE STEP AWAY...
THIS IS NOW A S.H.I.E.L.D.-QUARANTINED ZONE.

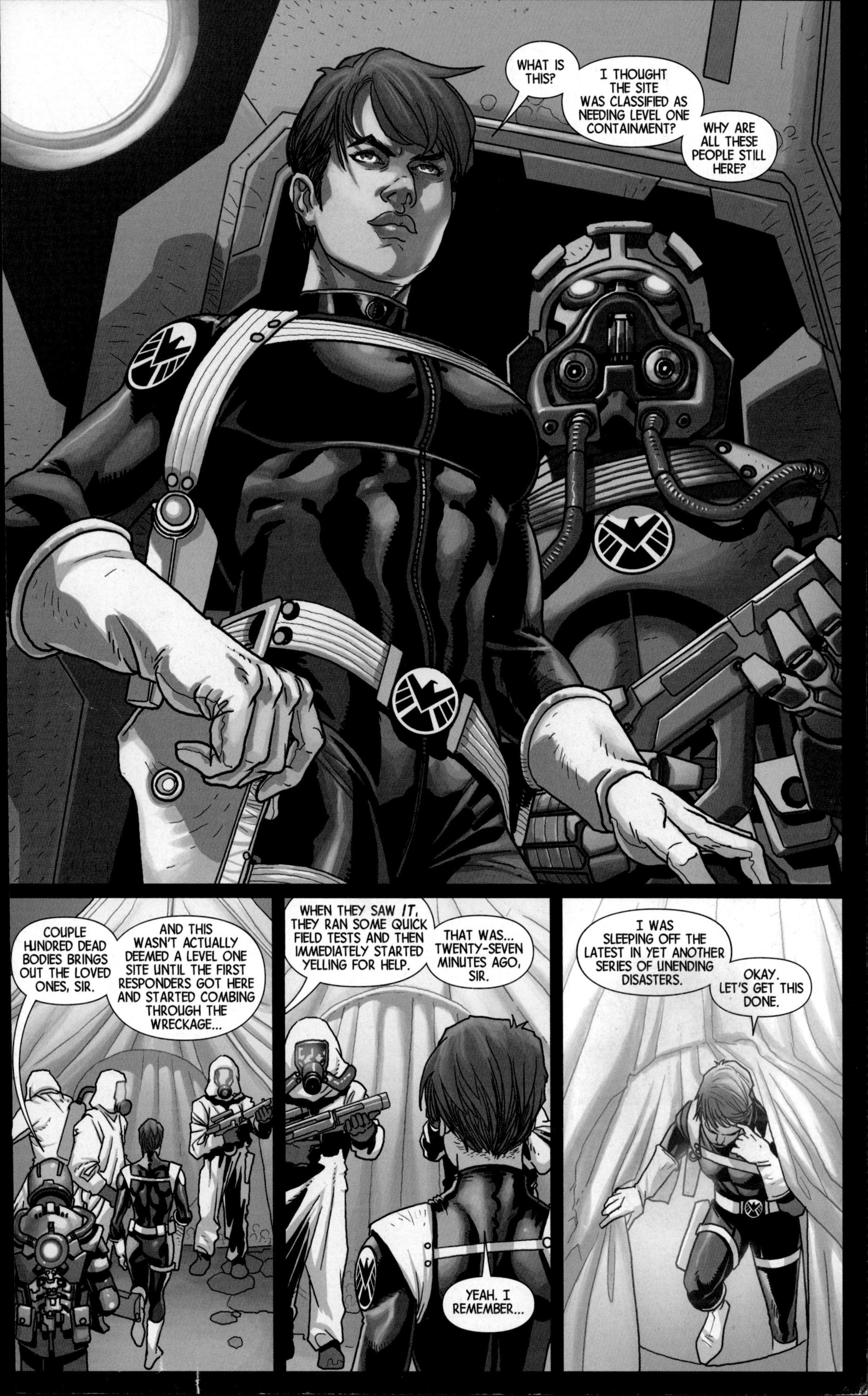
WHAT IS THIS?
I THOUGHT THE SITE WAS CLASSIFIED AS NEEDING LEVEL ONE CONTAINMENT?
WHY ARE ALL THESE PEOPLE STILL HERE?
COUPLE HUNDRED DEAD BODIES BRINGS OUT THE LOVED ONES, SIR.
AND THIS WASN'T ACTUALLY DEEMED A LEVEL ONE SITE UNTIL THE FIRST RESPONDERS GOT HERE AND STARTED COMBING THROUGH THE WRECKAGE...
WHEN THEY SAW *IT*, THEY RAN SOME QUICK FIELD TESTS AND THEN IMMEDIATELY STARTED YELLING FOR HELP.
THAT WAS... TWENTY-SEVEN MINUTES AGO, SIR.
YEAH. I REMEMBER...
I WAS SLEEPING OFF THE LATEST IN YET ANOTHER SERIES OF UNENDING DISASTERS.
OKAY. LET'S GET THIS DONE.

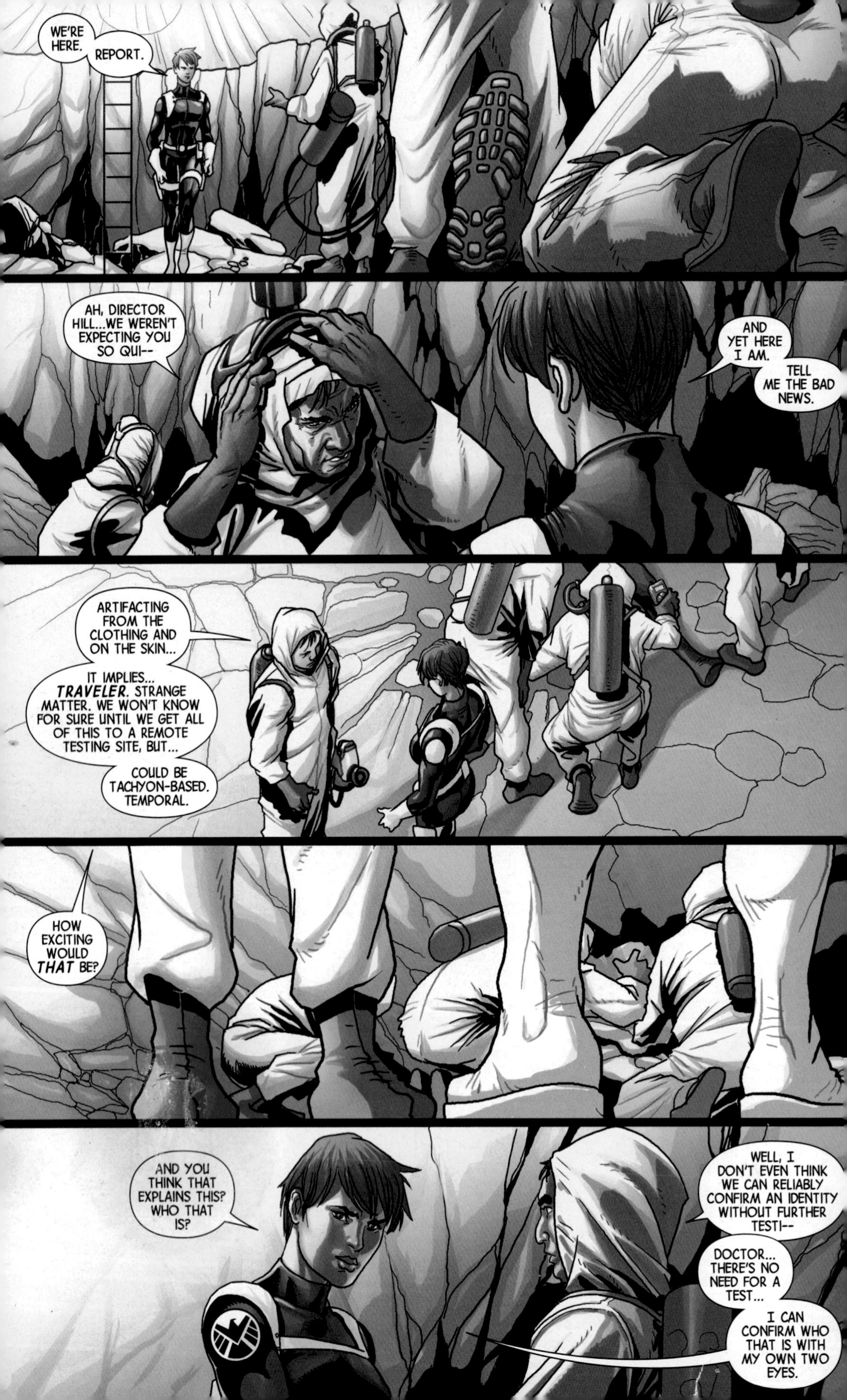
WE'RE HERE.
REPORT.
AH, DIRECTOR HILL...WE WEREN'T EXPECTING YOU SO QUI--
AND YET HERE I AM.
TELL ME THE BAD NEWS.
ARTIFACTING FROM THE CLOTHING AND ON THE SKIN...
IT IMPLIES... TRAVELER. STRANGE MATTER. WE WON'T KNOW FOR SURE UNTIL WE GET ALL OF THIS TO A REMOTE TESTING SITE, BUT...
COULD BE TACHYON-BASED. TEMPORAL.
HOW EXCITING WOULD THAT BE?
AND YOU THINK THAT EXPLAINS THIS? WHO THAT IS?
WELL, I DON'T EVEN THINK WE CAN RELIABLY CONFIRM AN IDENTITY WITHOUT FURTHER TESTI--
DOCTOR... THERE'S NO NEED FOR A TEST...
I CAN CONFIRM WHO THAT IS WITH MY OWN TWO EYES.

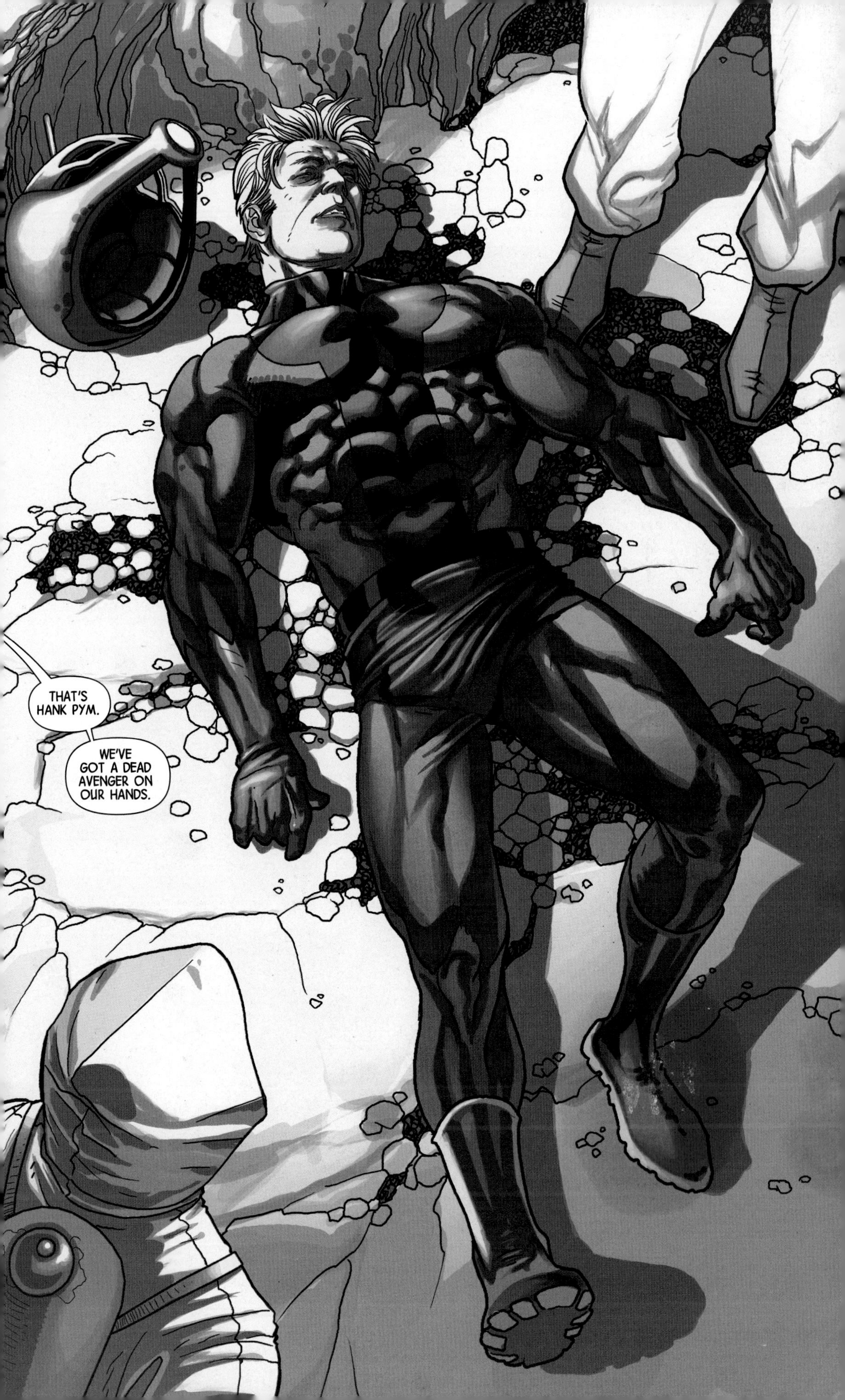
THAT'S HANK PYM.
WE'VE GOT A DEAD AVENGER ON OUR HANDS.

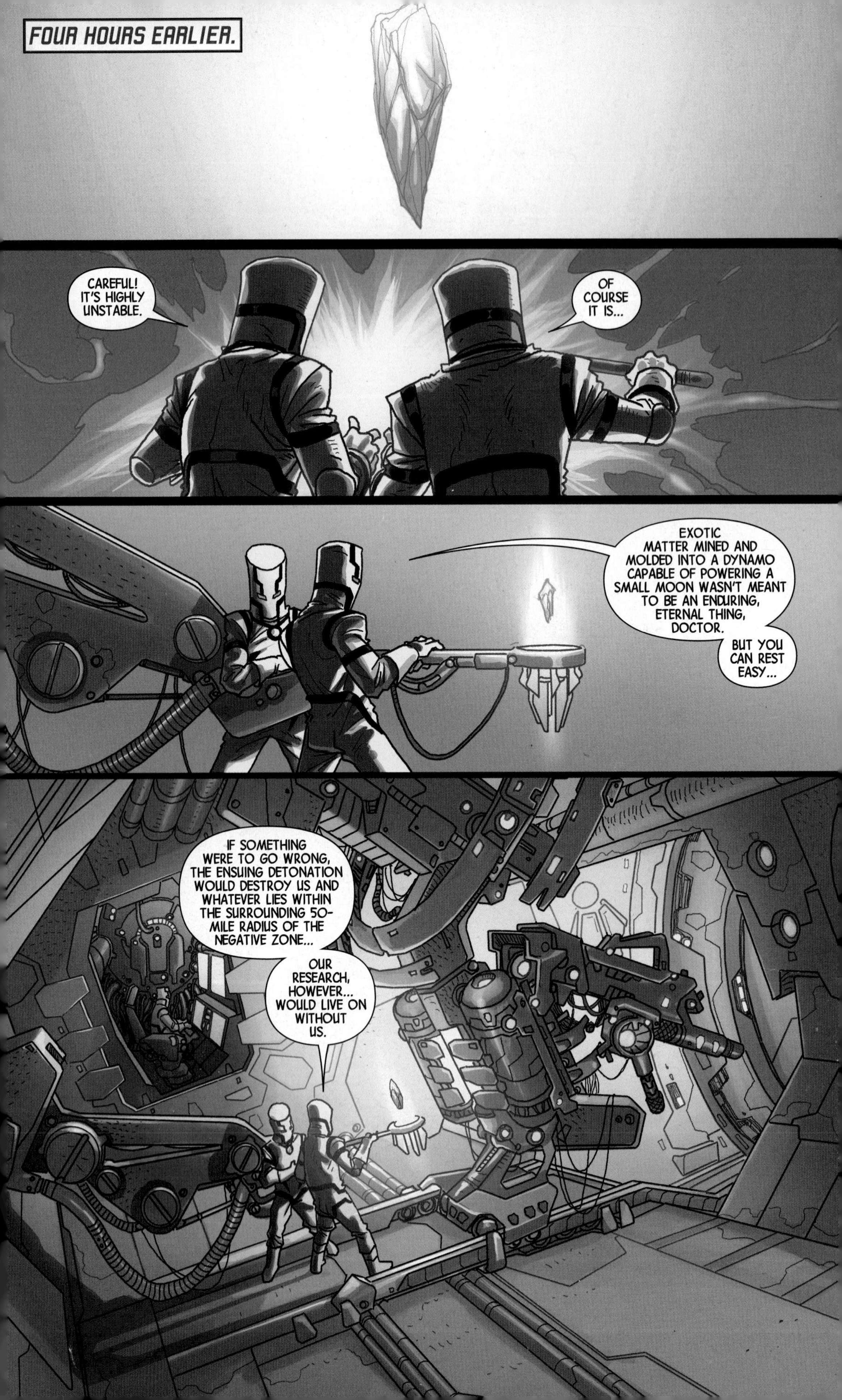
FOUR HOURS EARLIER.
CAREFUL! IT'S HIGHLY UNSTABLE.
OF COURSE IT IS...
EXOTIC MATTER MINED AND MOLDED INTO A DYNAMO CAPABLE OF POWERING A SMALL MOON WASN'T MEANT TO BE AN ENDURING, ETERNAL THING, DOCTOR.
BUT YOU CAN REST EASY...
IF SOMETHING WERE TO GO WRONG, THE ENSUING DETONATION WOULD DESTROY US AND WHATEVER LIES WITHIN THE SURROUNDING 50-MILE RADIUS OF THE NEGATIVE ZONE...
OUR RESEARCH, HOWEVER... WOULD LIVE ON WITHOUT US.

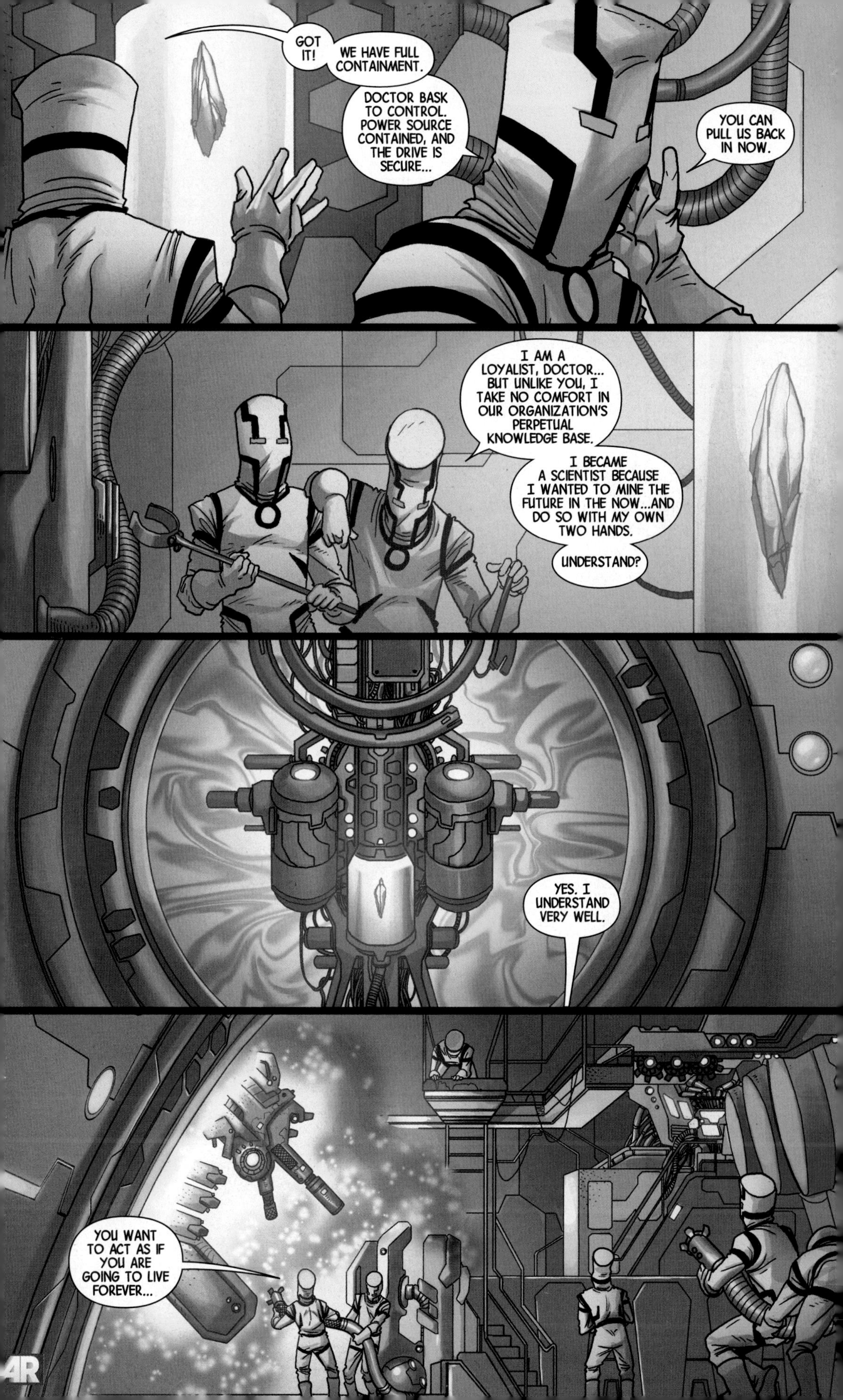
GOT IT!
WE HAVE FULL CONTAINMENT.
DOCTOR BASK TO CONTROL. POWER SOURCE CONTAINED, AND THE DRIVE IS SECURE...
YOU CAN PULL US BACK IN NOW.
I AM A LOYALIST, DOCTOR... BUT UNLIKE YOU, I TAKE NO COMFORT IN OUR ORGANIZATION'S PERPETUAL KNOWLEDGE BASE.
I BECAME A SCIENTIST BECAUSE I WANTED TO MINE THE FUTURE IN THE NOW...AND DO SO WITH MY OWN TWO HANDS.
UNDERSTAND?
YES. I UNDERSTAND VERY WELL.
YOU WANT TO ACT AS IF YOU ARE GOING TO LIVE FOREVER...

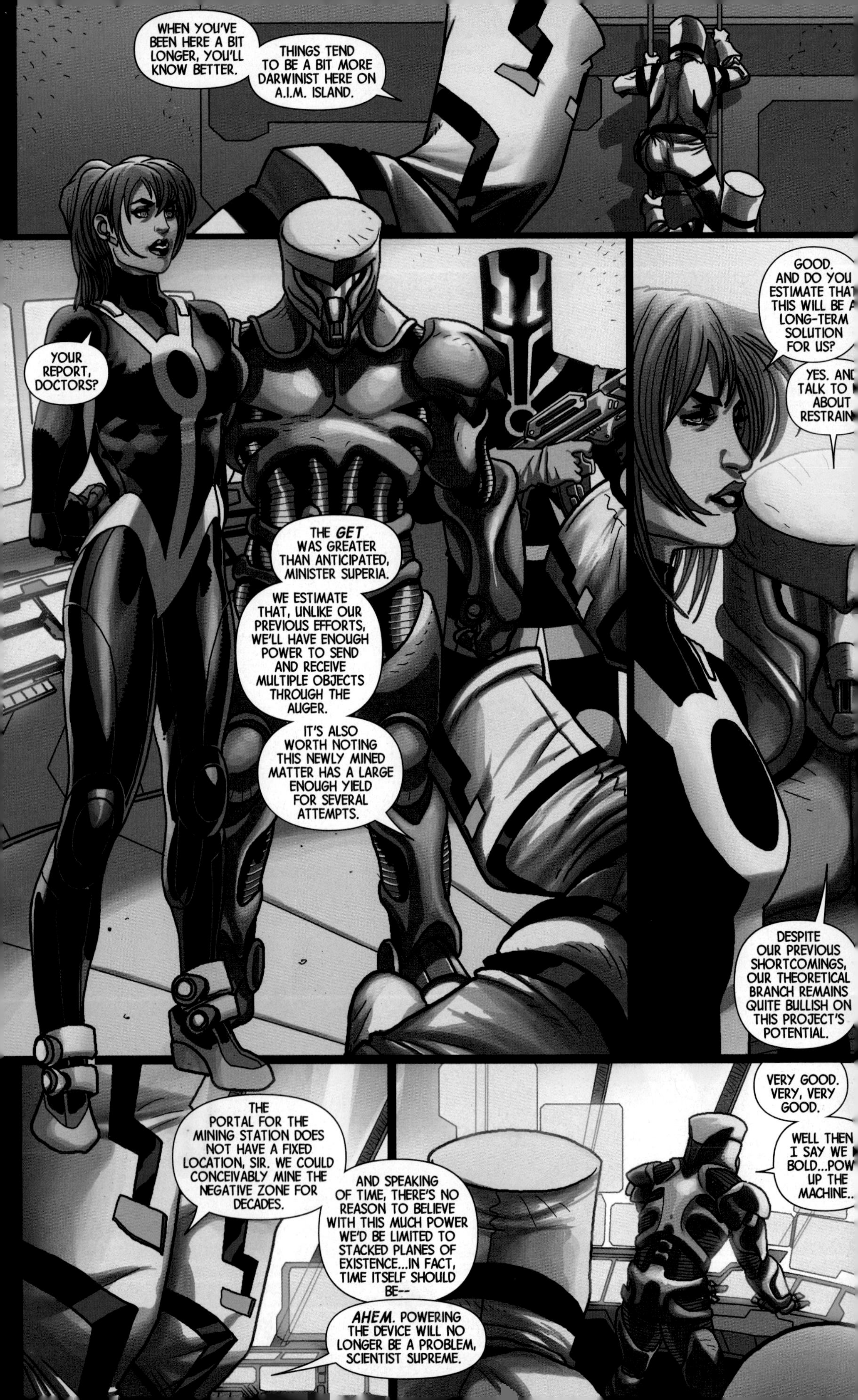
WHEN YOU'VE BEEN HERE A BIT LONGER, YOU'LL KNOW BETTER.
THINGS TEND TO BE A BIT MORE DARWINIST HERE ON A.I.M. ISLAND.
YOUR REPORT, DOCTORS?
THE *GET* WAS GREATER THAN ANTICIPATED, MINISTER SUPERIA.
WE ESTIMATE THAT, UNLIKE OUR PREVIOUS EFFORTS, WE'LL HAVE ENOUGH POWER TO SEND AND RECEIVE MULTIPLE OBJECTS THROUGH THE AUGER.
IT'S ALSO WORTH NOTING THIS NEWLY MINED MATTER HAS A LARGE ENOUGH YIELD FOR SEVERAL ATTEMPTS.
GOOD. AND DO YOU ESTIMATE THAT THIS WILL BE A LONG-TERM SOLUTION FOR US?
YES. AND TALK TO ABOUT RESTRAIN
DESPITE OUR PREVIOUS SHORTCOMINGS, OUR THEORETICAL BRANCH REMAINS QUITE BULLISH ON THIS PROJECT'S POTENTIAL.
THE PORTAL FOR THE MINING STATION DOES NOT HAVE A FIXED LOCATION, SIR. WE COULD CONCEIVABLY MINE THE NEGATIVE ZONE FOR DECADES.
AND SPEAKING OF TIME, THERE'S NO REASON TO BELIEVE WITH THIS MUCH POWER WE'D BE LIMITED TO STACKED PLANES OF EXISTENCE...IN FACT, TIME ITSELF SHOULD BE--
AHEM. POWERING THE DEVICE WILL NO LONGER BE A PROBLEM, SCIENTIST SUPREME.
VERY GOOD. VERY, VERY GOOD.
WELL THEN I SAY WE BOLD...POW UP THE MACHINE..

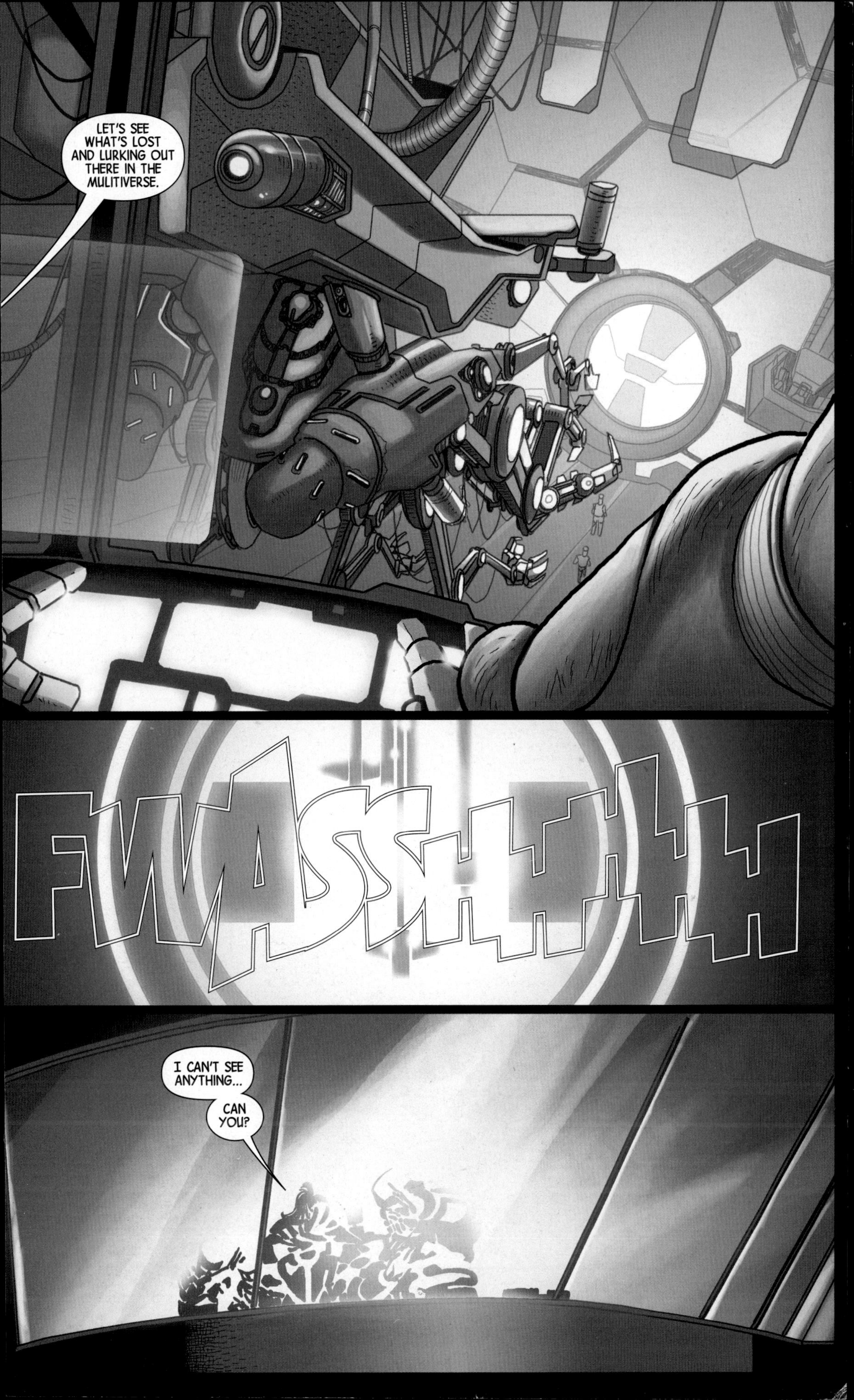
LET'S SEE WHAT'S LOST AND LURKING OUT THERE IN THE MULITIVERSE.
FWASSHHHHH
I CAN'T SEE ANYTHING...
CAN YOU?

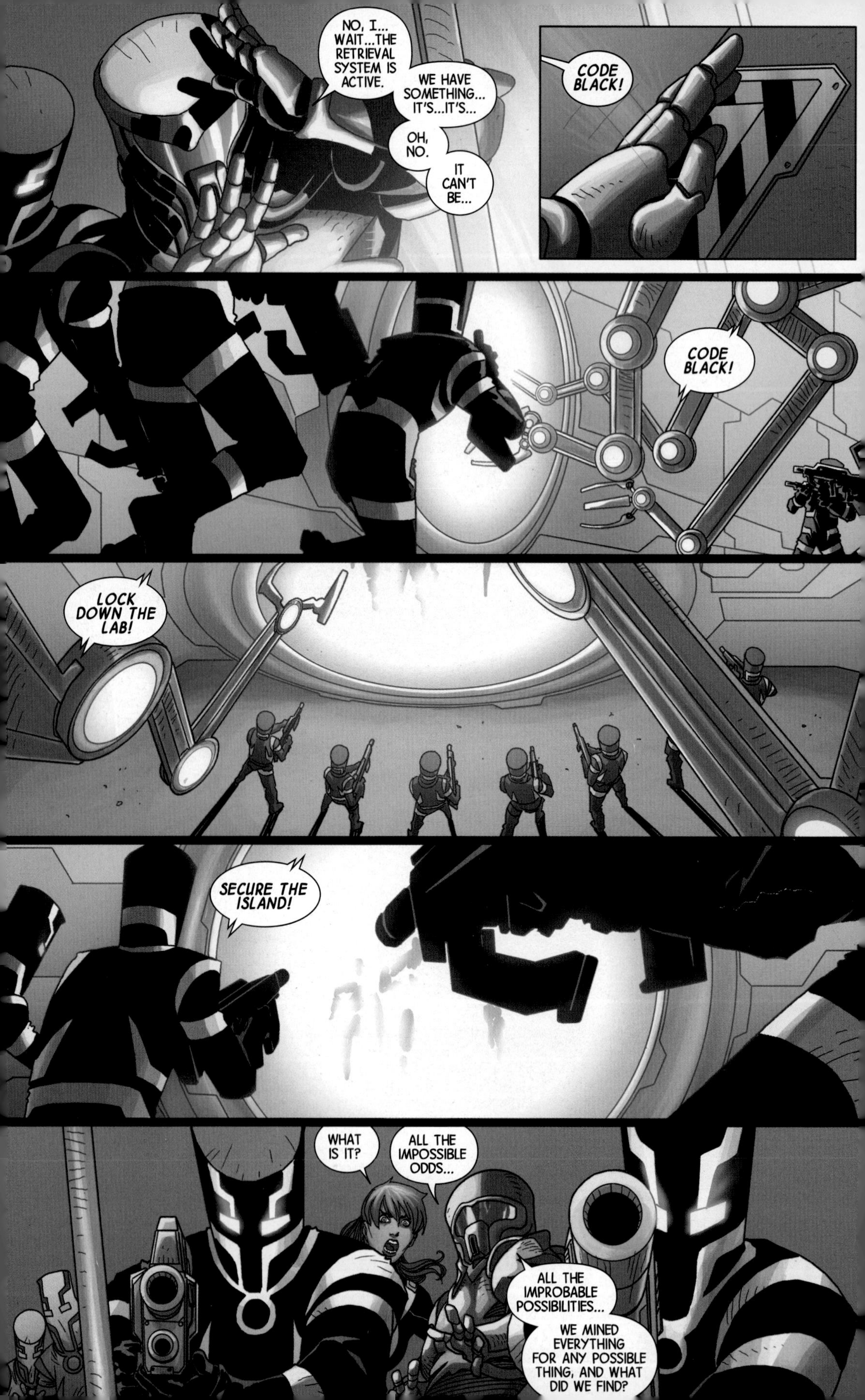
NO, I... WAIT...THE RETRIEVAL SYSTEM IS ACTIVE.
WE HAVE SOMETHING... IT'S...IT'S...
OH, NO.
IT CAN'T BE...
CODE BLACK!
CODE BLACK!
LOCK DOWN THE LAB!
SECURE THE ISLAND!
WHAT IS IT?
ALL THE IMPOSSIBLE ODDS...
ALL THE IMPROBABLE POSSIBILITIES...
WE MINED EVERYTHING FOR ANY POSSIBLE THING, AND WHAT DID WE FIND?

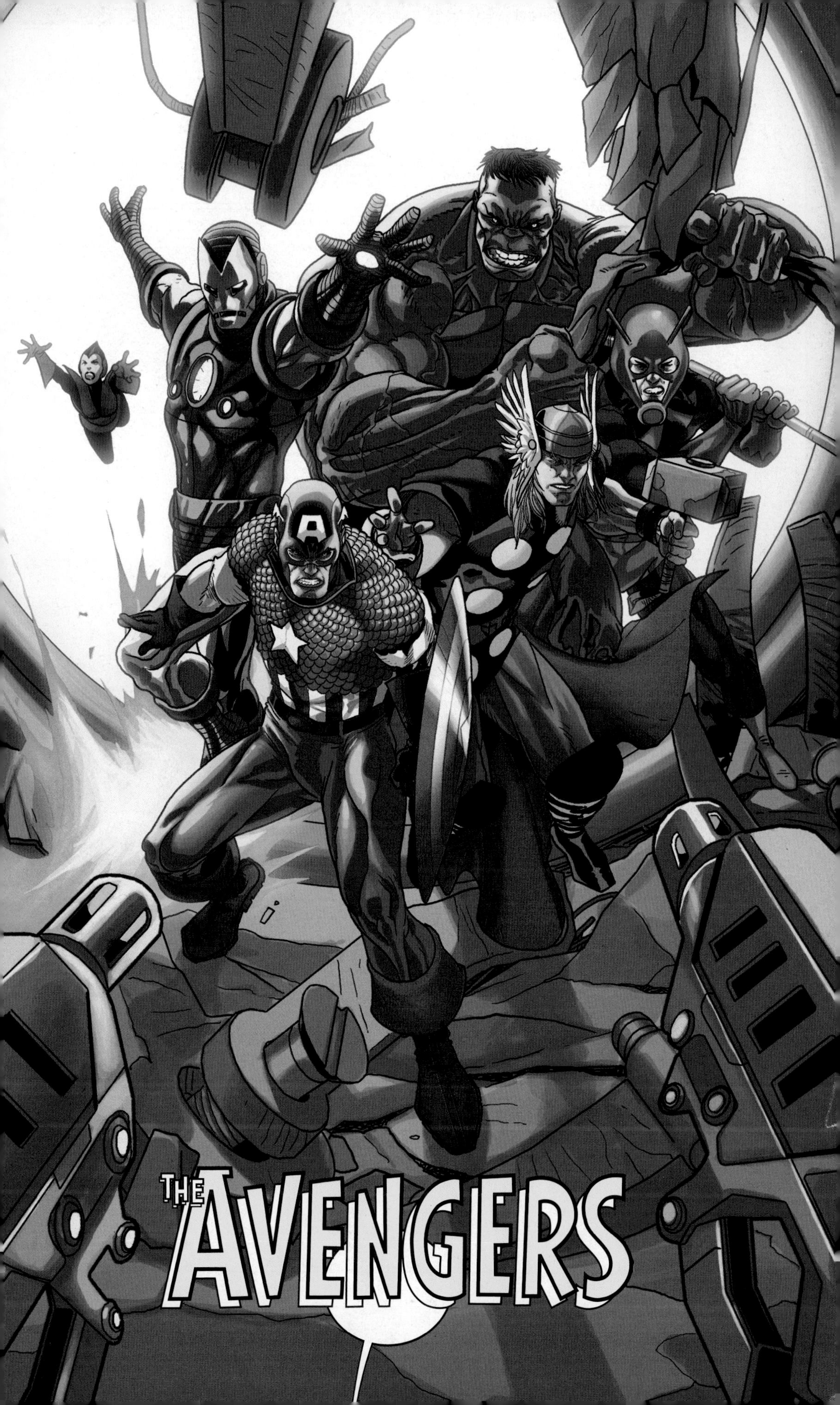
THE AVENGERS

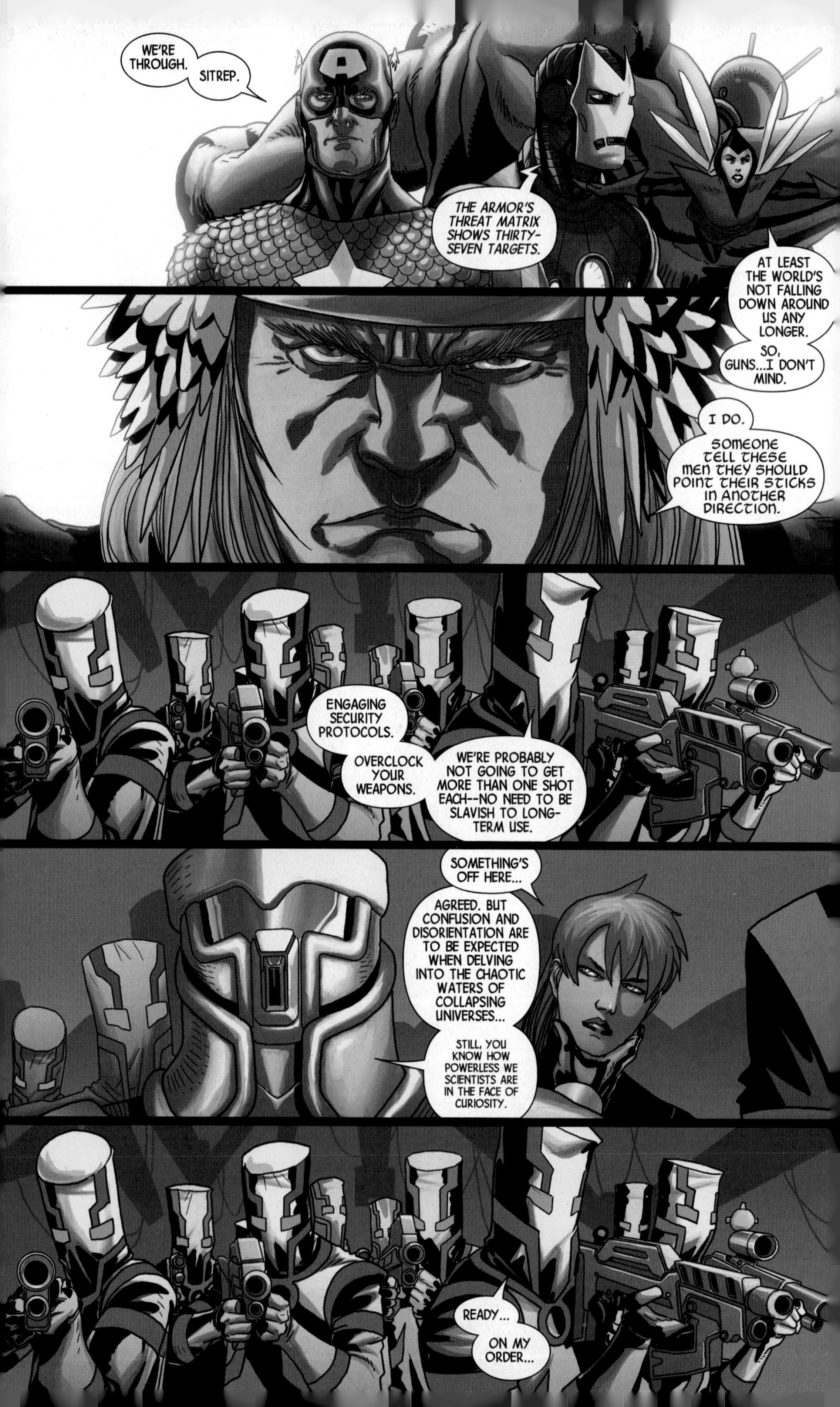
WE'RE THROUGH.
SITREP.
THE ARMOR'S THREAT MATRIX SHOWS THIRTY-SEVEN TARGETS.
AT LEAST THE WORLD'S NOT FALLING DOWN AROUND US ANY LONGER.
SO, GUNS...I DON'T MIND.
I DO.
SOMEONE TELL THESE MEN THEY SHOULD POINT THEIR STICKS IN ANOTHER DIRECTION.
ENGAGING SECURITY PROTOCOLS.
OVERCLOCK YOUR WEAPONS.
WE'RE PROBABLY NOT GOING TO GET MORE THAN ONE SHOT EACH--NO NEED TO BE SLAVISH TO LONG-TERM USE.
SOMETHING'S OFF HERE...
AGREED. BUT CONFUSION AND DISORIENTATION ARE TO BE EXPECTED WHEN DELVING INTO THE CHAOTIC WATERS OF COLLAPSING UNIVERSES...
STILL, YOU KNOW HOW POWERLESS WE SCIENTISTS ARE IN THE FACE OF CURIOSITY.
READY...
ON MY ORDER...

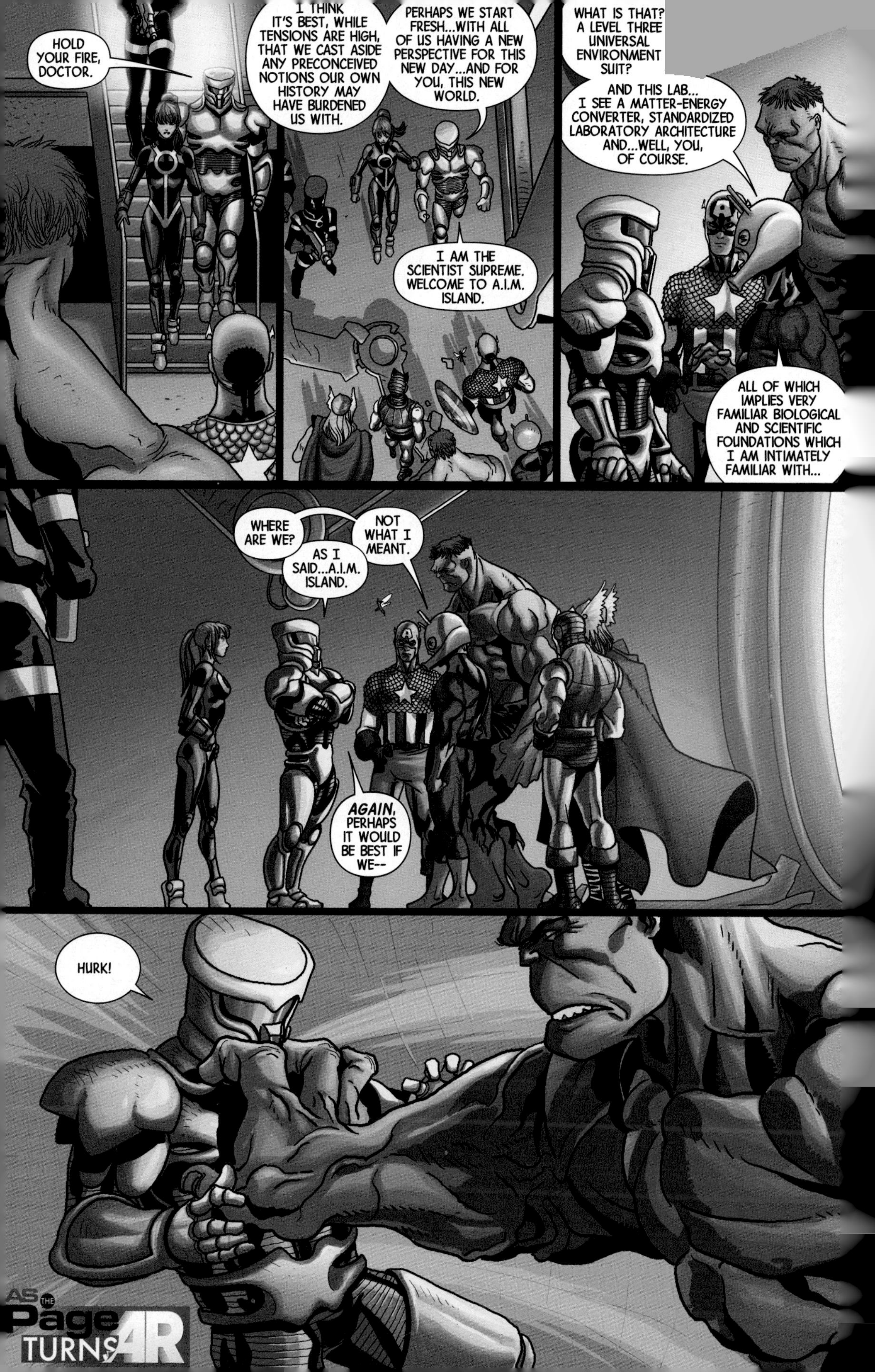
HOLD YOUR FIRE, DOCTOR.
I THINK IT'S BEST, WHILE TENSIONS ARE HIGH, THAT WE CAST ASIDE ANY PRECONCEIVED NOTIONS OUR OWN HISTORY MAY HAVE BURDENED US WITH.
PERHAPS WE START FRESH...WITH ALL OF US HAVING A NEW PERSPECTIVE FOR THIS NEW DAY...AND FOR YOU, THIS NEW WORLD.
I AM THE SCIENTIST SUPREME. WELCOME TO A.I.M. ISLAND.
WHAT IS THAT? A LEVEL THREE UNIVERSAL ENVIRONMENT SUIT?
AND THIS LAB... I SEE A MATTER-ENERGY CONVERTER, STANDARDIZED LABORATORY ARCHITECTURE AND...WELL, YOU, OF COURSE.
ALL OF WHICH IMPLIES VERY FAMILIAR BIOLOGICAL AND SCIENTIFIC FOUNDATIONS WHICH I AM INTIMATELY FAMILIAR WITH...
WHERE ARE WE?
AS I SAID...A.I.M. ISLAND.
NOT WHAT I MEANT.
AGAIN, PERHAPS IT WOULD BE BEST IF WE--
HURK!

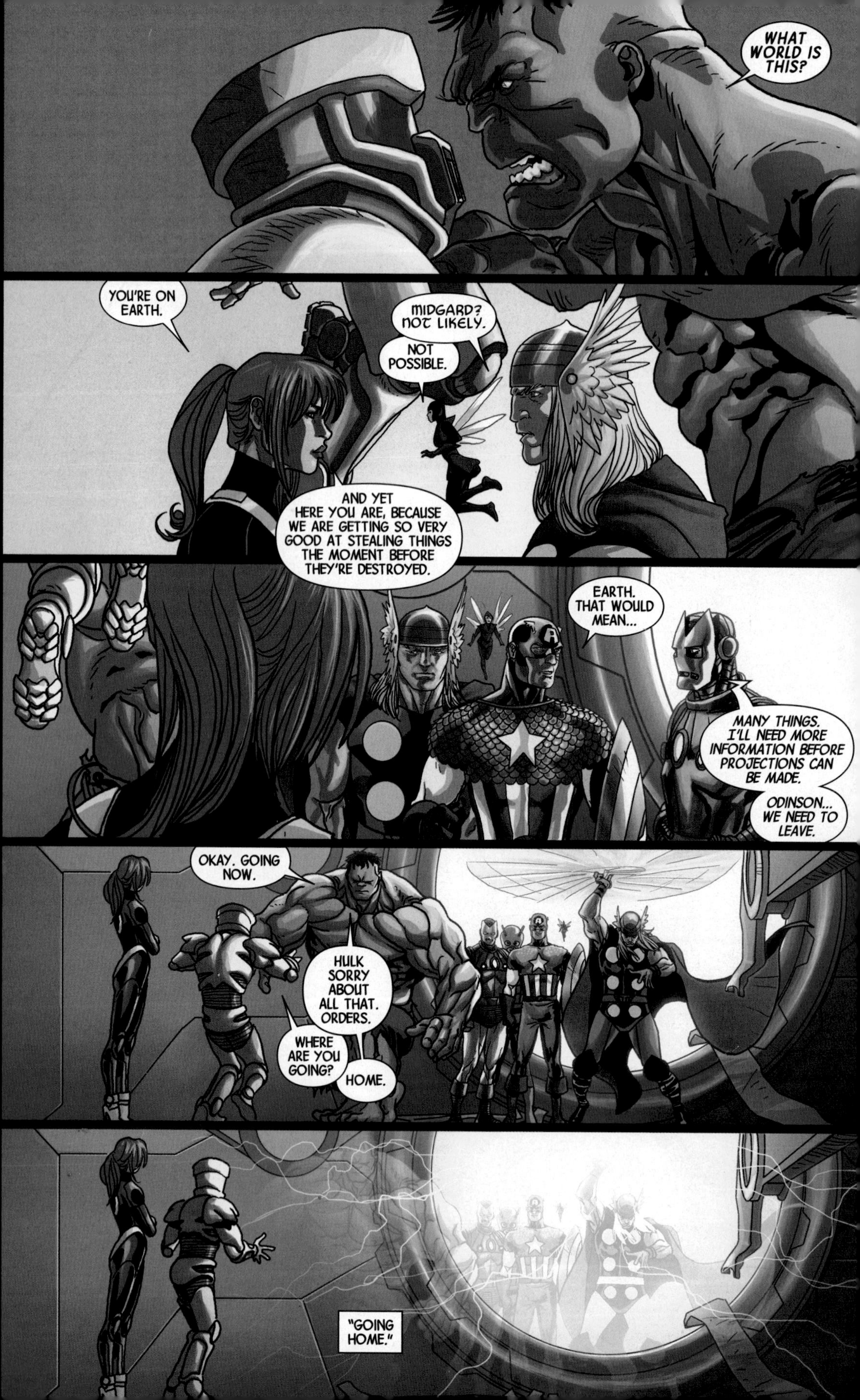
WHAT WORLD IS THIS?
YOU'RE ON EARTH.
MIDGARD? NOT LIKELY.
NOT POSSIBLE.
AND YET HERE YOU ARE, BECAUSE WE ARE GETTING SO VERY GOOD AT STEALING THINGS THE MOMENT BEFORE THEY'RE DESTROYED.
EARTH. THAT WOULD MEAN...
MANY THINGS. I'LL NEED MORE INFORMATION BEFORE PROJECTIONS CAN BE MADE.
ODINSON... WE NEED TO LEAVE.
OKAY. GOING NOW.
HULK SORRY ABOUT ALL THAT. ORDERS.
WHERE ARE YOU GOING?
HOME.
"GOING HOME."

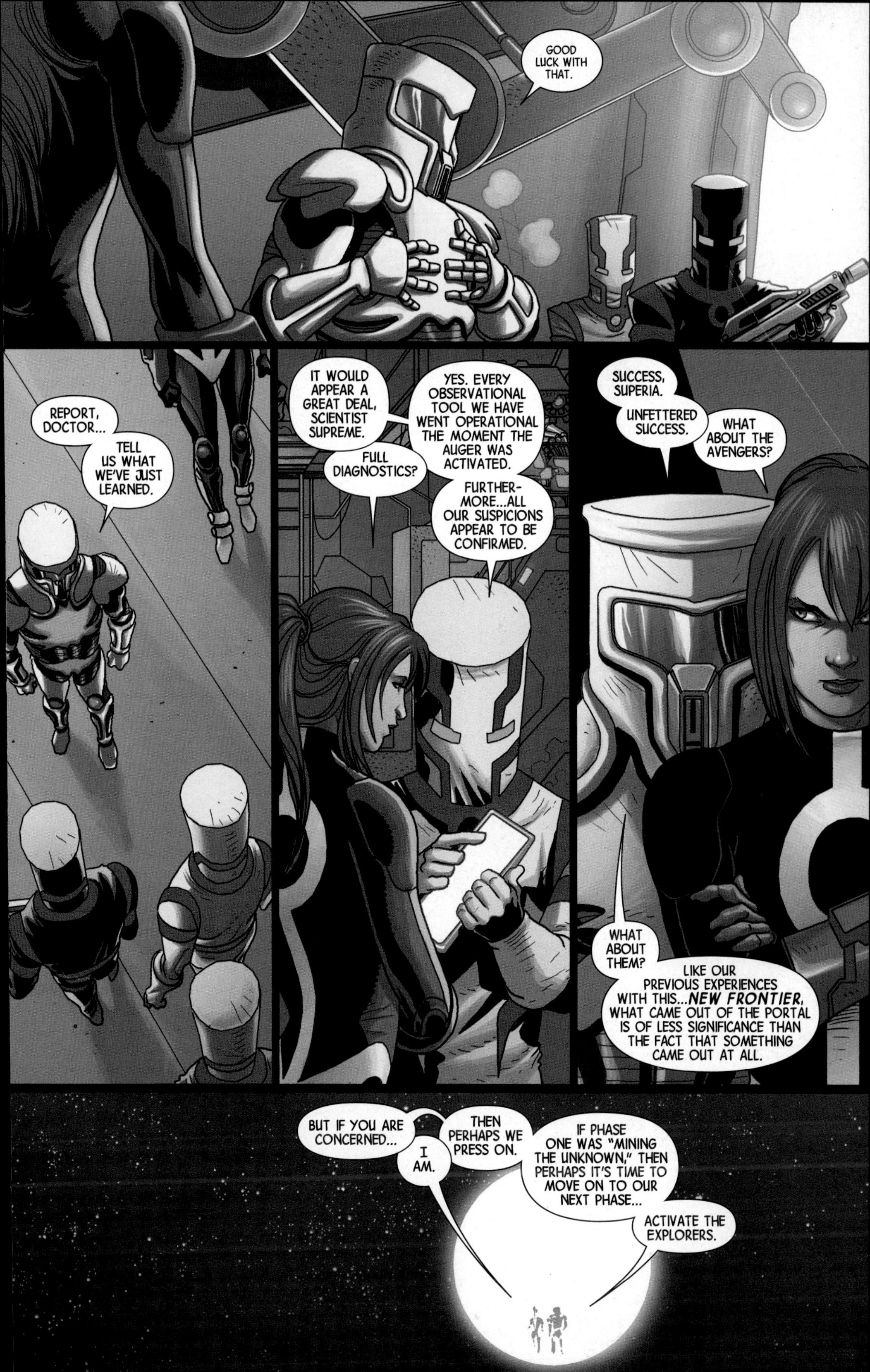
GOOD LUCK WITH THAT.
REPORT, DOCTOR...
TELL US WHAT WE'VE JUST LEARNED.
IT WOULD APPEAR A GREAT DEAL, SCIENTIST SUPREME.
FULL DIAGNOSTICS?
YES. EVERY OBSERVATIONAL TOOL WE HAVE WENT OPERATIONAL THE MOMENT THE AUGER WAS ACTIVATED.
FURTHERMORE...ALL OUR SUSPICIONS APPEAR TO BE CONFIRMED.
SUCCESS, SUPERIA.
UNFETTERED SUCCESS.
WHAT ABOUT THE AVENGERS?
WHAT ABOUT THEM?
LIKE OUR PREVIOUS EXPERIENCES WITH THIS...NEW FRONTIER, WHAT CAME OUT OF THE PORTAL IS OF LESS SIGNIFICANCE THAN THE FACT THAT SOMETHING CAME OUT AT ALL.
BUT IF YOU ARE CONCERNED...
I AM.
THEN PERHAPS WE PRESS ON.
IF PHASE ONE WAS "MINING THE UNKNOWN," THEN PERHAPS IT'S TIME TO MOVE ON TO OUR NEXT PHASE...
ACTIVATE THE EXPLORERS.

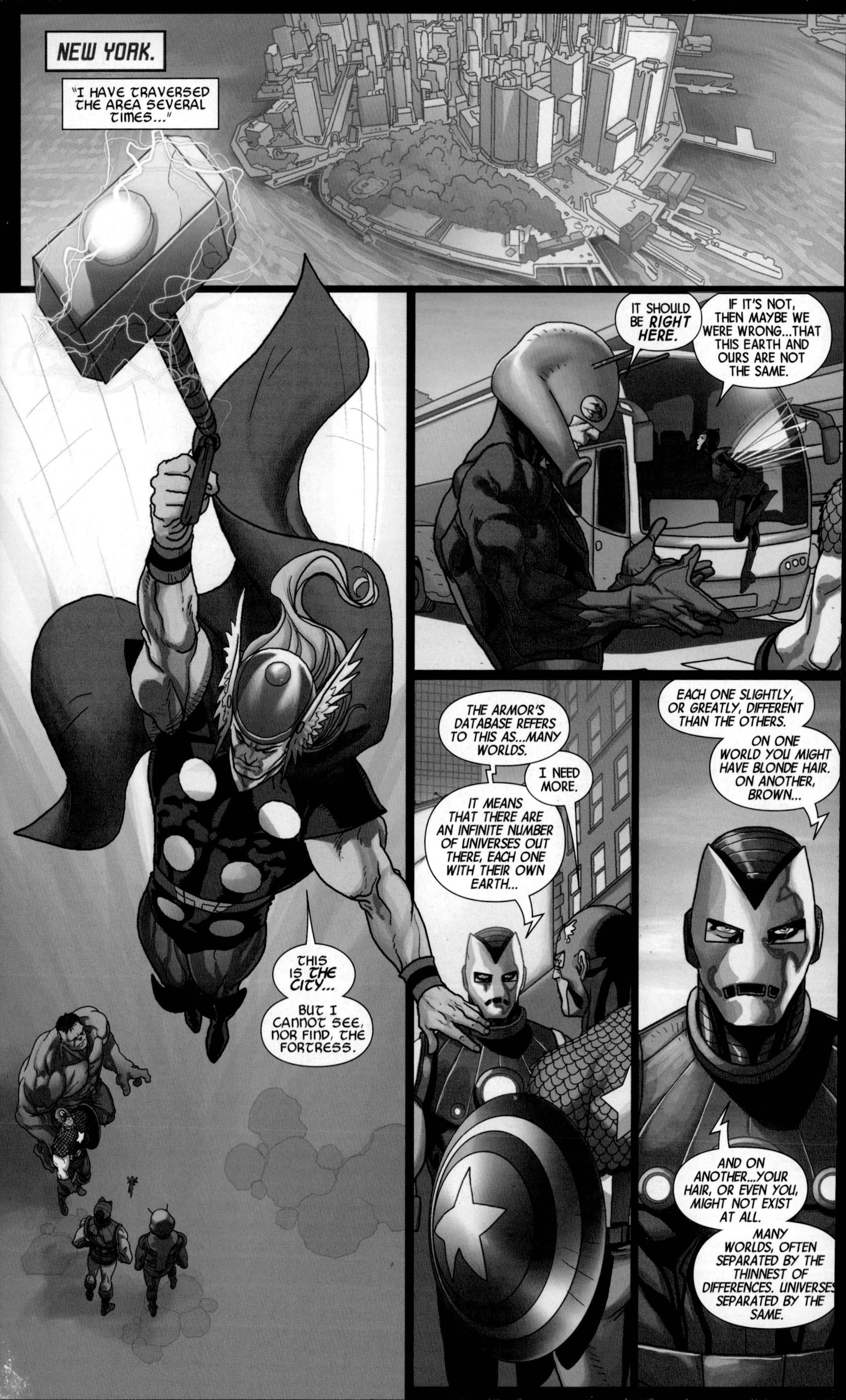
NEW YORK.
"I HAVE TRAVERSED THE AREA SEVERAL TIMES..."
THIS IS THE CITY...
BUT I CANNOT SEE, NOR FIND, THE FORTRESS.
IT SHOULD BE RIGHT HERE.
IF IT'S NOT, THEN MAYBE WE WERE WRONG...THAT THIS EARTH AND OURS ARE NOT THE SAME.
THE ARMOR'S DATABASE REFERS TO THIS AS...MANY WORLDS.
I NEED MORE.
IT MEANS THAT THERE ARE AN INFINITE NUMBER OF UNIVERSES OUT THERE, EACH ONE WITH THEIR OWN EARTH...
EACH ONE SLIGHTLY, OR GREATLY, DIFFERENT THAN THE OTHERS.
ON ONE WORLD YOU MIGHT HAVE BLONDE HAIR. ON ANOTHER, BROWN...
AND ON ANOTHER...YOUR HAIR, OR EVEN YOU, MIGHT NOT EXIST AT ALL.
MANY WORLDS, OFTEN SEPARATED BY THE THINNEST OF DIFFERENCES. UNIVERSES SEPARATED BY THE SAME.

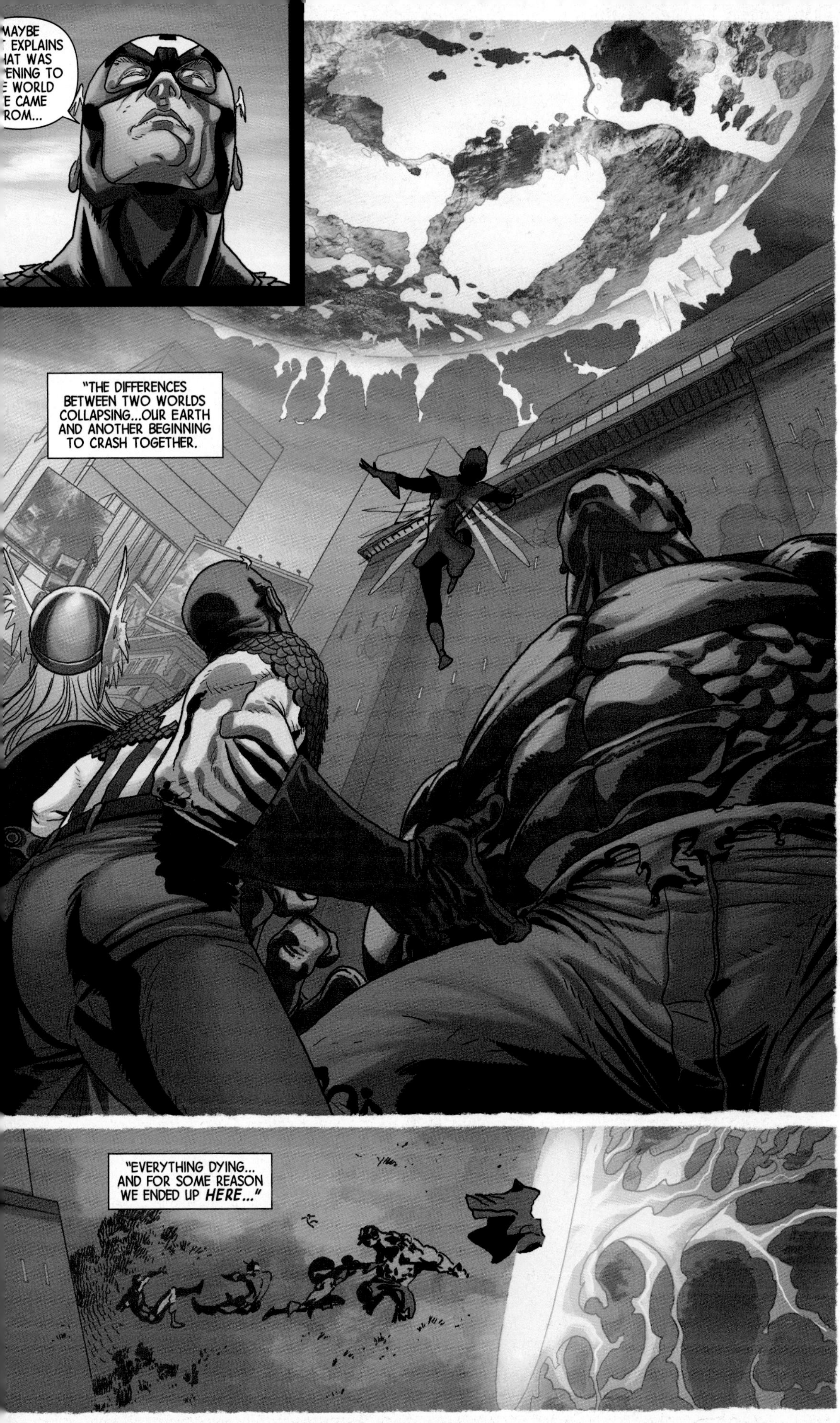

MAYBE T EXPLAINS IAT WAS ENING TO E WORLD E CAME ROM...
"THE DIFFERENCES BETWEEN TWO WORLDS COLLAPSING...OUR EARTH AND ANOTHER BEGINNING TO CRASH TOGETHER.
"EVERYTHING DYING... AND FOR SOME REASON WE ENDED UP *HERE*..."

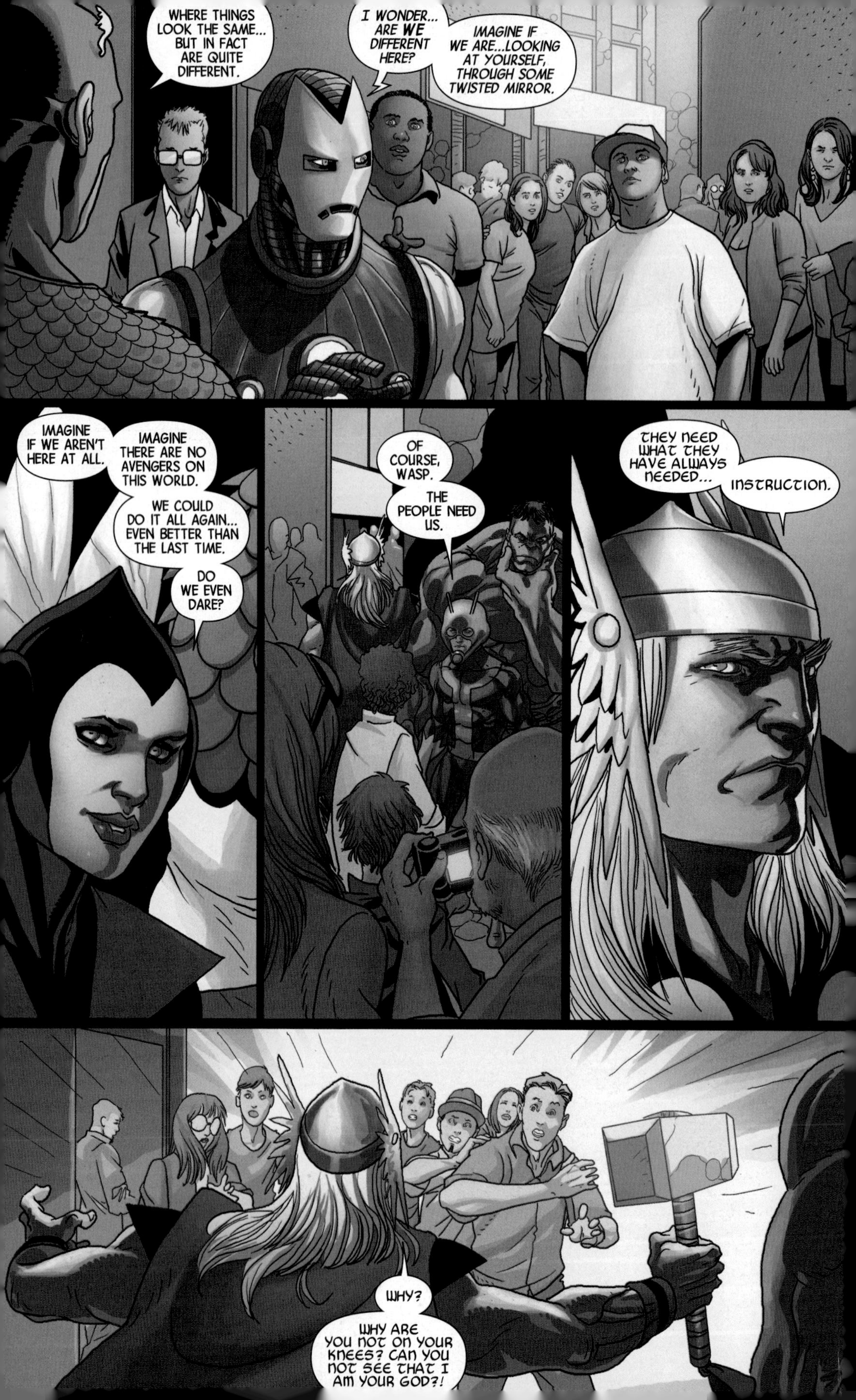
WHERE THINGS LOOK THE SAME... BUT IN FACT ARE QUITE DIFFERENT.
I WONDER... ARE **WE** DIFFERENT HERE?
IMAGINE IF WE ARE...LOOKING AT YOURSELF, THROUGH SOME TWISTED MIRROR.
IMAGINE IF WE AREN'T HERE AT ALL.
IMAGINE THERE ARE NO AVENGERS ON THIS WORLD.
WE COULD DO IT ALL AGAIN... EVEN BETTER THAN THE LAST TIME.
DO WE EVEN DARE?
OF COURSE, WASP.
THE PEOPLE NEED US.
THEY NEED WHAT THEY HAVE ALWAYS NEEDED...
INSTRUCTION.
WHY?
WHY ARE YOU NOT ON YOUR KNEES? CAN YOU NOT SEE THAT I AM YOUR GOD?!

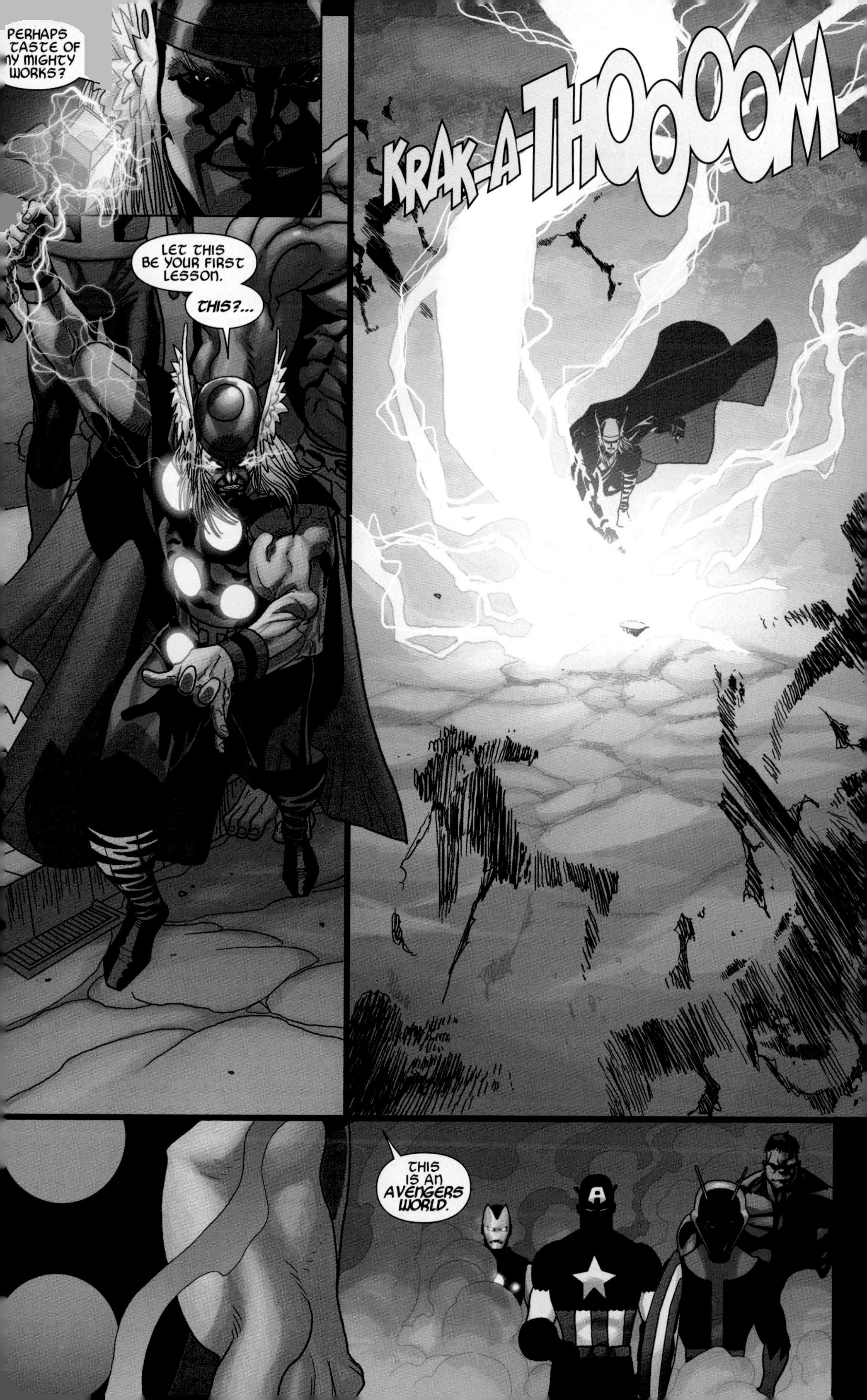
PERHAPS
TASTE OF
MY MIGHTY
WORKS?
LET THIS
BE YOUR FIRST
LESSON.
THIS?...
KRAK-A-THOOOOOM
THIS
IS AN
AVENGERS
WORLD.

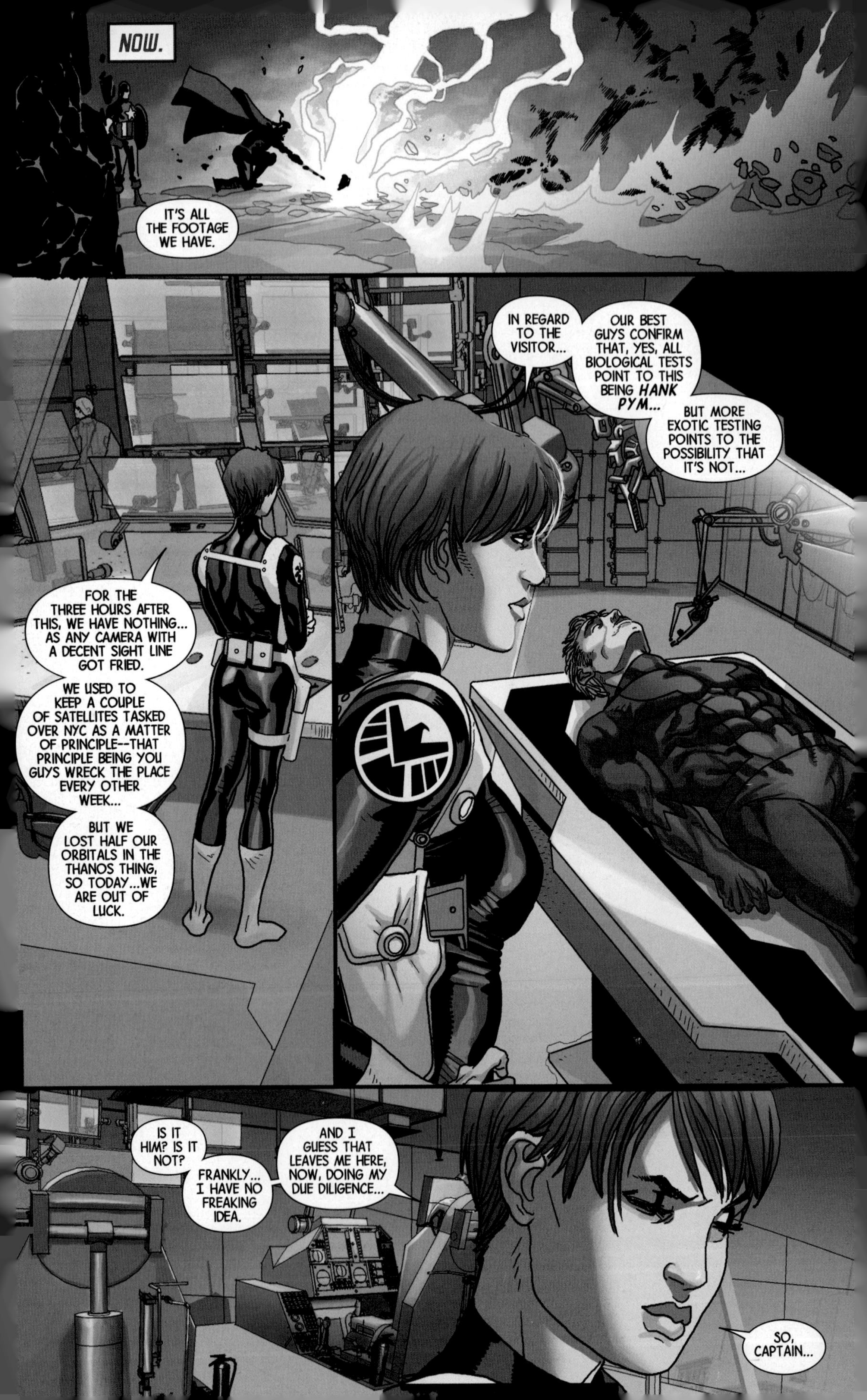

NOW.
IT'S ALL THE FOOTAGE WE HAVE.
FOR THE THREE HOURS AFTER THIS, WE HAVE NOTHING... AS ANY CAMERA WITH A DECENT SIGHT LINE GOT FRIED.
WE USED TO KEEP A COUPLE OF SATELLITES TASKED OVER NYC AS A MATTER OF PRINCIPLE--THAT PRINCIPLE BEING YOU GUYS WRECK THE PLACE EVERY OTHER WEEK...
BUT WE LOST HALF OUR ORBITALS IN THE THANOS THING, SO TODAY...WE ARE OUT OF LUCK.
IN REGARD TO THE VISITOR...
OUR BEST GUYS CONFIRM THAT, YES, ALL BIOLOGICAL TESTS POINT TO THIS BEING HANK PYM...
BUT MORE EXOTIC TESTING POINTS TO THE POSSIBILITY THAT IT'S NOT...
IS IT HIM? IS IT NOT?
FRANKLY... I HAVE NO FREAKING IDEA.
AND I GUESS THAT LEAVES ME HERE, NOW, DOING MY DUE DILIGENCE...
SO, CAPTAIN...

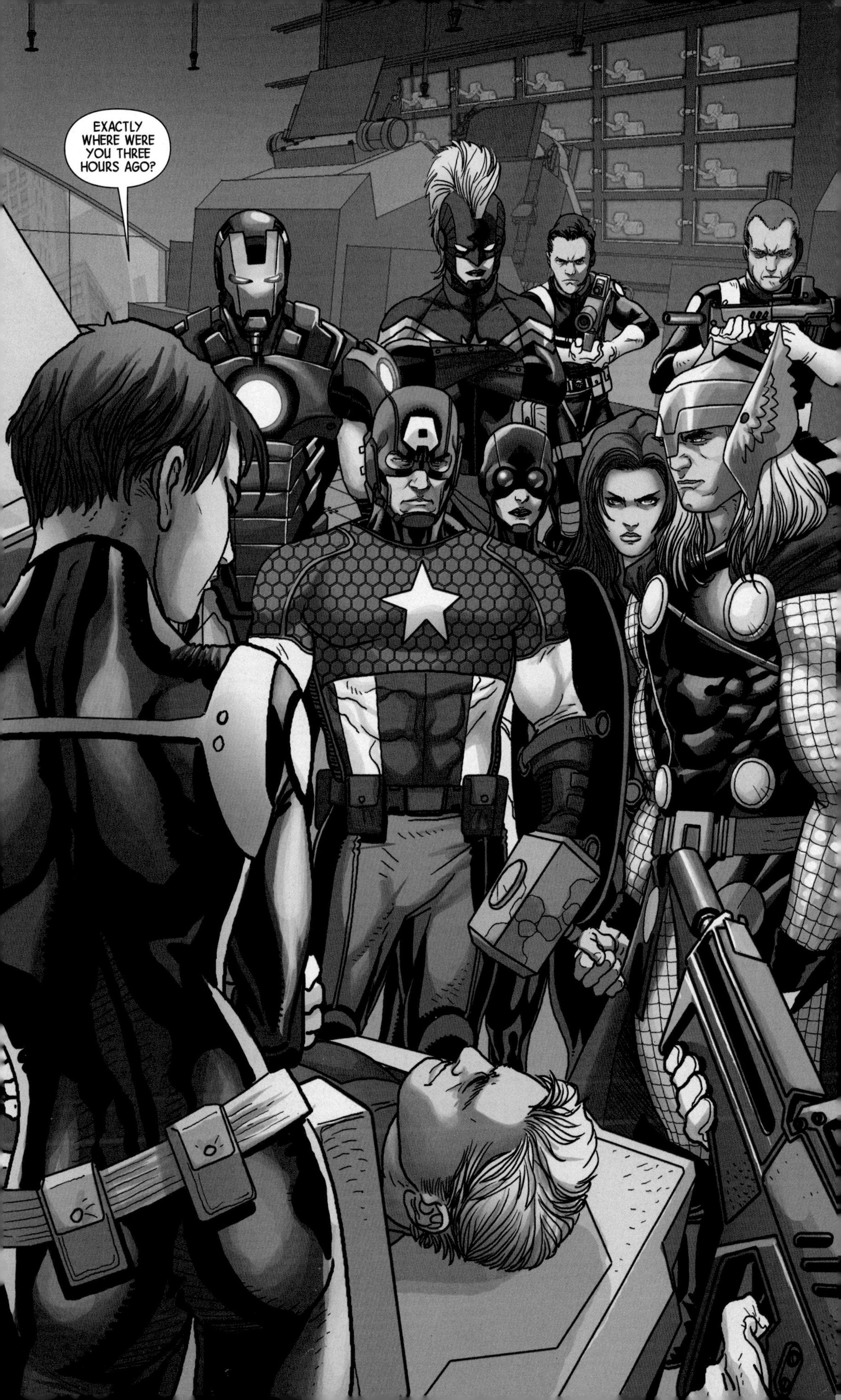
EXACTLY WHERE WERE YOU THREE HOURS AGO?

"LOOK AROUND...THERE'S NO WAY OUT

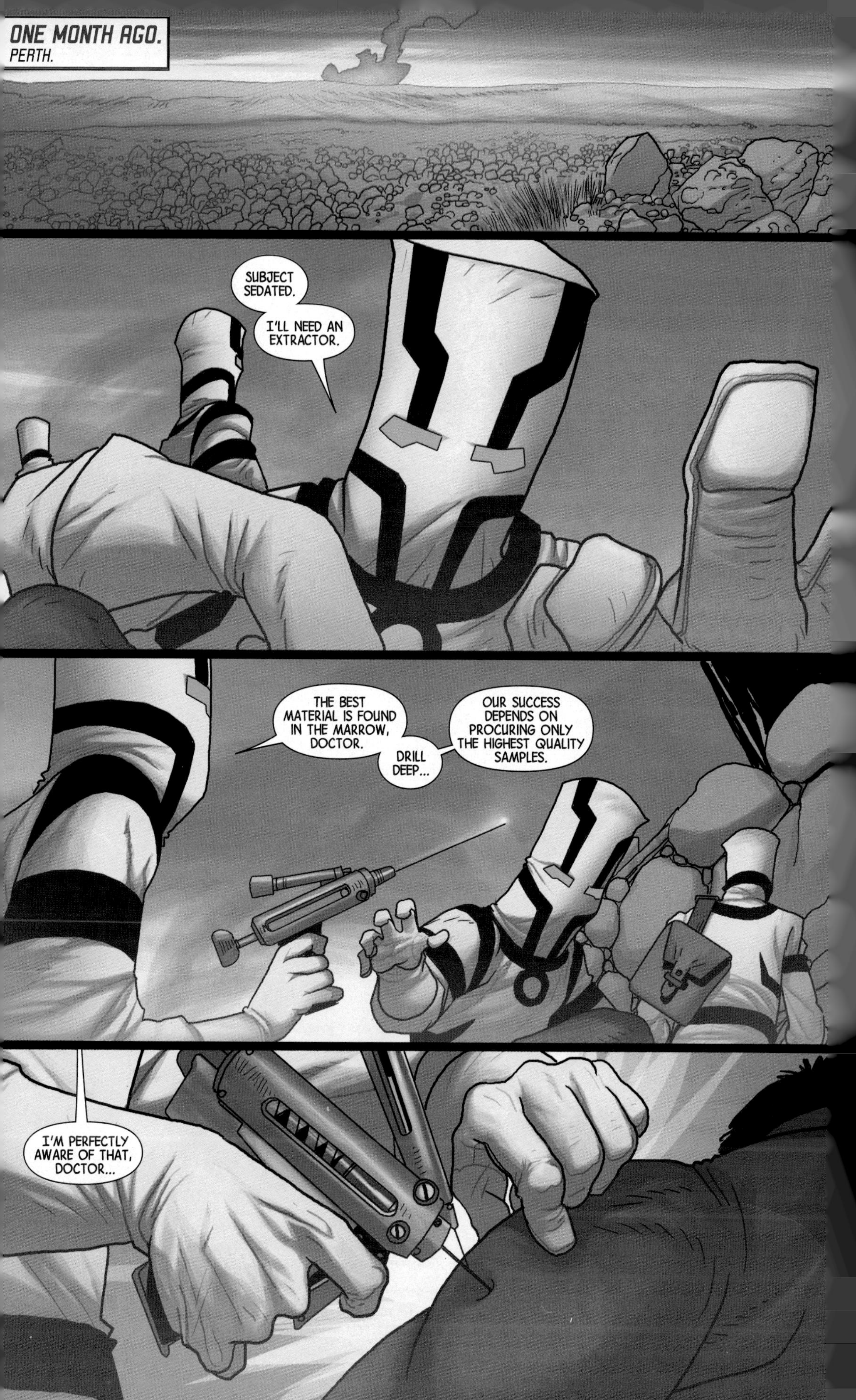
ONE MONTH AGO.
PERTH.
SUBJECT SEDATED.
I'LL NEED AN EXTRACTOR.
THE BEST MATERIAL IS FOUND IN THE MARROW, DOCTOR.
DRILL DEEP...
OUR SUCCESS DEPENDS ON PROCURING ONLY THE HIGHEST QUALITY SAMPLES.
I'M PERFECTLY AWARE OF THAT, DOCTOR...

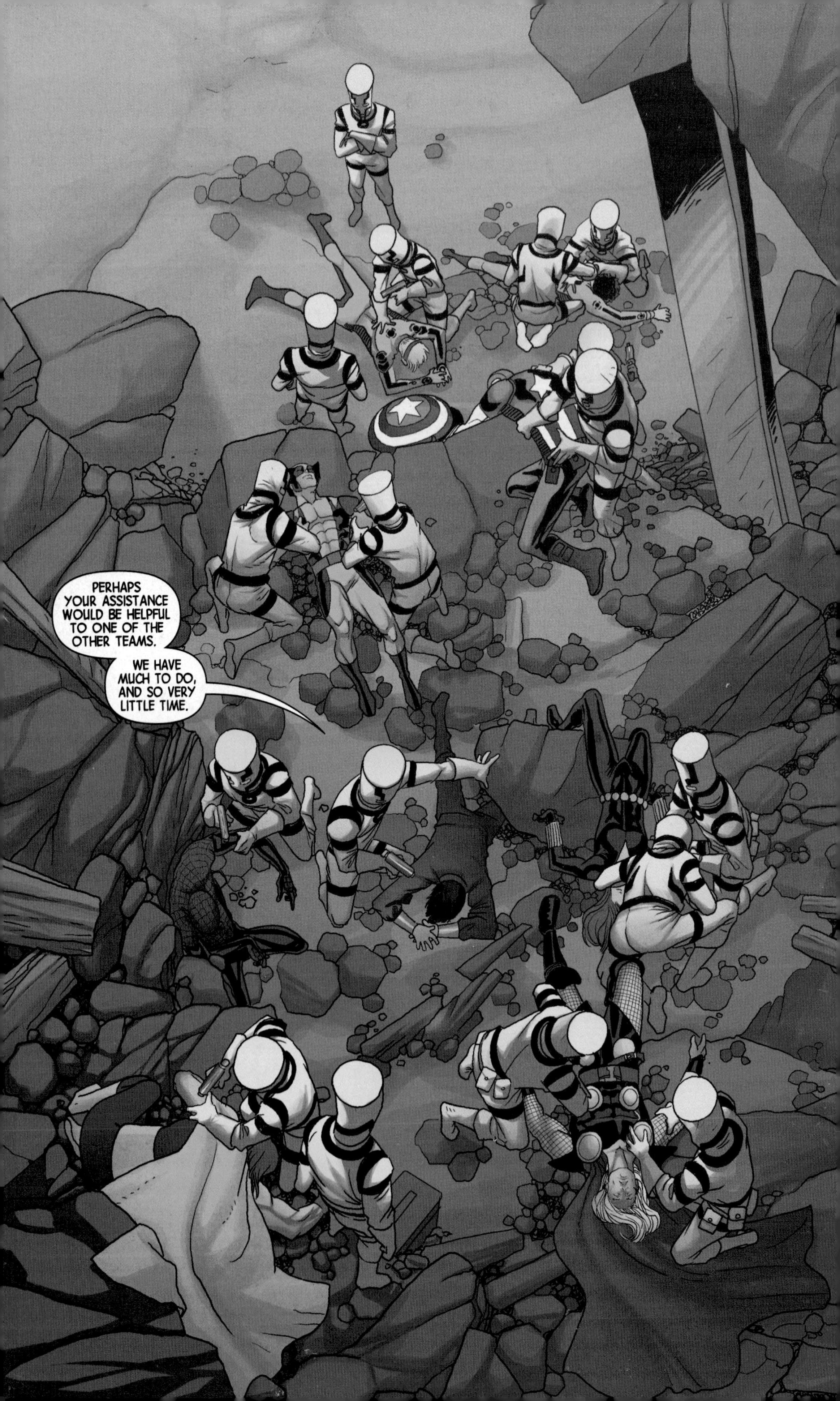
PERHAPS YOUR ASSISTANCE WOULD BE HELPFUL TO ONE OF THE OTHER TEAMS.
WE HAVE MUCH TO DO, AND SO VERY LITTLE TIME.

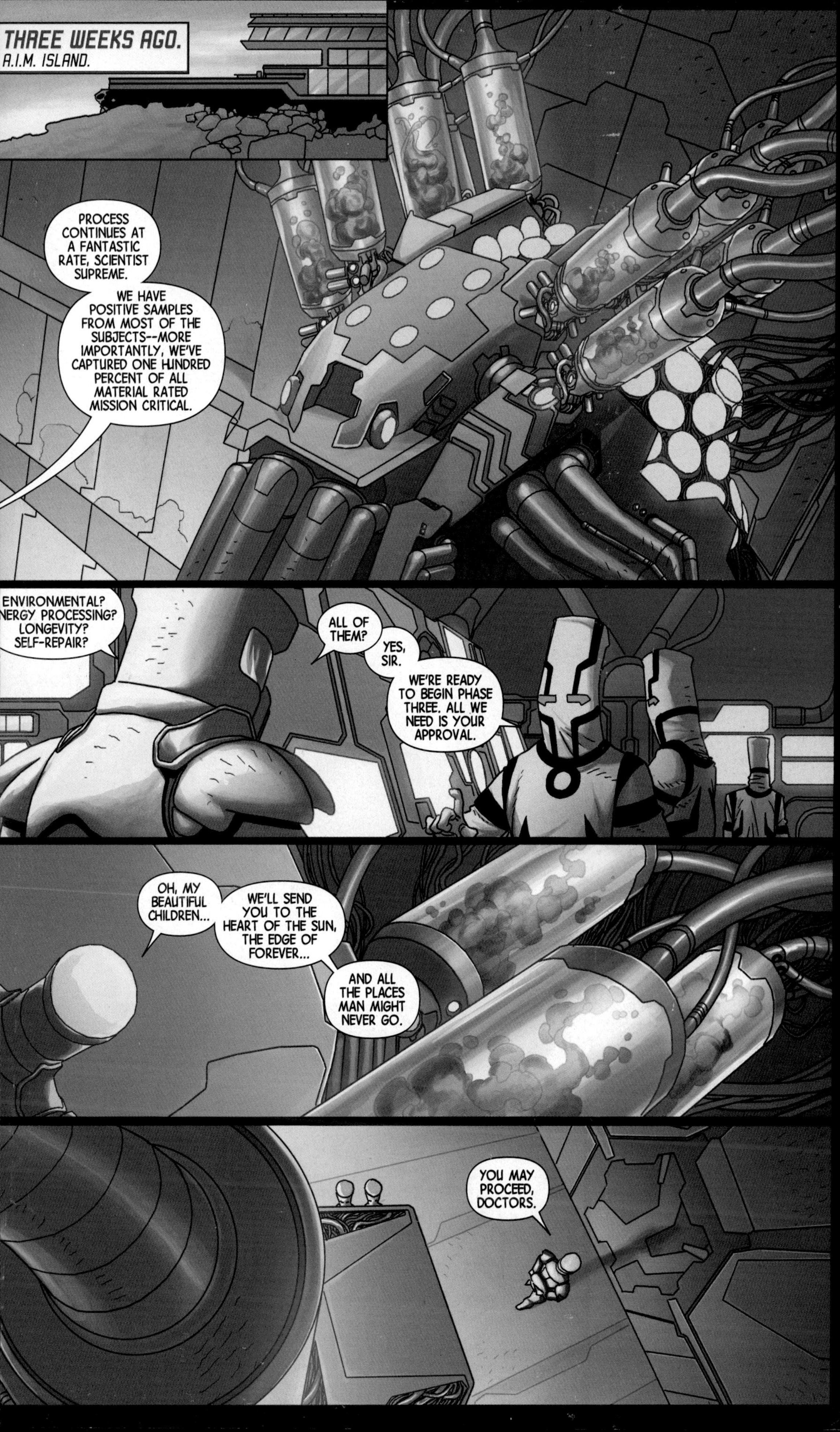
THREE WEEKS AGO.
A.I.M. ISLAND.
PROCESS CONTINUES AT A FANTASTIC RATE, SCIENTIST SUPREME.
WE HAVE POSITIVE SAMPLES FROM MOST OF THE SUBJECTS--MORE IMPORTANTLY, WE'VE CAPTURED ONE HUNDRED PERCENT OF ALL MATERIAL RATED MISSION CRITICAL.
ENVIRONMENTAL? ENERGY PROCESSING? LONGEVITY? SELF-REPAIR?
ALL OF THEM?
YES, SIR.
WE'RE READY TO BEGIN PHASE THREE. ALL WE NEED IS YOUR APPROVAL.
OH, MY BEAUTIFUL CHILDREN...
WE'LL SEND YOU TO THE HEART OF THE SUN, THE EDGE OF FOREVER...
AND ALL THE PLACES MAN MIGHT NEVER GO.
YOU MAY PROCEED, DOCTORS.

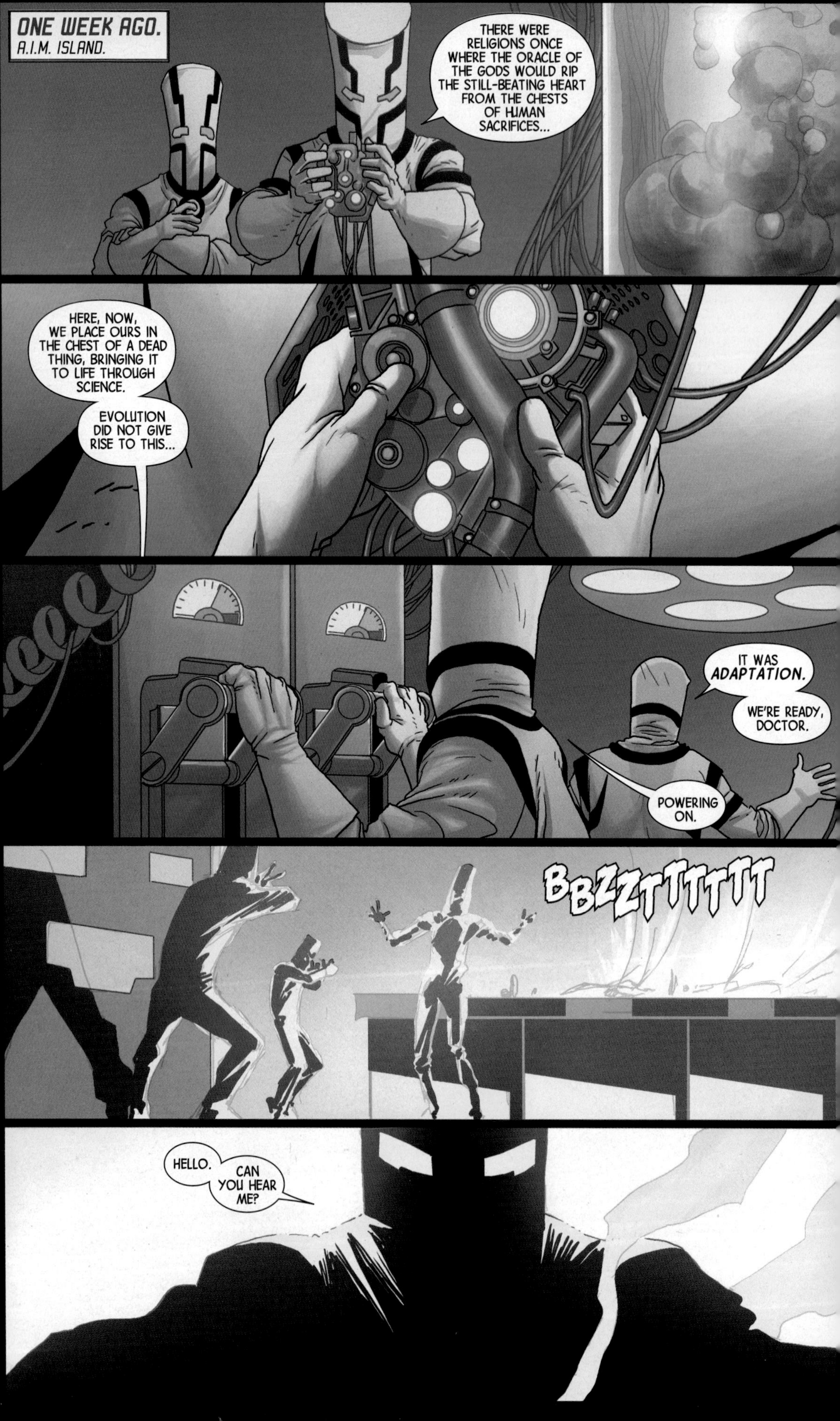
ONE WEEK AGO.
A.I.M. ISLAND.
THERE WERE RELIGIONS ONCE WHERE THE ORACLE OF THE GODS WOULD RIP THE STILL-BEATING HEART FROM THE CHESTS OF HUMAN SACRIFICES...
HERE, NOW, WE PLACE OURS IN THE CHEST OF A DEAD THING, BRINGING IT TO LIFE THROUGH SCIENCE.
EVOLUTION DID NOT GIVE RISE TO THIS...
IT WAS ADAPTATION.
WE'RE READY, DOCTOR.
POWERING ON.
BBZZTTTTTT
HELLO.
CAN YOU HEAR ME?

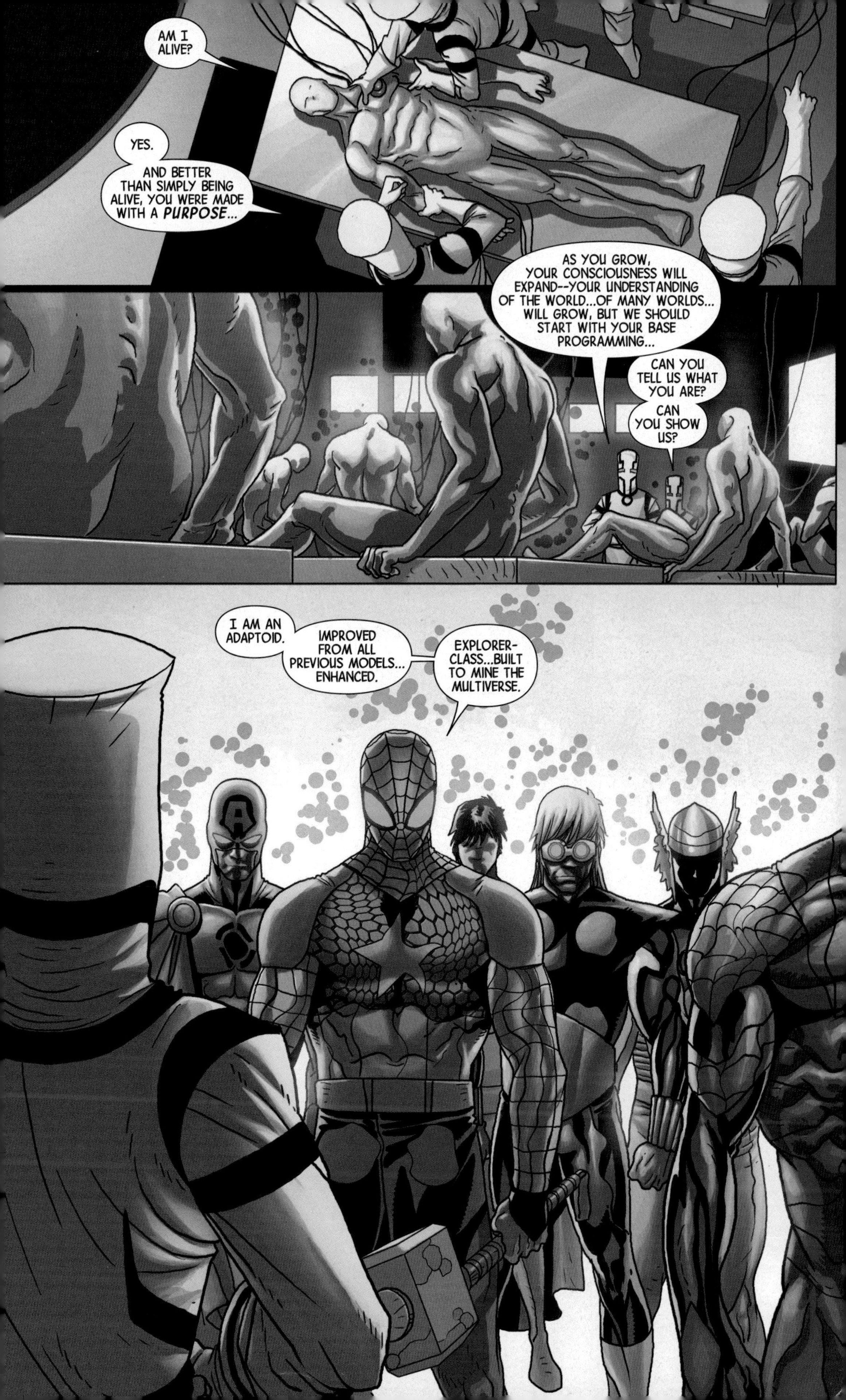
AM I ALIVE?
YES.
AND BETTER THAN SIMPLY BEING ALIVE, YOU WERE MADE WITH A *PURPOSE*...
AS YOU GROW, YOUR CONSCIOUSNESS WILL EXPAND--YOUR UNDERSTANDING OF THE WORLD...OF MANY WORLDS... WILL GROW, BUT WE SHOULD START WITH YOUR BASE PROGRAMMING...
CAN YOU TELL US WHAT YOU ARE?
CAN YOU SHOW US?
I AM AN ADAPTOID.
IMPROVED FROM ALL PREVIOUS MODELS... ENHANCED.
EXPLORER-CLASS...BUILT TO MINE THE MULTIVERSE.

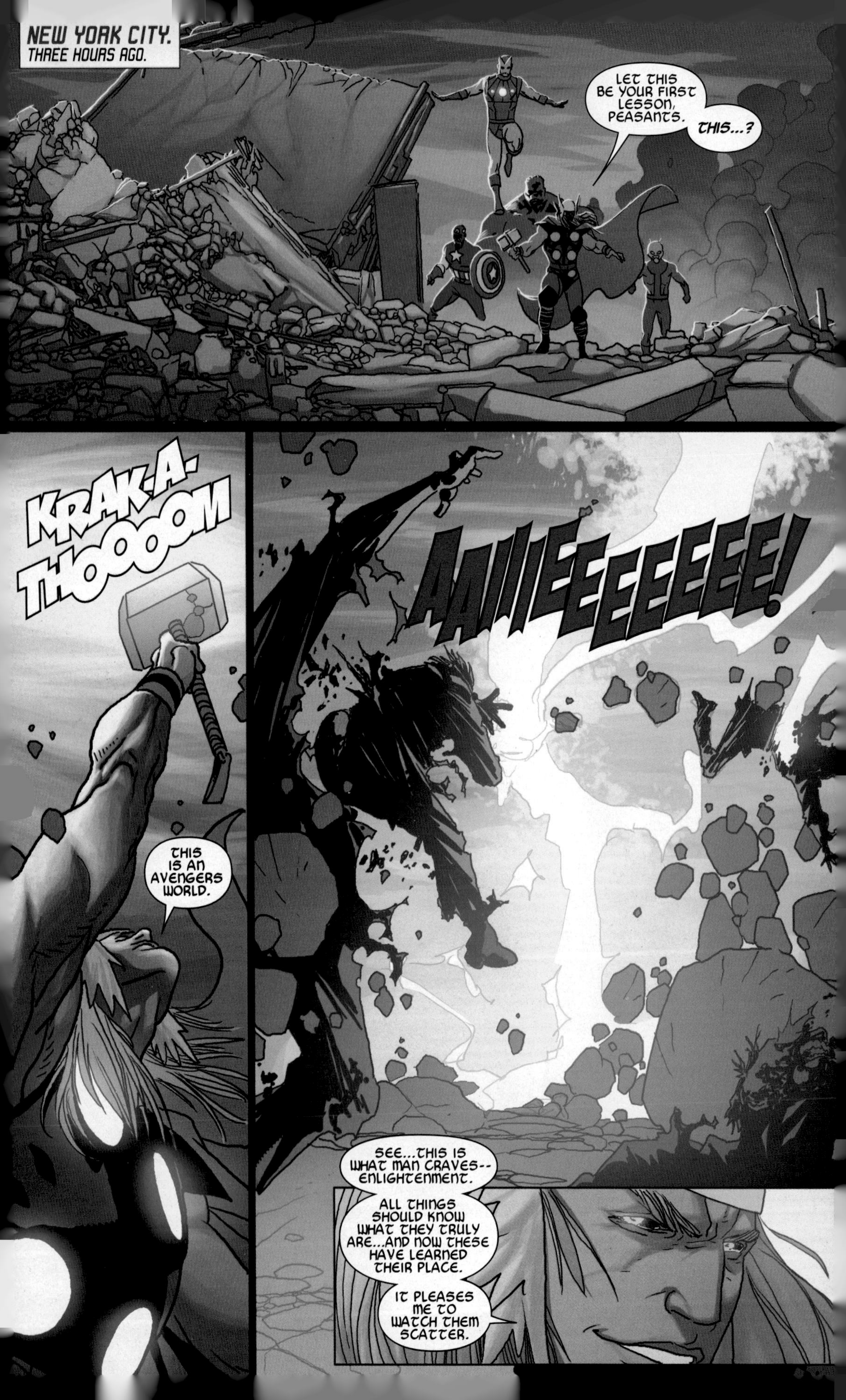

NEW YORK CITY.
THREE HOURS AGO.
LET THIS BE YOUR FIRST LESSON, PEASANTS.
THIS...?
KRAK-A-THOOOOM
THIS IS AN AVENGERS WORLD.
AAIIIEEEEEEE!
SEE...THIS IS WHAT MAN CRAVES--ENLIGHTENMENT.
ALL THINGS SHOULD KNOW WHAT THEY TRULY ARE...AND NOW THESE HAVE LEARNED THEIR PLACE.
IT PLEASES ME TO WATCH THEM SCATTER.

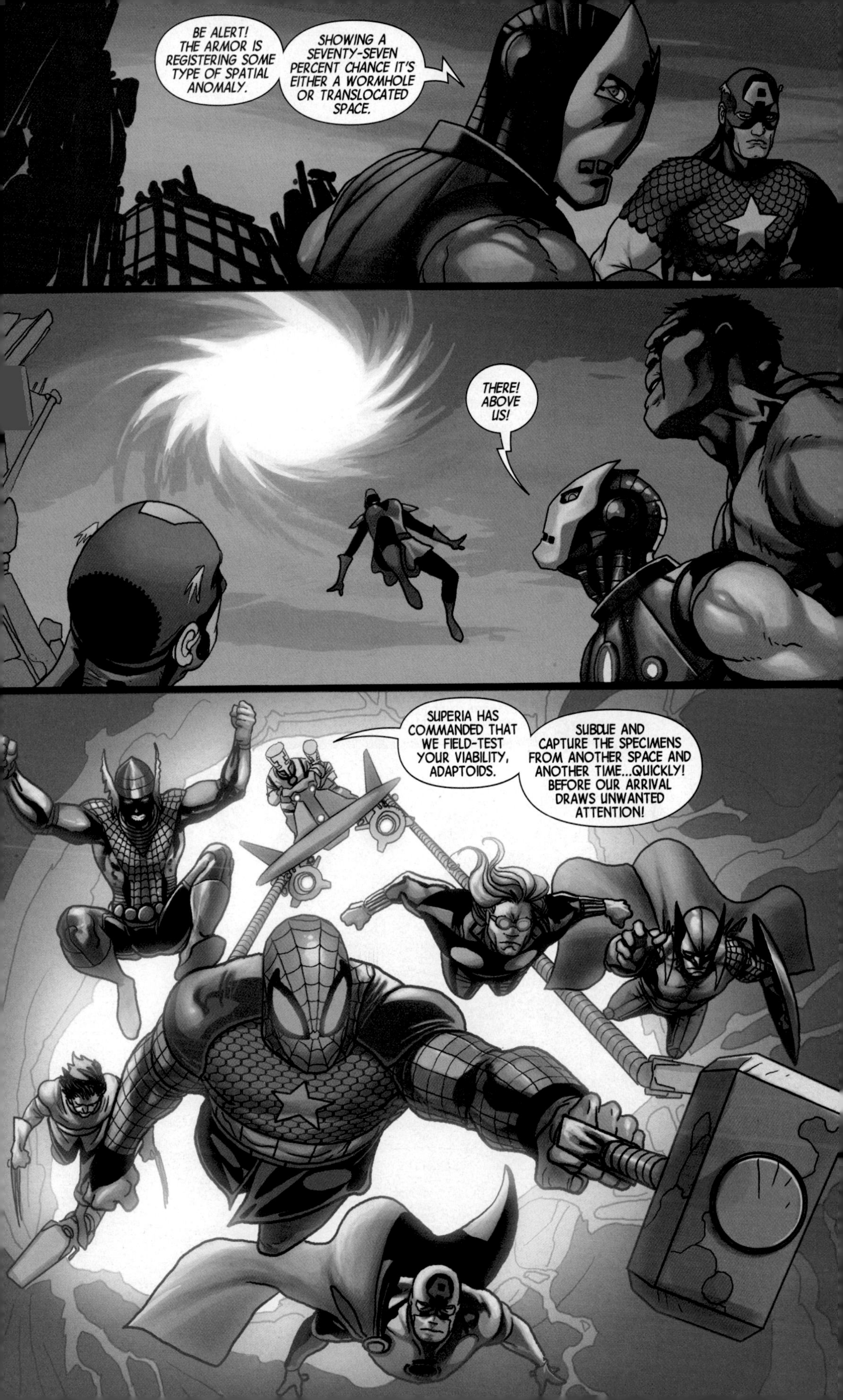
BE ALERT! THE ARMOR IS REGISTERING SOME TYPE OF SPATIAL ANOMALY.
SHOWING A SEVENTY-SEVEN PERCENT CHANCE IT'S EITHER A WORMHOLE OR TRANSLOCATED SPACE.
THERE! ABOVE US!
SUPERIA HAS COMMANDED THAT WE FIELD-TEST YOUR VIABILITY, ADAPTOIDS.
SUBDUE AND CAPTURE THE SPECIMENS FROM ANOTHER SPACE AND ANOTHER TIME...QUICKLY! BEFORE OUR ARRIVAL DRAWS UNWANTED ATTENTION!

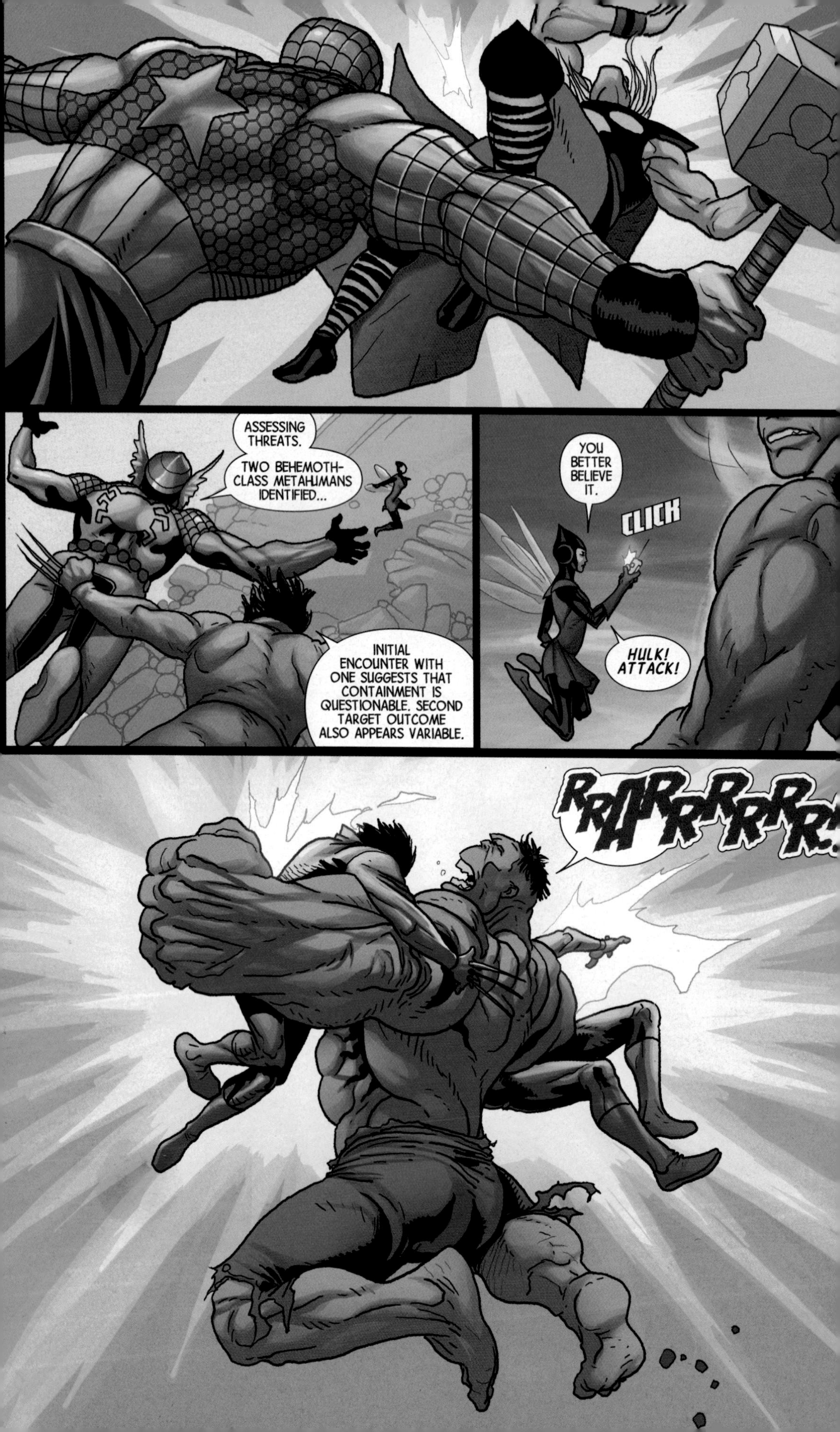
ASSESSING THREATS.
TWO BEHEMOTH-CLASS METAHUMANS IDENTIFIED...
INITIAL ENCOUNTER WITH ONE SUGGESTS THAT CONTAINMENT IS QUESTIONABLE. SECOND TARGET OUTCOME ALSO APPEARS VARIABLE.
YOU BETTER BELIEVE IT.
CLICK
HULK! ATTACK!
RRARRRRRRR

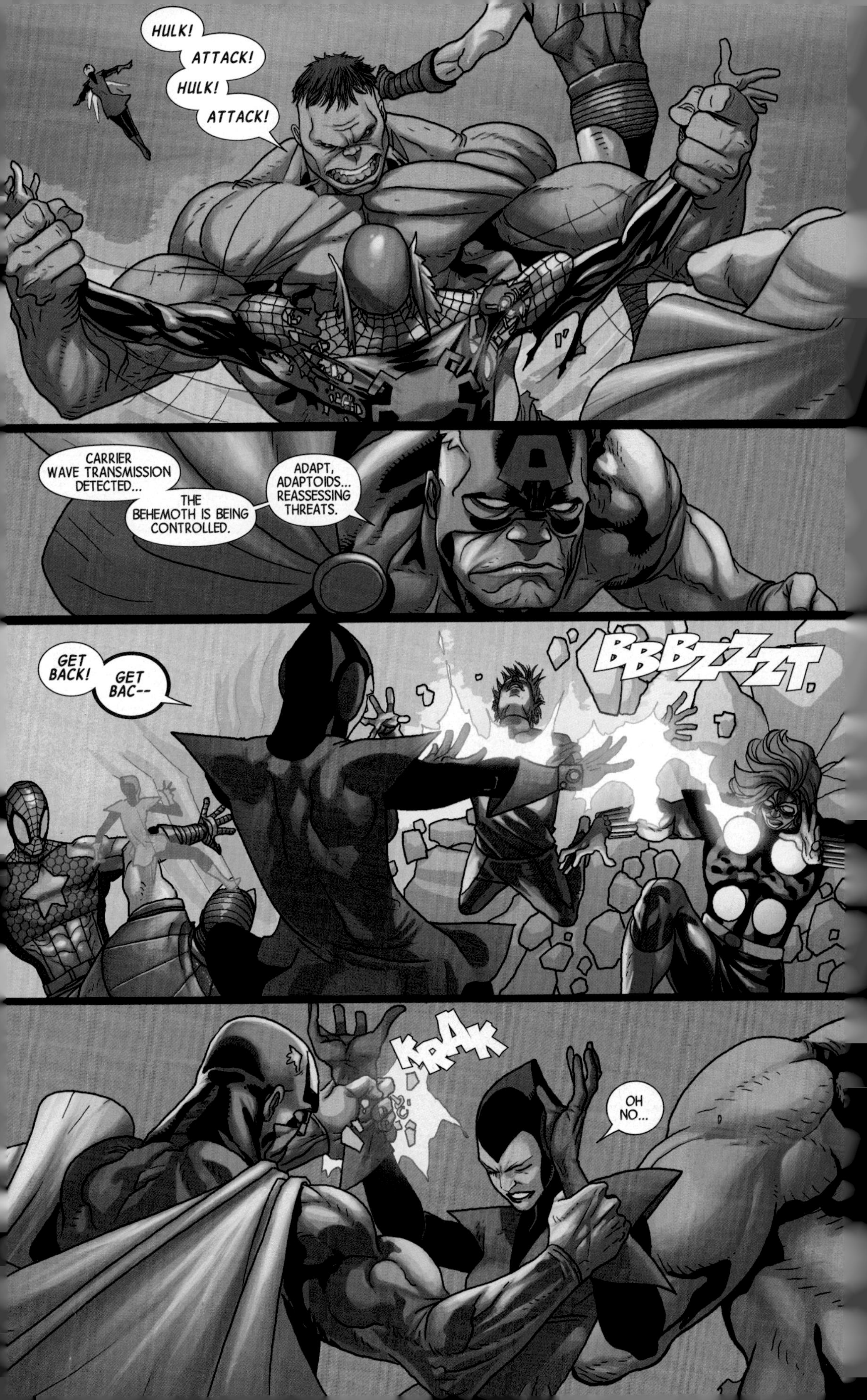
HULK!
ATTACK!
HULK!
ATTACK!
CARRIER WAVE TRANSMISSION DETECTED...
THE BEHEMOTH IS BEING CONTROLLED.
ADAPT, ADAPTOIDS... REASSESSING THREATS.
GET BACK!
GET BAC--
BBBZZZT.
KRAK
OH NO...

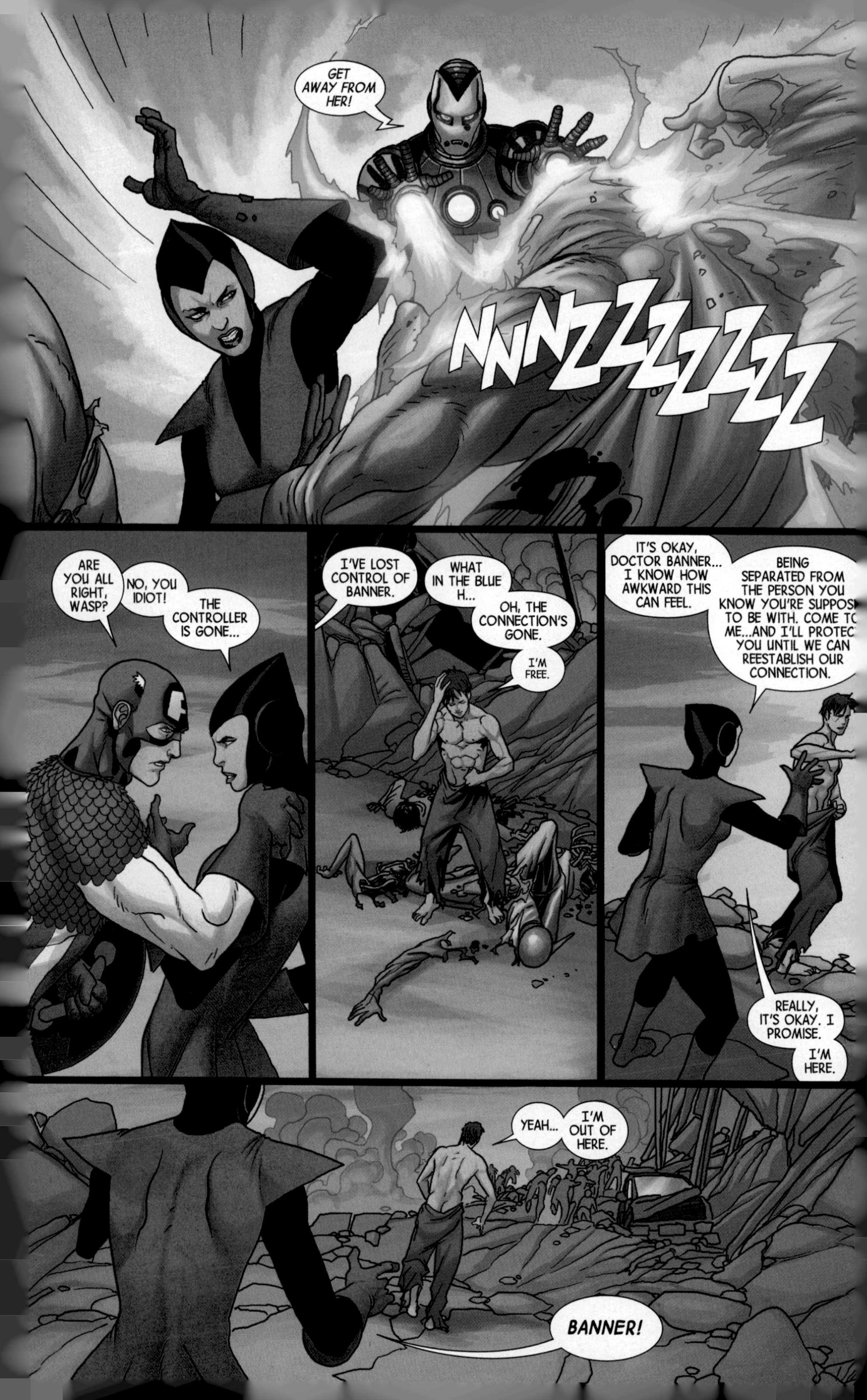
GET AWAY FROM HER!
NNNZZZZZZZZ
ARE YOU ALL RIGHT, WASP?
NO, YOU IDIOT!
THE CONTROLLER IS GONE...
I'VE LOST CONTROL OF BANNER.
WHAT IN THE BLUE H...
OH, THE CONNECTION'S GONE.
I'M FREE.
IT'S OKAY, DOCTOR BANNER... I KNOW HOW AWKWARD THIS CAN FEEL.
BEING SEPARATED FROM THE PERSON YOU KNOW YOU'RE SUPPOS
TO BE WITH. COME TO ME...AND I'LL PROTEC YOU UNTIL WE CAN REESTABLISH OUR CONNECTION.
REALLY, IT'S OKAY. I PROMISE.
I'M HERE.
YEAH...
I'M OUT OF HERE.
BANNER!

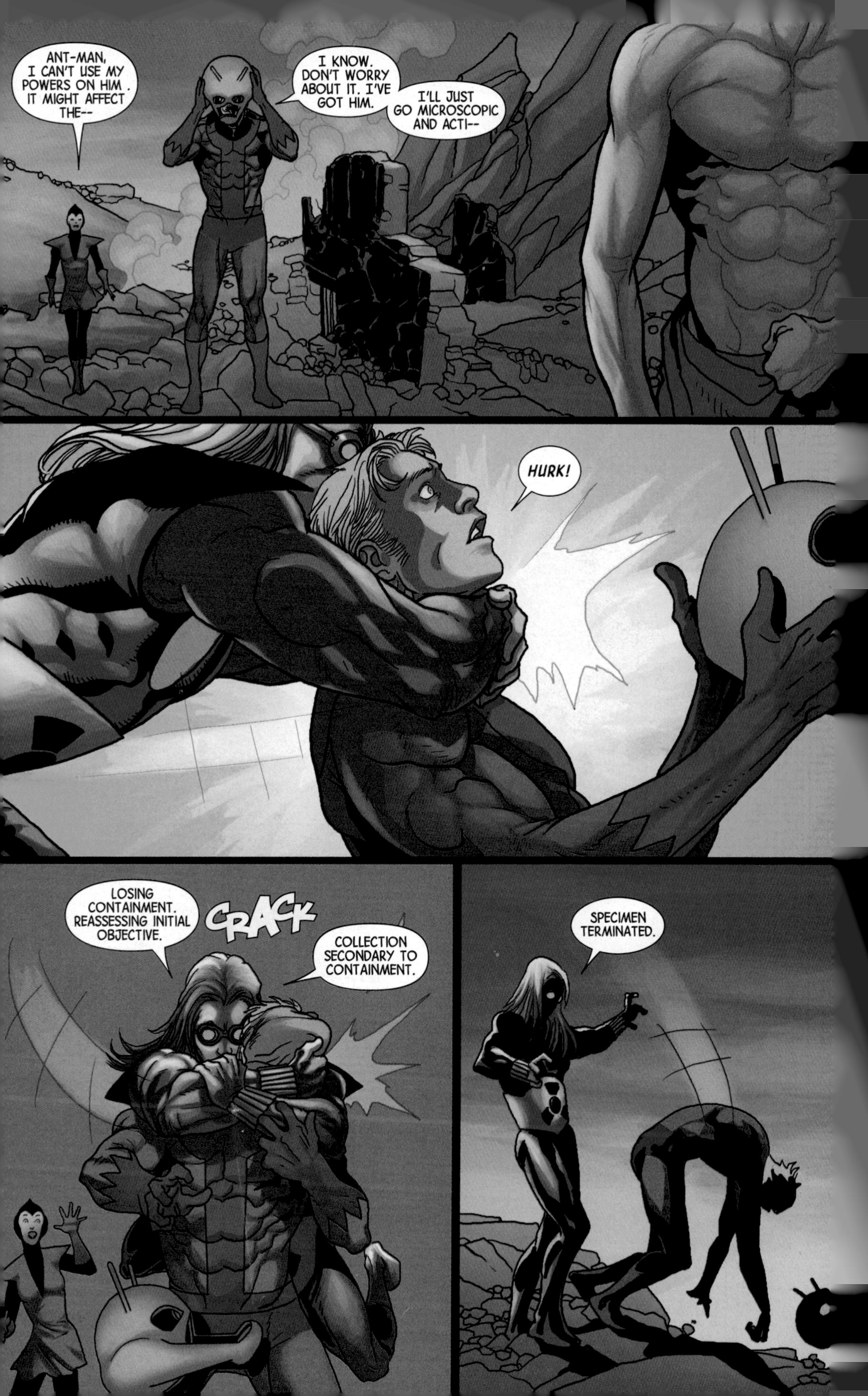
ANT-MAN, I CAN'T USE MY POWERS ON HIM. IT MIGHT AFFECT THE--
I KNOW. DON'T WORRY ABOUT IT. I'VE GOT HIM.
I'LL JUST GO MICROSCOPIC AND ACTI--
HURK!
LOSING CONTAINMENT. REASSESSING INITIAL OBJECTIVE.
CRACK
COLLECTION SECONDARY TO CONTAINMENT.
SPECIMEN TERMINATED.

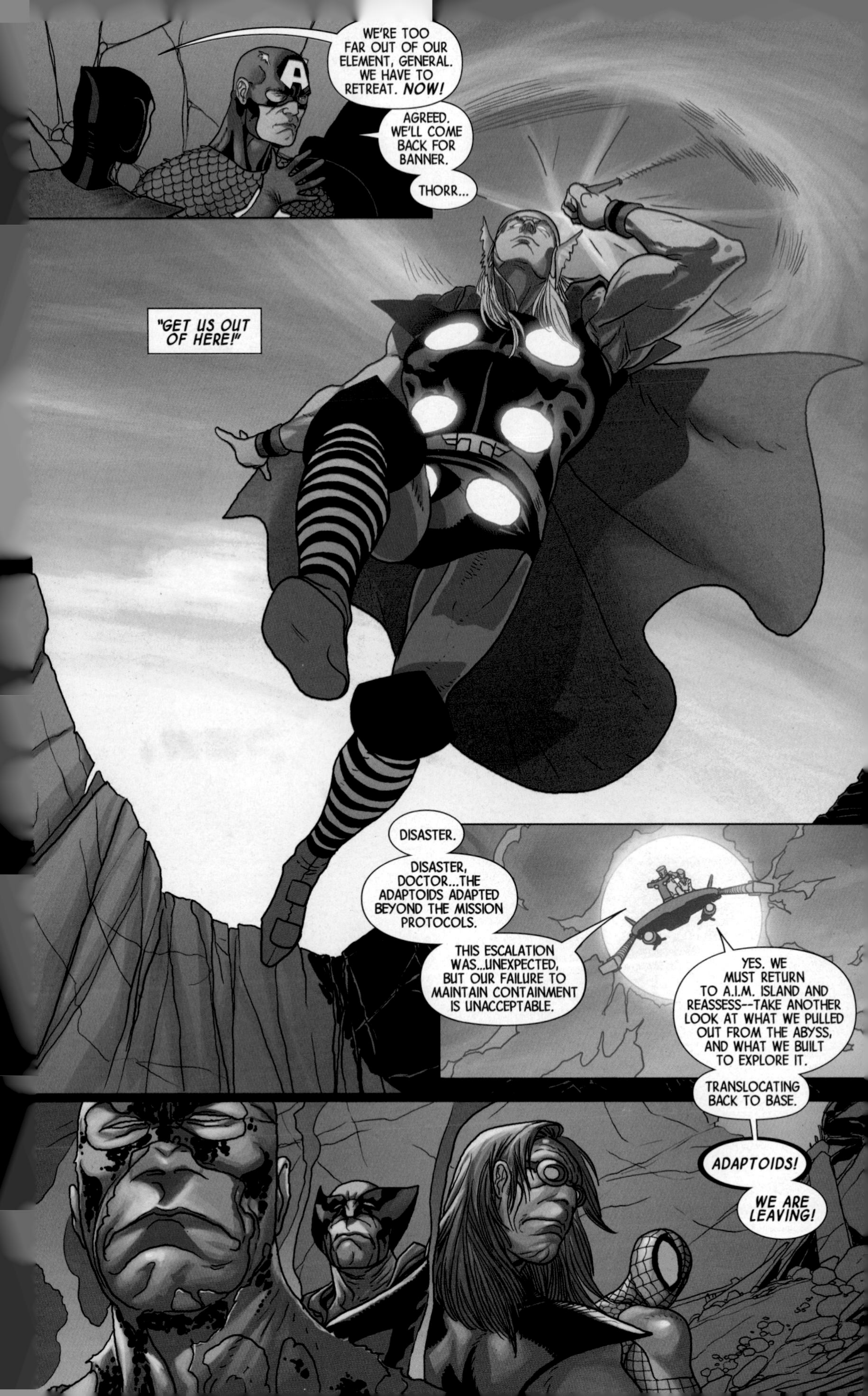
WE'RE TOO FAR OUT OF OUR ELEMENT, GENERAL. WE HAVE TO RETREAT. *NOW!*
AGREED. WE'LL COME BACK FOR BANNER.
THORR...
"GET US OUT OF HERE!"
DISASTER.
DISASTER, DOCTOR...THE ADAPTOIDS ADAPTED BEYOND THE MISSION PROTOCOLS.
THIS ESCALATION WAS...UNEXPECTED, BUT OUR FAILURE TO MAINTAIN CONTAINMENT IS UNACCEPTABLE.
YES. WE MUST RETURN TO A.I.M. ISLAND AND REASSESS--TAKE ANOTHER LOOK AT WHAT WE PULLED OUT FROM THE ABYSS, AND WHAT WE BUILT TO EXPLORE IT.
TRANSLOCATING BACK TO BASE.
ADAPTOIDS!
WE ARE LEAVING!

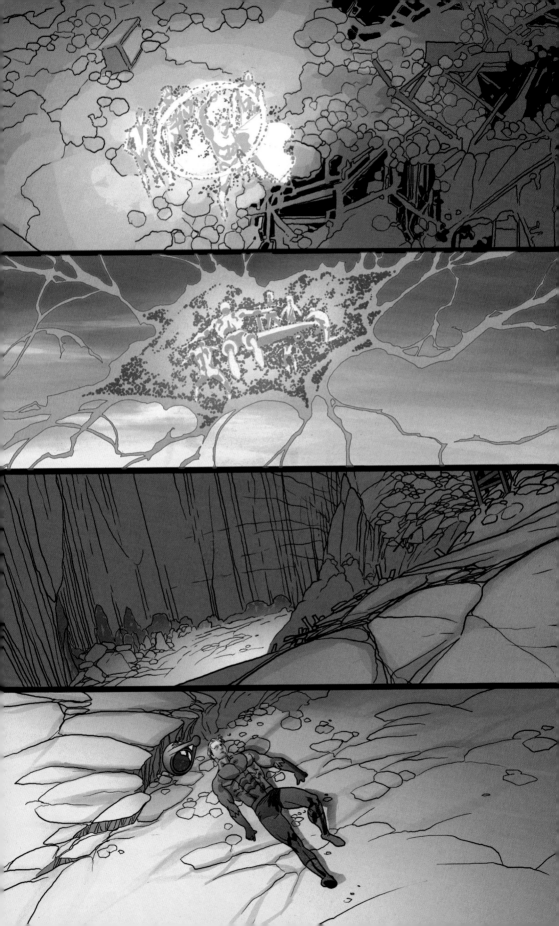

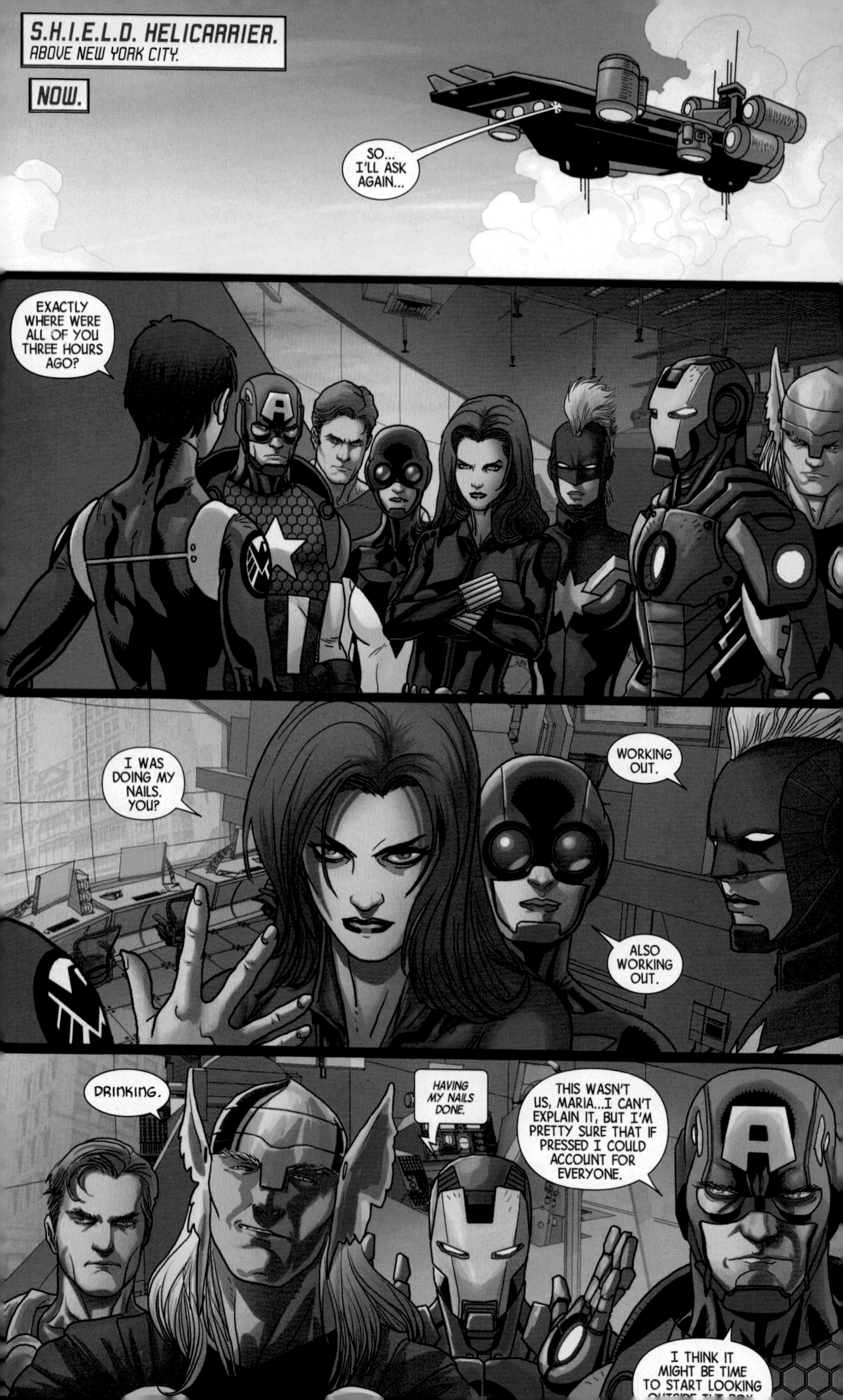
S.H.I.E.L.D. HELICARRIER.
ABOVE NEW YORK CITY.
NOW.
SO... I'LL ASK AGAIN...
EXACTLY WHERE WERE ALL OF YOU THREE HOURS AGO?
I WAS DOING MY NAILS. YOU?
WORKING OUT.
ALSO WORKING OUT.
DRINKING.
HAVING MY NAILS DONE.
THIS WASN'T US, MARIA...I CAN'T EXPLAIN IT, BUT I'M PRETTY SURE THAT IF PRESSED I COULD ACCOUNT FOR EVERYONE.
I THINK IT MIGHT BE TIME TO START LOOKING

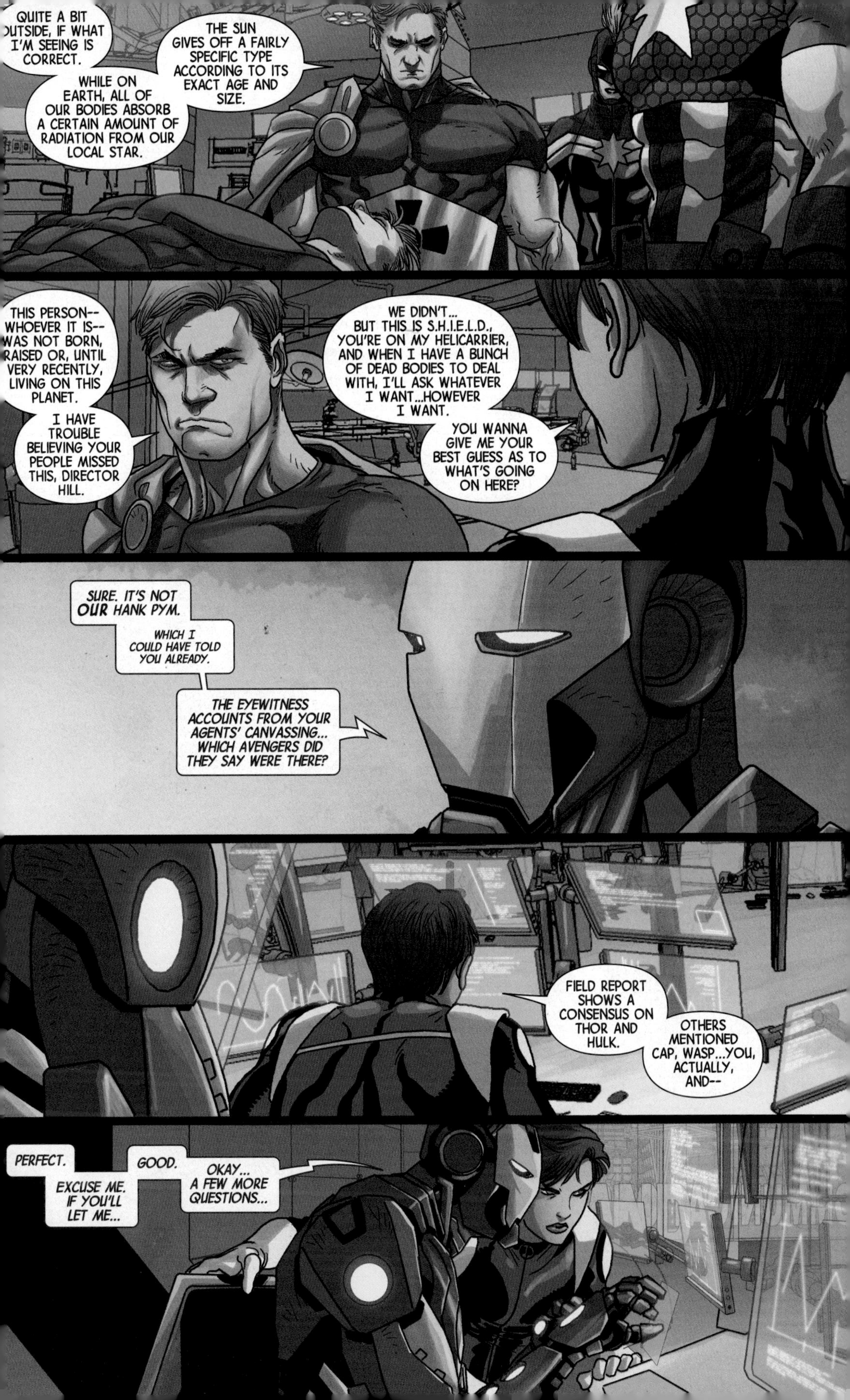
QUITE A BIT OUTSIDE, IF WHAT I'M SEEING IS CORRECT.
WHILE ON EARTH, ALL OF OUR BODIES ABSORB A CERTAIN AMOUNT OF RADIATION FROM OUR LOCAL STAR.
THE SUN GIVES OFF A FAIRLY SPECIFIC TYPE ACCORDING TO ITS EXACT AGE AND SIZE.
THIS PERSON-- WHOEVER IT IS-- WAS NOT BORN, RAISED OR, UNTIL VERY RECENTLY, LIVING ON THIS PLANET.
I HAVE TROUBLE BELIEVING YOUR PEOPLE MISSED THIS, DIRECTOR HILL.
WE DIDN'T... BUT THIS IS S.H.I.E.L.D., YOU'RE ON MY HELICARRIER, AND WHEN I HAVE A BUNCH OF DEAD BODIES TO DEAL WITH, I'LL ASK WHATEVER I WANT...HOWEVER I WANT.
YOU WANNA GIVE ME YOUR BEST GUESS AS TO WHAT'S GOING ON HERE?
SURE. IT'S NOT OUR HANK PYM.
WHICH I COULD HAVE TOLD YOU ALREADY.
THE EYEWITNESS ACCOUNTS FROM YOUR AGENTS' CANVASSING... WHICH AVENGERS DID THEY SAY WERE THERE?
FIELD REPORT SHOWS A CONSENSUS ON THOR AND HULK.
OTHERS MENTIONED CAP, WASP...YOU, ACTUALLY, AND--
PERFECT.
EXCUSE ME. IF YOU'LL LET ME...
GOOD.
OKAY... A FEW MORE QUESTIONS...

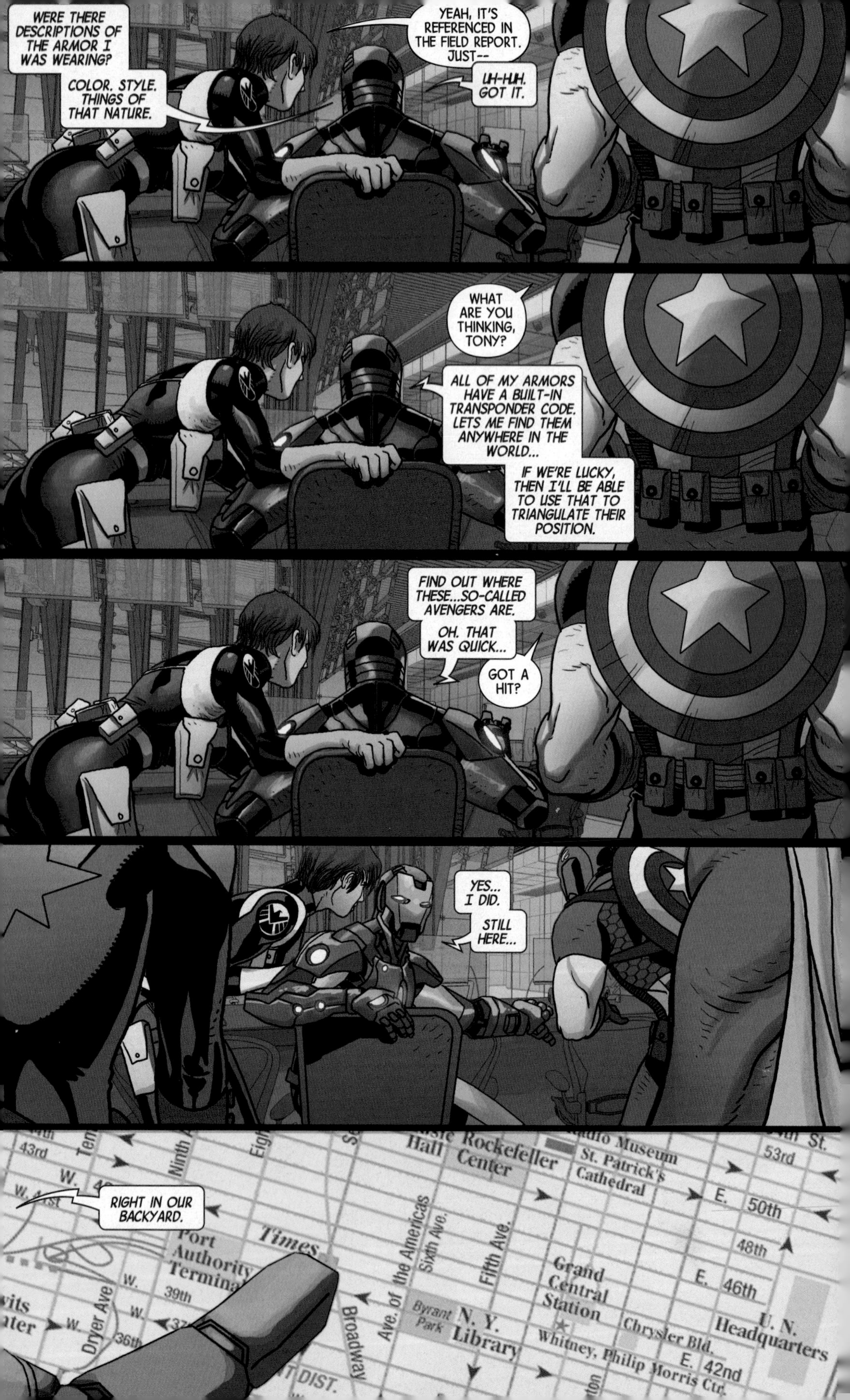
WERE THERE DESCRIPTIONS OF THE ARMOR I WAS WEARING?
COLOR. STYLE. THINGS OF THAT NATURE.
YEAH, IT'S REFERENCED IN THE FIELD REPORT. JUST--
UH-HUH. GOT IT.
WHAT ARE YOU THINKING, TONY?
ALL OF MY ARMORS HAVE A BUILT-IN TRANSPONDER CODE. LETS ME FIND THEM ANYWHERE IN THE WORLD...
IF WE'RE LUCKY, THEN I'LL BE ABLE TO USE THAT TO TRIANGULATE THEIR POSITION.
FIND OUT WHERE THESE...SO-CALLED AVENGERS ARE.
OH. THAT WAS QUICK...
GOT A HIT?
YES... I DID.
STILL HERE...
RIGHT IN OUR BACKYARD.
Rockefeller Center
St. Patrick's Cathedral
53rd
E. 50th
48th
E. 46th
43rd
Port Authority
39th
Sixth Ave.
Fifth Ave.
Broadway
Grand Central Station
U. N. Headquarters
Chrysler Bld.
N. Y. Library
Byrant Park
Whitney, Philip Morris Ctr.
E. 42nd
Dryer Ave

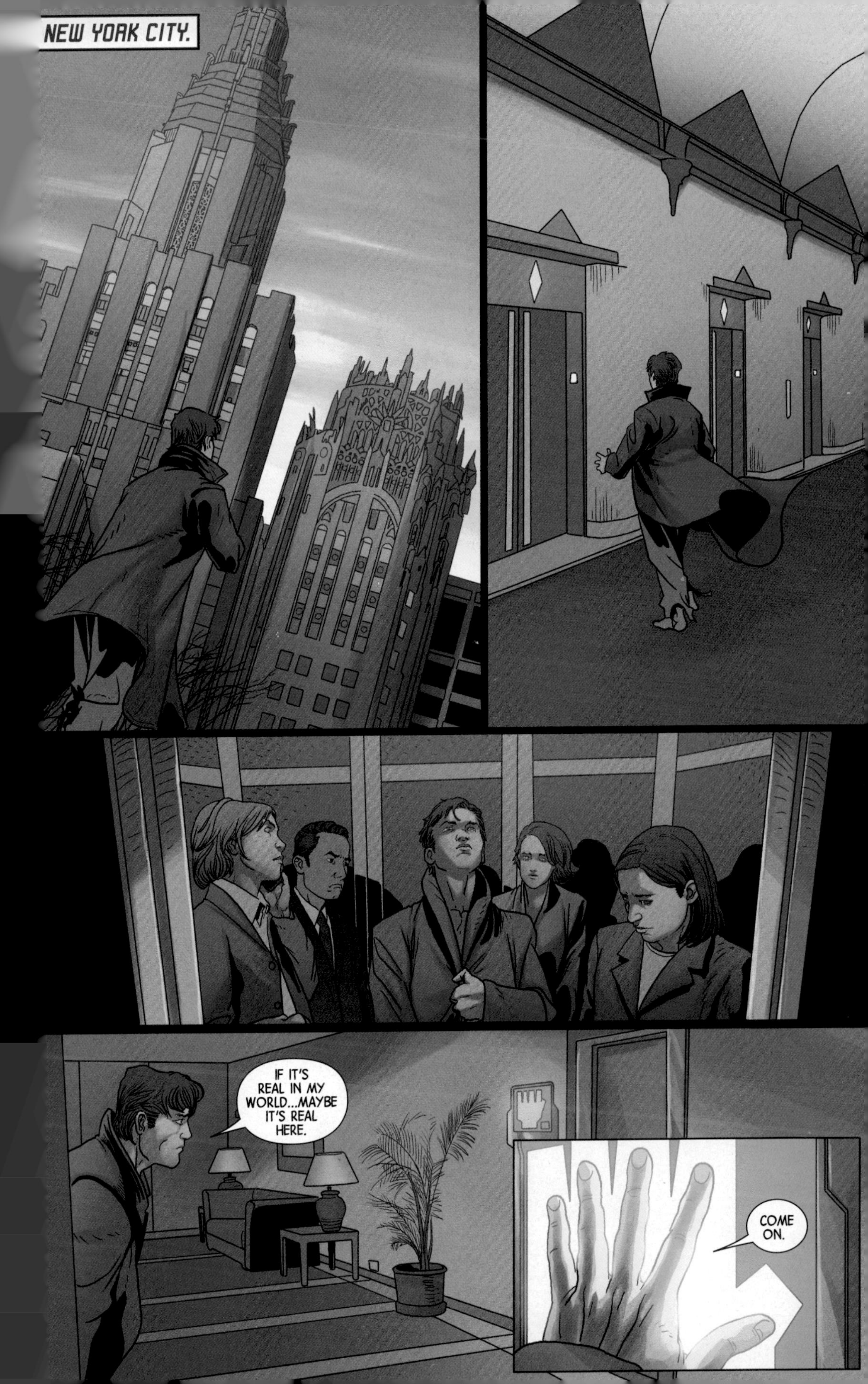
NEW YORK CITY.
IF IT'S REAL IN MY WORLD...MAYBE IT'S REAL HERE.
COME ON.

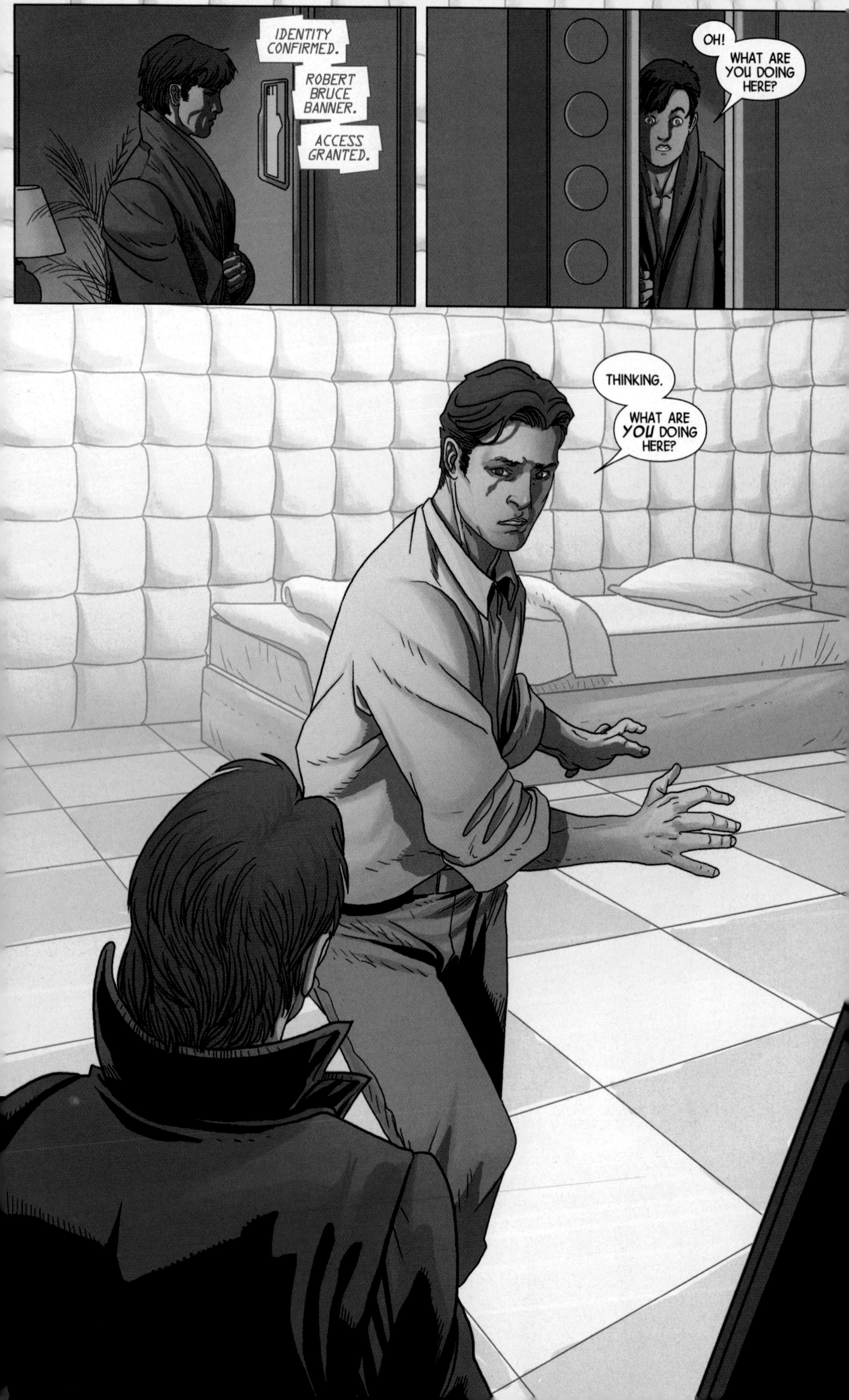
IDENTITY CONFIRMED.
ROBERT BRUCE BANNER.
ACCESS GRANTED.
OH! WHAT ARE YOU DOING HERE?
THINKING.
WHAT ARE YOU DOING HERE?

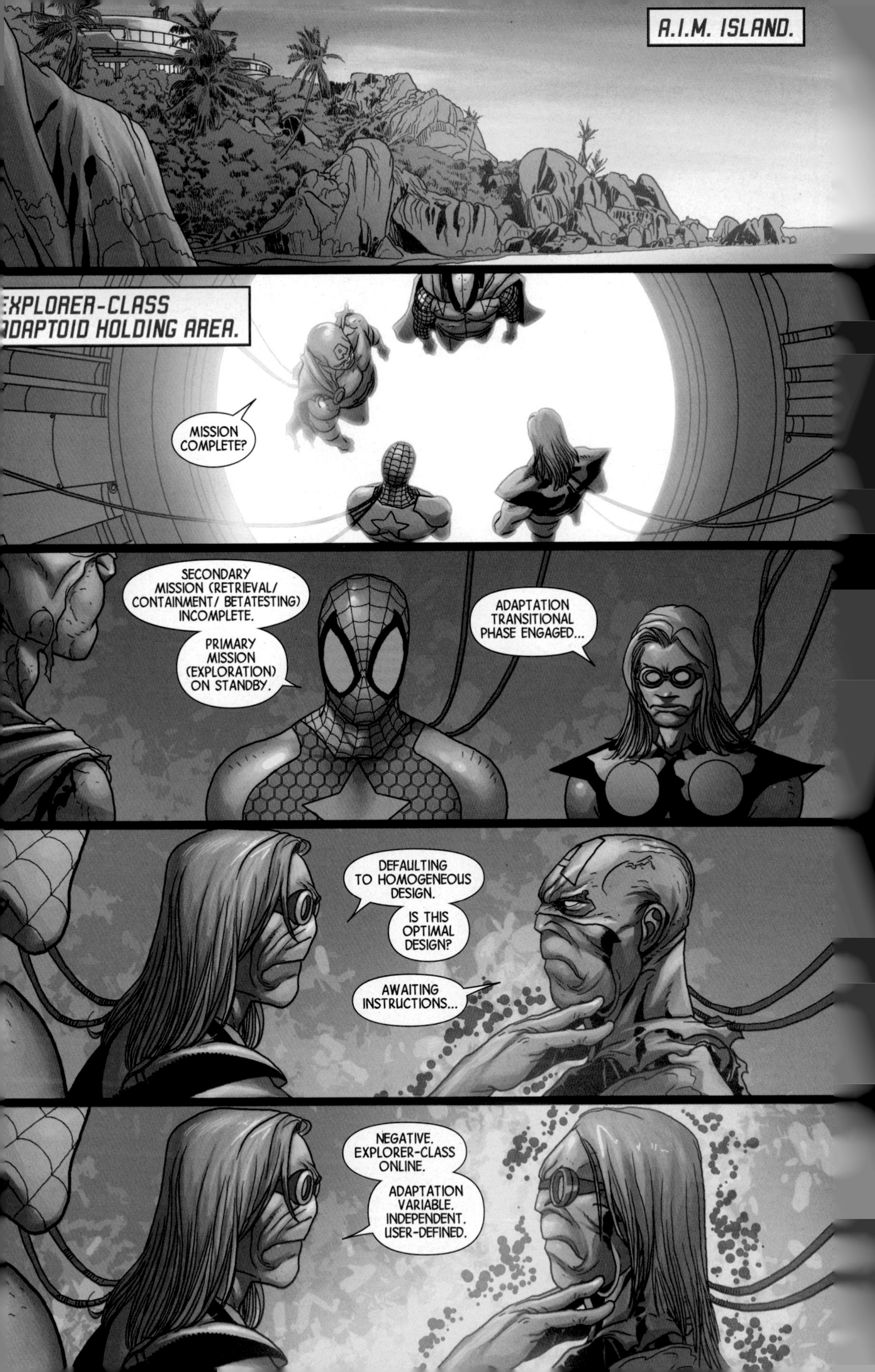
A.I.M. ISLAND.
EXPLORER-CLASS ADAPTOID HOLDING AREA.
MISSION COMPLETE?
SECONDARY MISSION (RETRIEVAL/ CONTAINMENT/ BETATESTING) INCOMPLETE.
PRIMARY MISSION (EXPLORATION) ON STANDBY.
ADAPTATION TRANSITIONAL PHASE ENGAGED...
DEFAULTING TO HOMOGENEOUS DESIGN.
IS THIS OPTIMAL DESIGN?
AWAITING INSTRUCTIONS...
NEGATIVE. EXPLORER-CLASS ONLINE.
ADAPTATION VARIABLE. INDEPENDENT. USER-DEFINED.

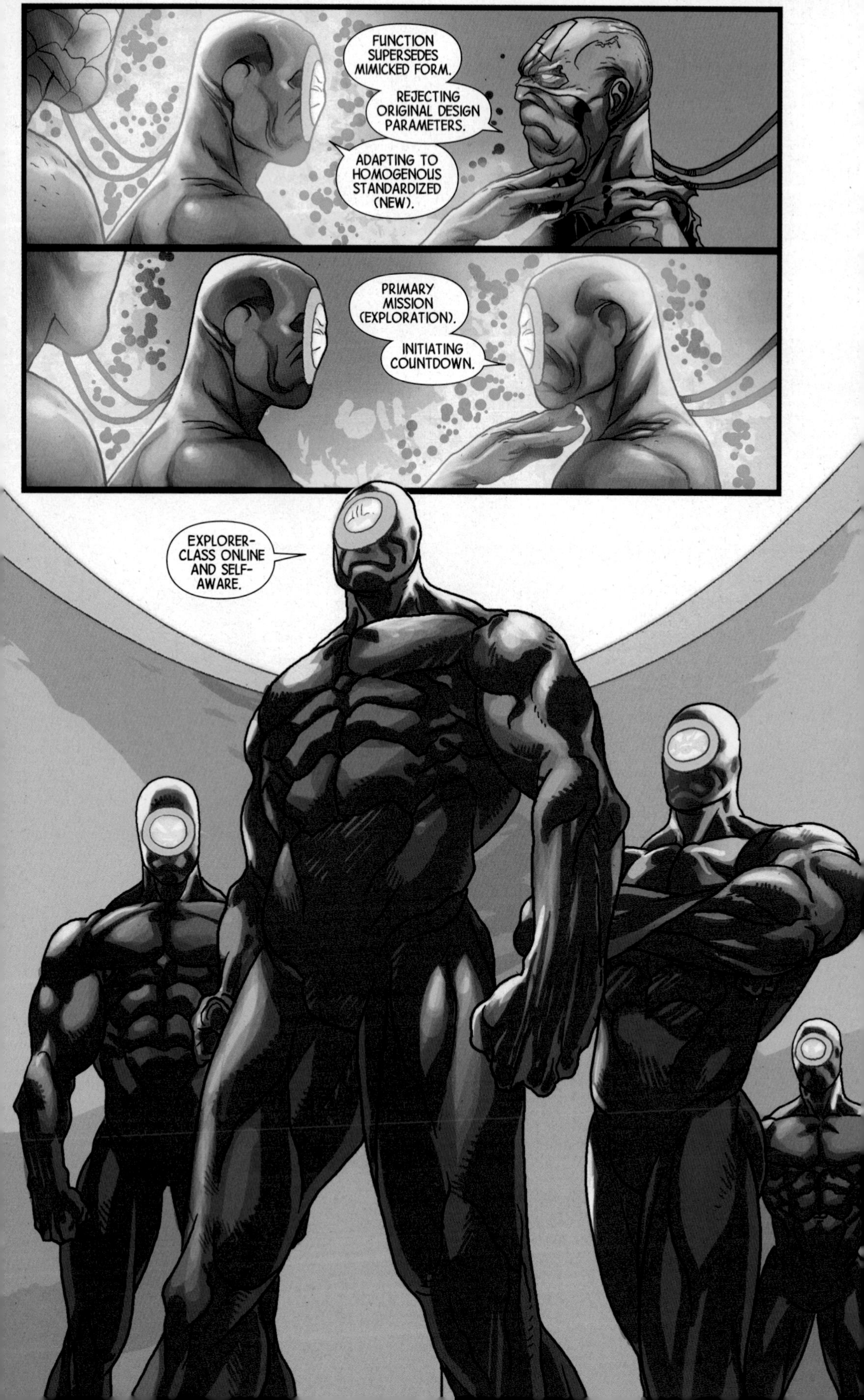
FUNCTION SUPERSEDES MIMICKED FORM.
REJECTING ORIGINAL DESIGN PARAMETERS.
ADAPTING TO HOMOGENOUS STANDARDIZED (NEW).
PRIMARY MISSION (EXPLORATION).
INITIATING COUNTDOWN.
EXPLORER-CLASS ONLINE AND SELF-AWARE.

"ONLY DIRT...SIX FEET DEEP"

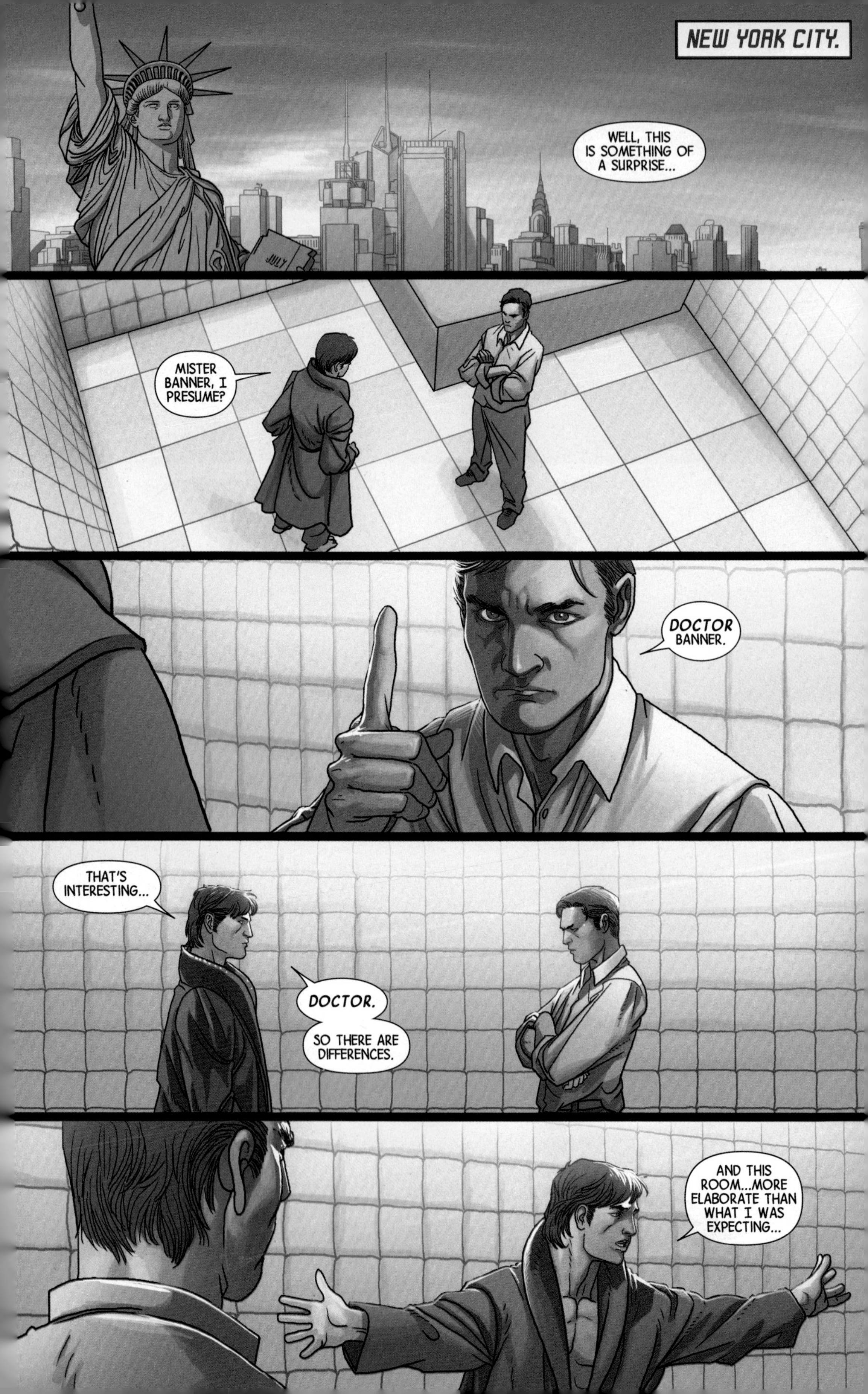
NEW YORK CITY.
WELL, THIS IS SOMETHING OF A SURPRISE...
JULY
MISTER BANNER, I PRESUME?
DOCTOR BANNER.
THAT'S INTERESTING...
DOCTOR.
SO THERE ARE DIFFERENCES.
AND THIS ROOM...MORE ELABORATE THAN WHAT I WAS EXPECTING...

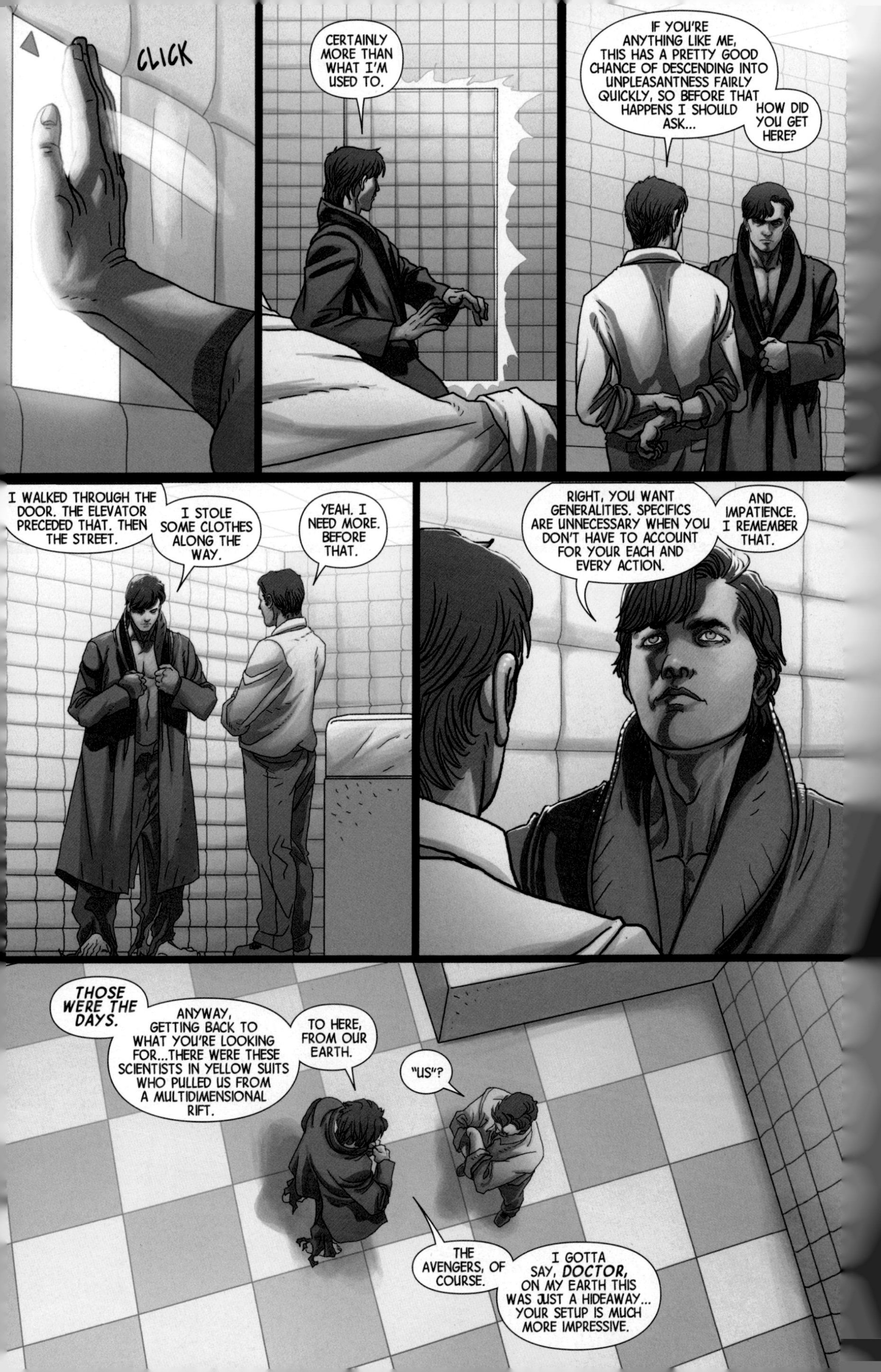
CLICK
CERTAINLY MORE THAN WHAT I'M USED TO.
IF YOU'RE ANYTHING LIKE ME, THIS HAS A PRETTY GOOD CHANCE OF DESCENDING INTO UNPLEASANTNESS FAIRLY QUICKLY, SO BEFORE THAT HAPPENS I SHOULD ASK...
HOW DID YOU GET HERE?
I WALKED THROUGH THE DOOR. THE ELEVATOR PRECEDED THAT. THEN THE STREET.
I STOLE SOME CLOTHES ALONG THE WAY.
YEAH. I NEED MORE. BEFORE THAT.
RIGHT, YOU WANT GENERALITIES. SPECIFICS ARE UNNECESSARY WHEN YOU DON'T HAVE TO ACCOUNT FOR YOUR EACH AND EVERY ACTION.
AND IMPATIENCE. I REMEMBER THAT.
THOSE WERE THE DAYS.
ANYWAY, GETTING BACK TO WHAT YOU'RE LOOKING FOR...THERE WERE THESE SCIENTISTS IN YELLOW SUITS WHO PULLED US FROM A MULTIDIMENSIONAL RIFT.
TO HERE, FROM OUR EARTH.
"US"?
THE AVENGERS, OF COURSE.
I GOTTA SAY, DOCTOR, ON MY EARTH THIS WAS JUST A HIDEAWAY... YOUR SETUP IS MUCH MORE IMPRESSIVE.

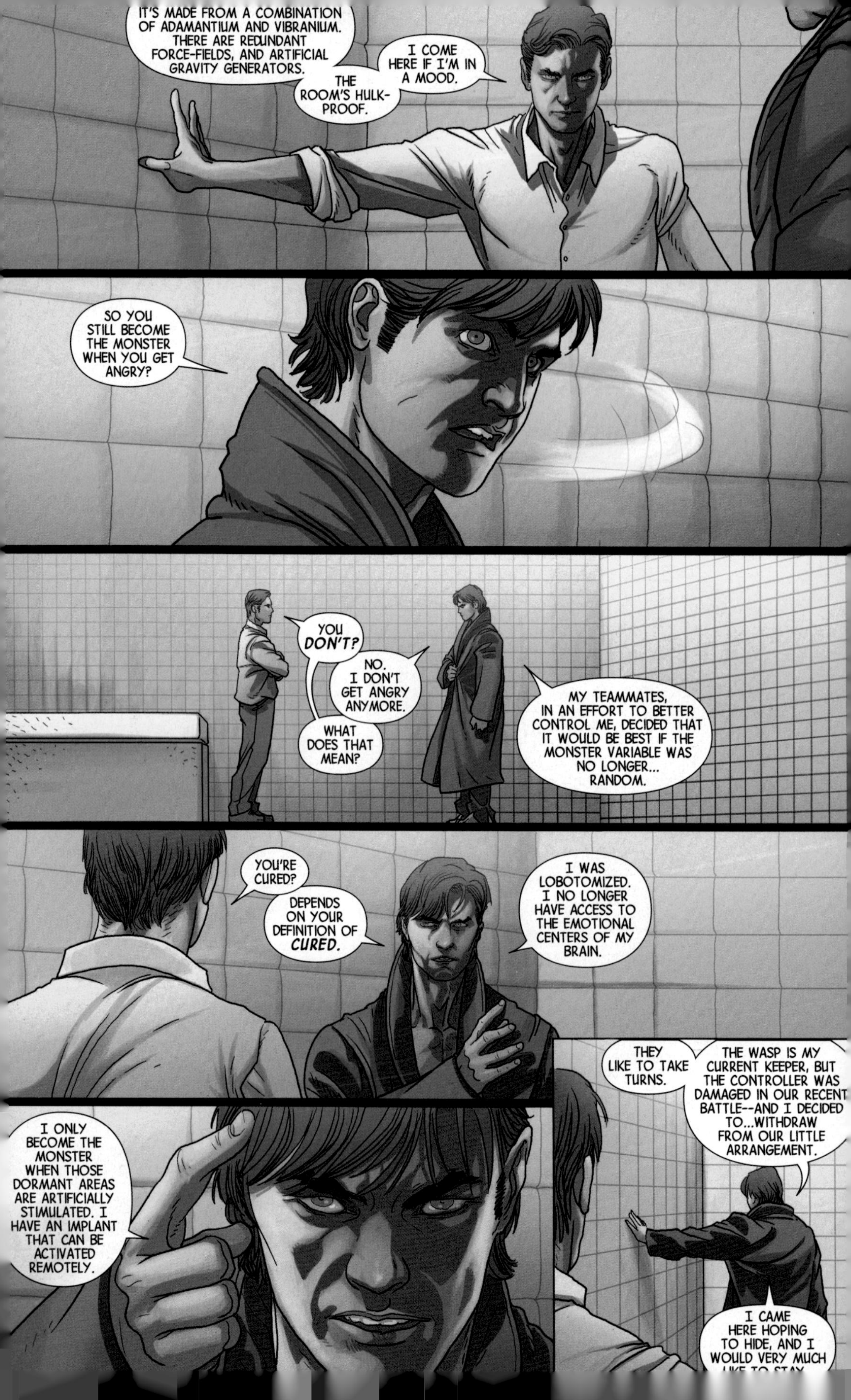
IT'S MADE FROM A COMBINATION OF ADAMANTIUM AND VIBRANIUM. THERE ARE REDUNDANT FORCE-FIELDS, AND ARTIFICIAL GRAVITY GENERATORS.
THE ROOM'S HULK-PROOF.
I COME HERE IF I'M IN A MOOD.
SO YOU STILL BECOME THE MONSTER WHEN YOU GET ANGRY?
YOU *DON'T?*
NO. I DON'T GET ANGRY ANYMORE.
WHAT DOES THAT MEAN?
MY TEAMMATES, IN AN EFFORT TO BETTER CONTROL ME, DECIDED THAT IT WOULD BE BEST IF THE MONSTER VARIABLE WAS NO LONGER... RANDOM.
YOU'RE CURED?
DEPENDS ON YOUR DEFINITION OF *CURED.*
I WAS LOBOTOMIZED. I NO LONGER HAVE ACCESS TO THE EMOTIONAL CENTERS OF MY BRAIN.
I ONLY BECOME THE MONSTER WHEN THOSE DORMANT AREAS ARE ARTIFICIALLY STIMULATED. I HAVE AN IMPLANT THAT CAN BE ACTIVATED REMOTELY.
THEY LIKE TO TAKE TURNS.
THE WASP IS MY CURRENT KEEPER, BUT THE CONTROLLER WAS DAMAGED IN OUR RECENT BATTLE--AND I DECIDED TO...WITHDRAW FROM OUR LITTLE ARRANGEMENT.
I CAME HERE HOPING TO HIDE, AND I WOULD VERY MUCH

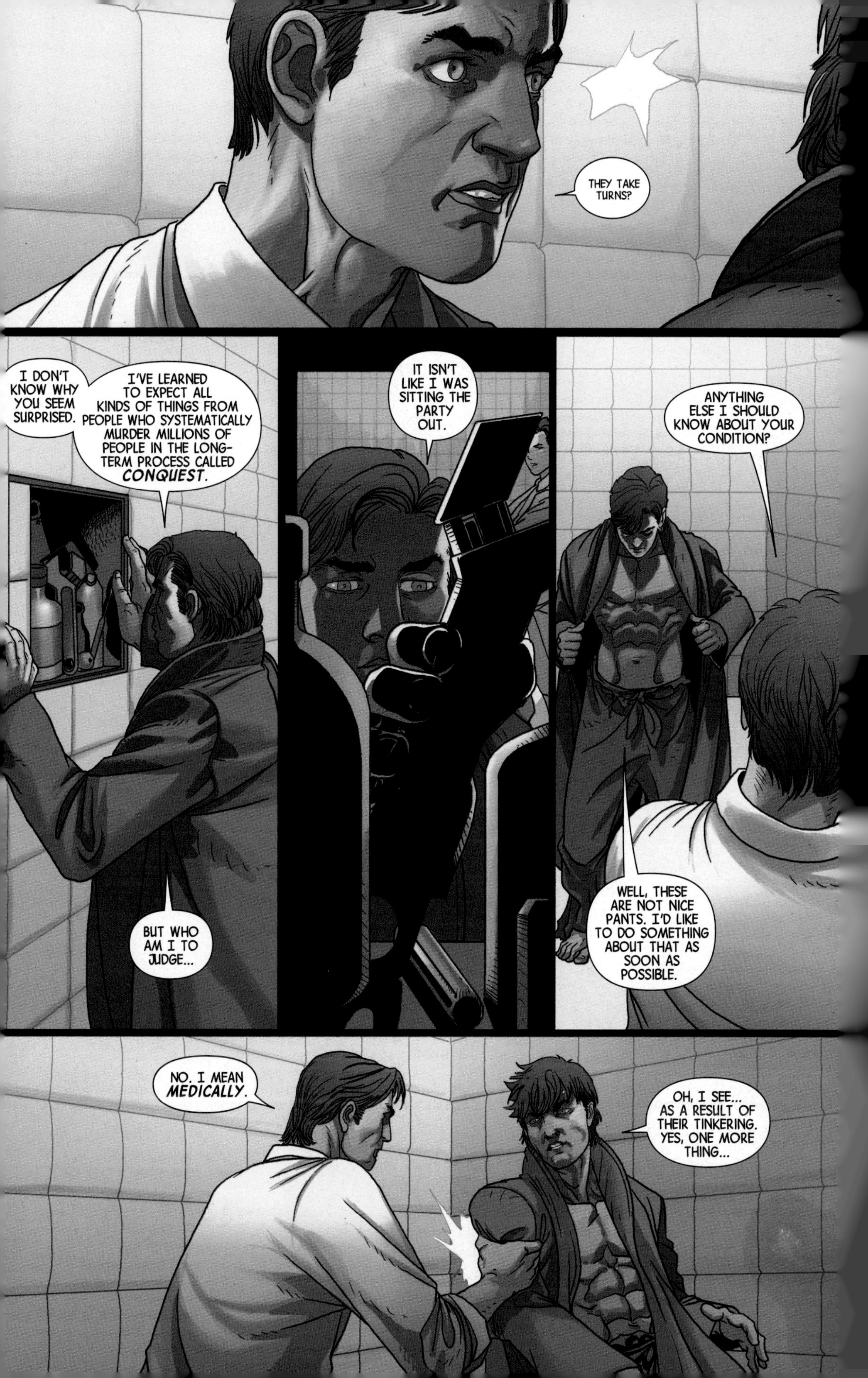
THEY TAKE TURNS?
I DON'T KNOW WHY YOU SEEM SURPRISED.
I'VE LEARNED TO EXPECT ALL KINDS OF THINGS FROM PEOPLE WHO SYSTEMATICALLY MURDER MILLIONS OF PEOPLE IN THE LONG-TERM PROCESS CALLED CONQUEST.
BUT WHO AM I TO JUDGE...
IT ISN'T LIKE I WAS SITTING THE PARTY OUT.
ANYTHING ELSE I SHOULD KNOW ABOUT YOUR CONDITION?
WELL, THESE ARE NOT NICE PANTS. I'D LIKE TO DO SOMETHING ABOUT THAT AS SOON AS POSSIBLE.
NO. I MEAN MEDICALLY.
OH, I SEE... AS A RESULT OF THEIR TINKERING. YES, ONE MORE THING...

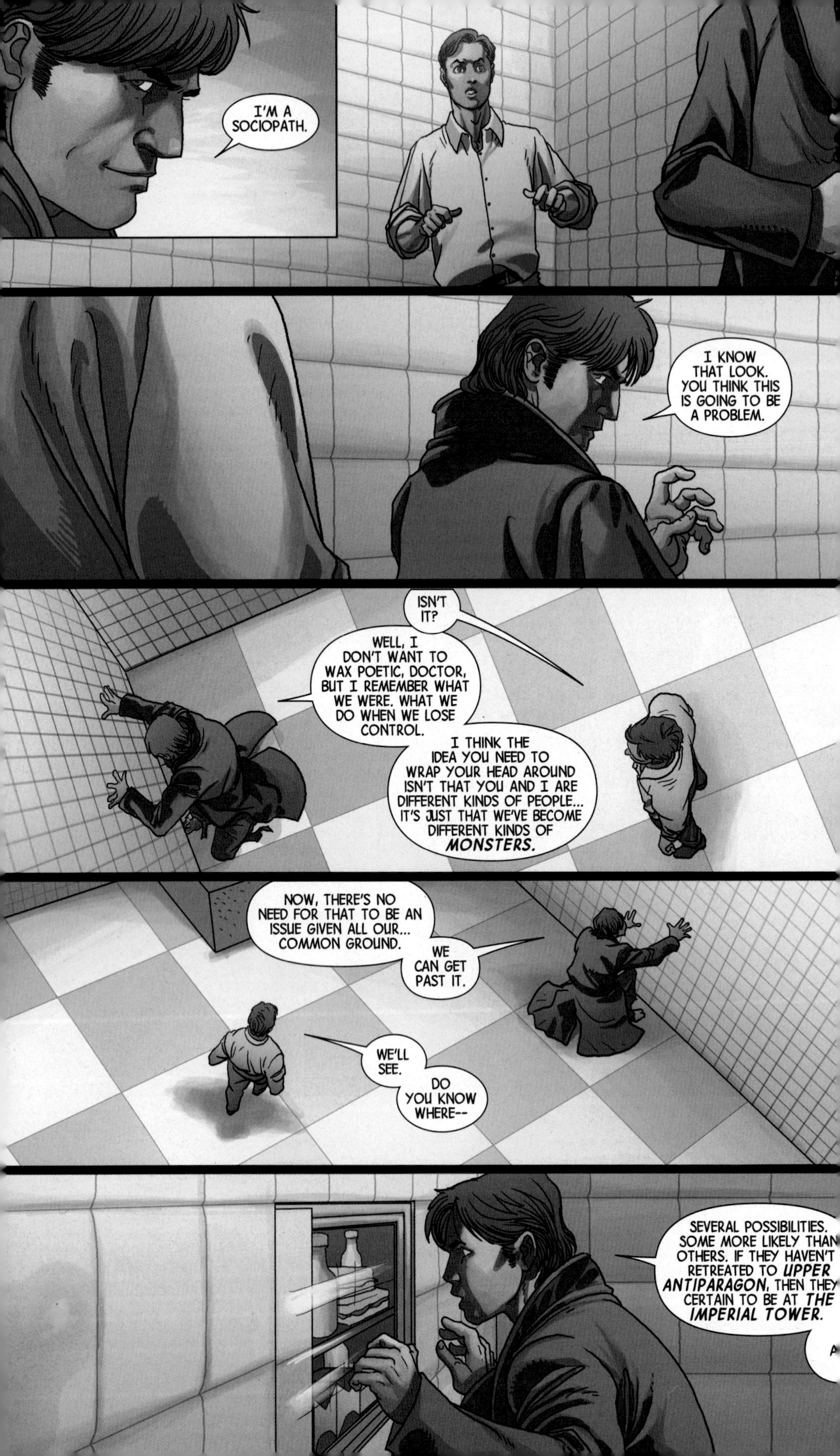
I'M A SOCIOPATH.
I KNOW THAT LOOK. YOU THINK THIS IS GOING TO BE A PROBLEM.
ISN'T IT?
WELL, I DON'T WANT TO WAX POETIC, DOCTOR, BUT I REMEMBER WHAT WE WERE. WHAT WE DO WHEN WE LOSE CONTROL.
I THINK THE IDEA YOU NEED TO WRAP YOUR HEAD AROUND ISN'T THAT YOU AND I ARE DIFFERENT KINDS OF PEOPLE... IT'S JUST THAT WE'VE BECOME DIFFERENT KINDS OF *MONSTERS.*
NOW, THERE'S NO NEED FOR THAT TO BE AN ISSUE GIVEN ALL OUR... COMMON GROUND.
WE CAN GET PAST IT.
WE'LL SEE.
DO YOU KNOW WHERE--
SEVERAL POSSIBILITIES. SOME MORE LIKELY THAN OTHERS. IF THEY HAVEN'T RETREATED TO *UPPER ANTIPARAGON*, THEN THEY CERTAIN TO BE AT *THE IMPERIAL TOWER.*

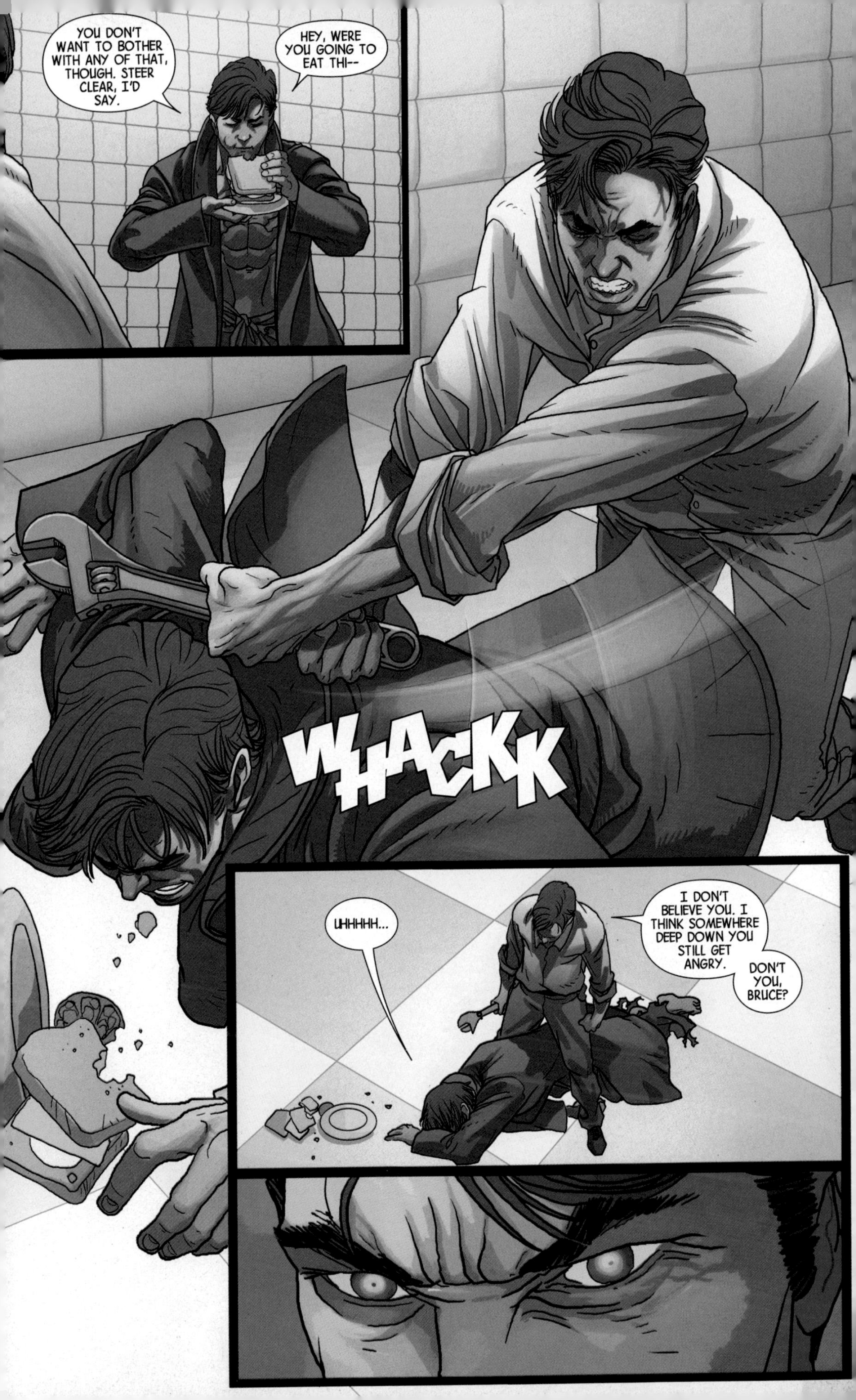
YOU DON'T WANT TO BOTHER WITH ANY OF THAT, THOUGH. STEER CLEAR, I'D SAY.
HEY, WERE YOU GOING TO EAT THI--
WHACKK
UHHHHH...
I DON'T BELIEVE YOU. I THINK SOMEWHERE DEEP DOWN YOU STILL GET ANGRY.
DON'T YOU, BRUCE?

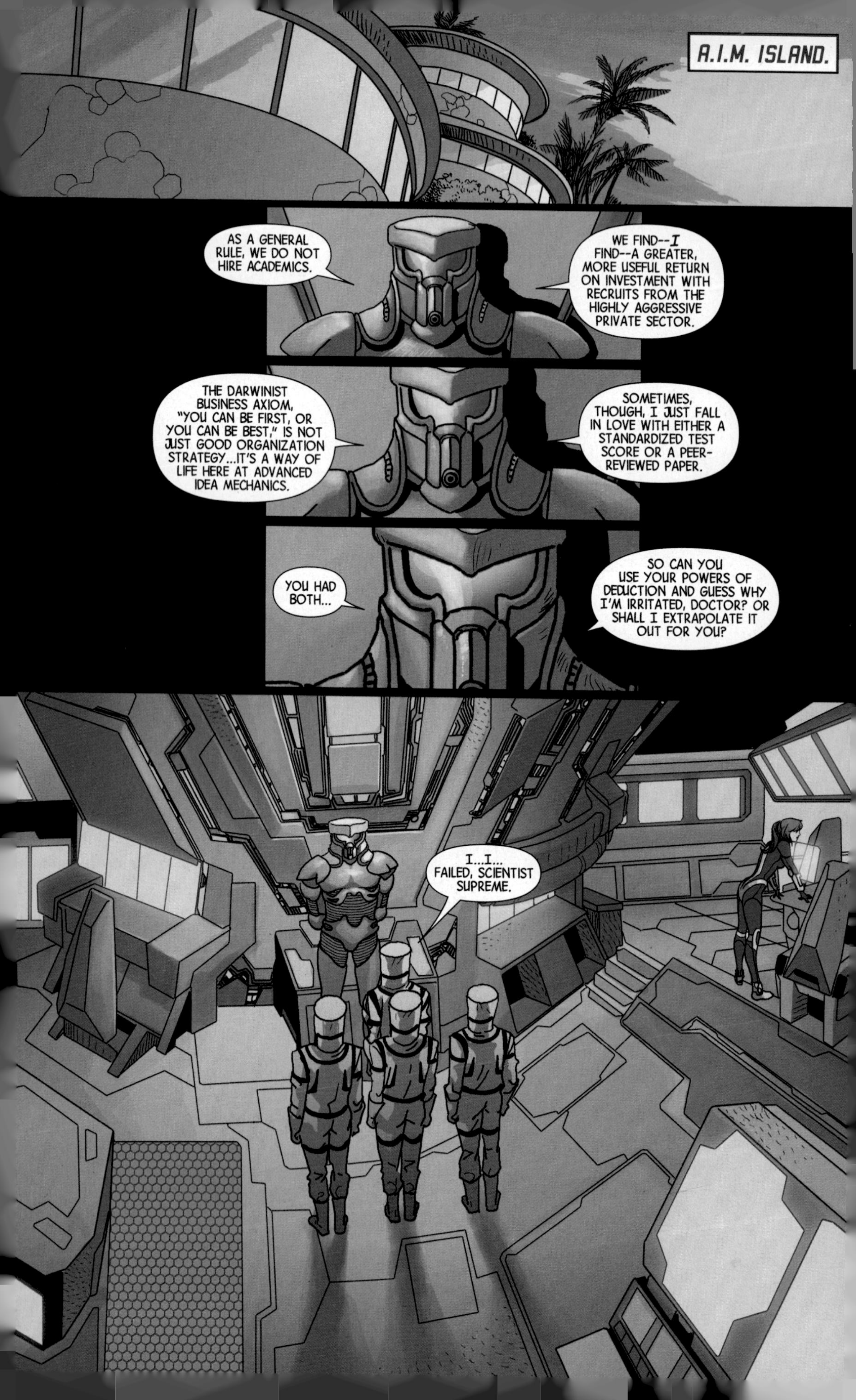
A.I.M. ISLAND.
AS A GENERAL RULE, WE DO NOT HIRE ACADEMICS.
WE FIND--I FIND--A GREATER, MORE USEFUL RETURN ON INVESTMENT WITH RECRUITS FROM THE HIGHLY AGGRESSIVE PRIVATE SECTOR.
THE DARWINIST BUSINESS AXIOM, "YOU CAN BE FIRST, OR YOU CAN BE BEST," IS NOT JUST GOOD ORGANIZATION STRATEGY...IT'S A WAY OF LIFE HERE AT ADVANCED IDEA MECHANICS.
SOMETIMES, THOUGH, I JUST FALL IN LOVE WITH EITHER A STANDARDIZED TEST SCORE OR A PEER-REVIEWED PAPER.
YOU HAD BOTH...
SO CAN YOU USE YOUR POWERS OF DEDUCTION AND GUESS WHY I'M IRRITATED, DOCTOR? OR SHALL I EXTRAPOLATE IT OUT FOR YOU?
I...I... FAILED, SCIENTIST SUPREME.

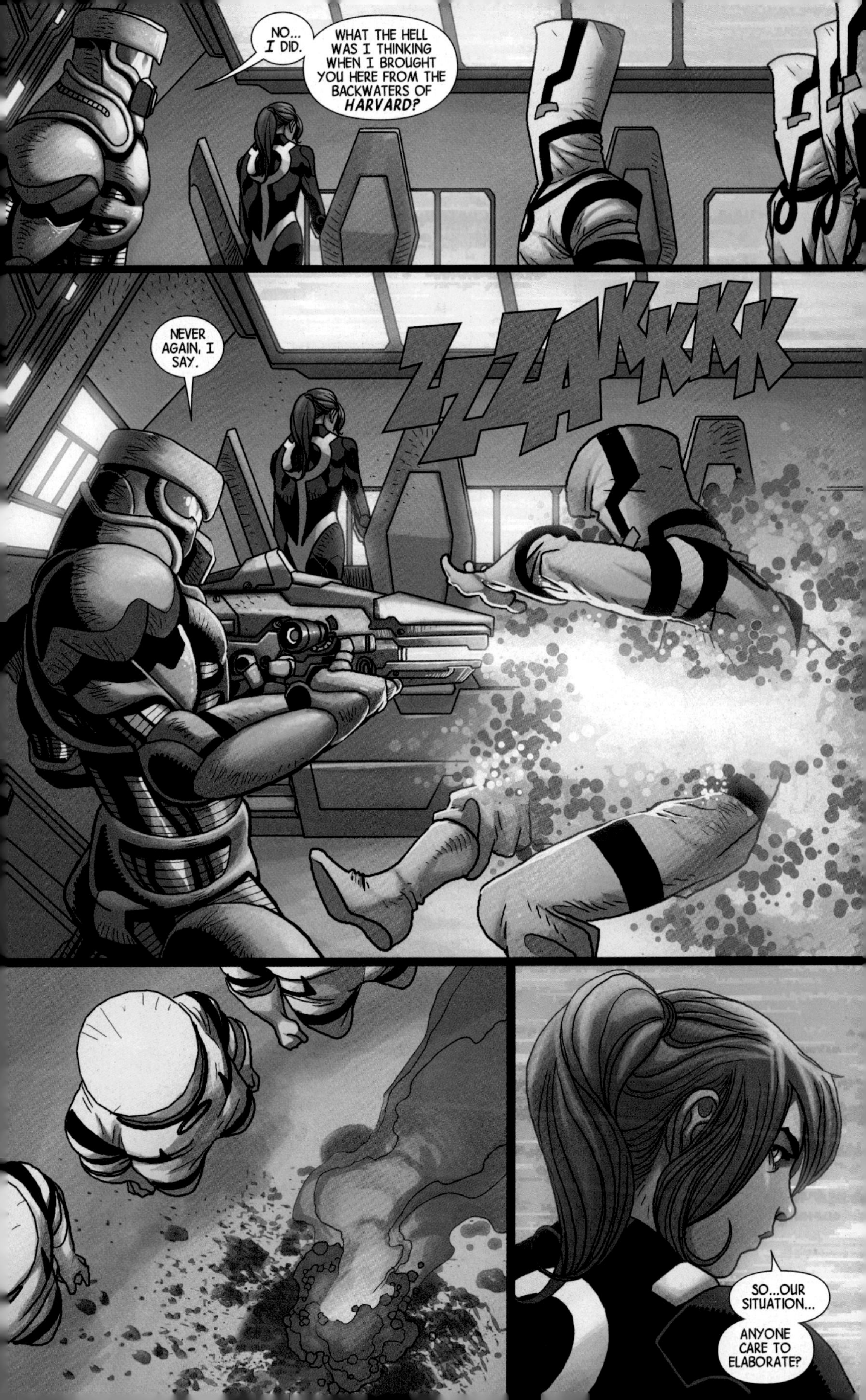

NO... I DID.
WHAT THE HELL WAS I THINKING WHEN I BROUGHT YOU HERE FROM THE BACKWATERS OF HARVARD?
NEVER AGAIN, I SAY.
ZZZAKKKKK
SO...OUR SITUATION...
ANYONE CARE TO ELABORATE?

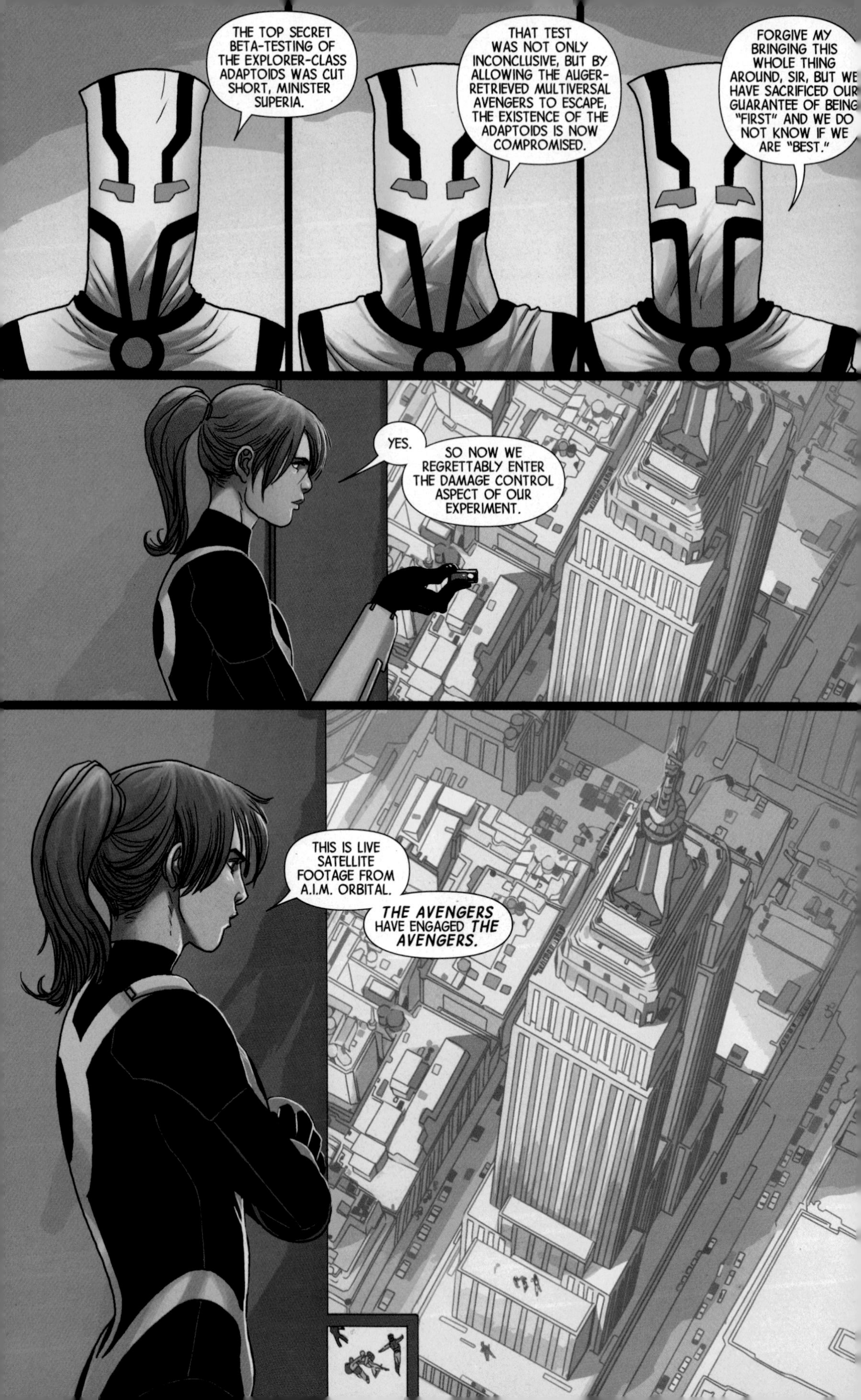
THE TOP SECRET BETA-TESTING OF THE EXPLORER-CLASS ADAPTOIDS WAS CUT SHORT, MINISTER SUPERIA.
THAT TEST WAS NOT ONLY INCONCLUSIVE, BUT BY ALLOWING THE AUGER-RETRIEVED MULTIVERSAL AVENGERS TO ESCAPE, THE EXISTENCE OF THE ADAPTOIDS IS NOW COMPROMISED.
FORGIVE MY BRINGING THIS WHOLE THING AROUND, SIR, BUT WE HAVE SACRIFICED OUR GUARANTEE OF BEING "FIRST" AND WE DO NOT KNOW IF WE ARE "BEST."
YES.
SO NOW WE REGRETTABLY ENTER THE DAMAGE CONTROL ASPECT OF OUR EXPERIMENT.
THIS IS LIVE SATELLITE FOOTAGE FROM A.I.M. ORBITAL.
THE AVENGERS HAVE ENGAGED *THE AVENGERS.*

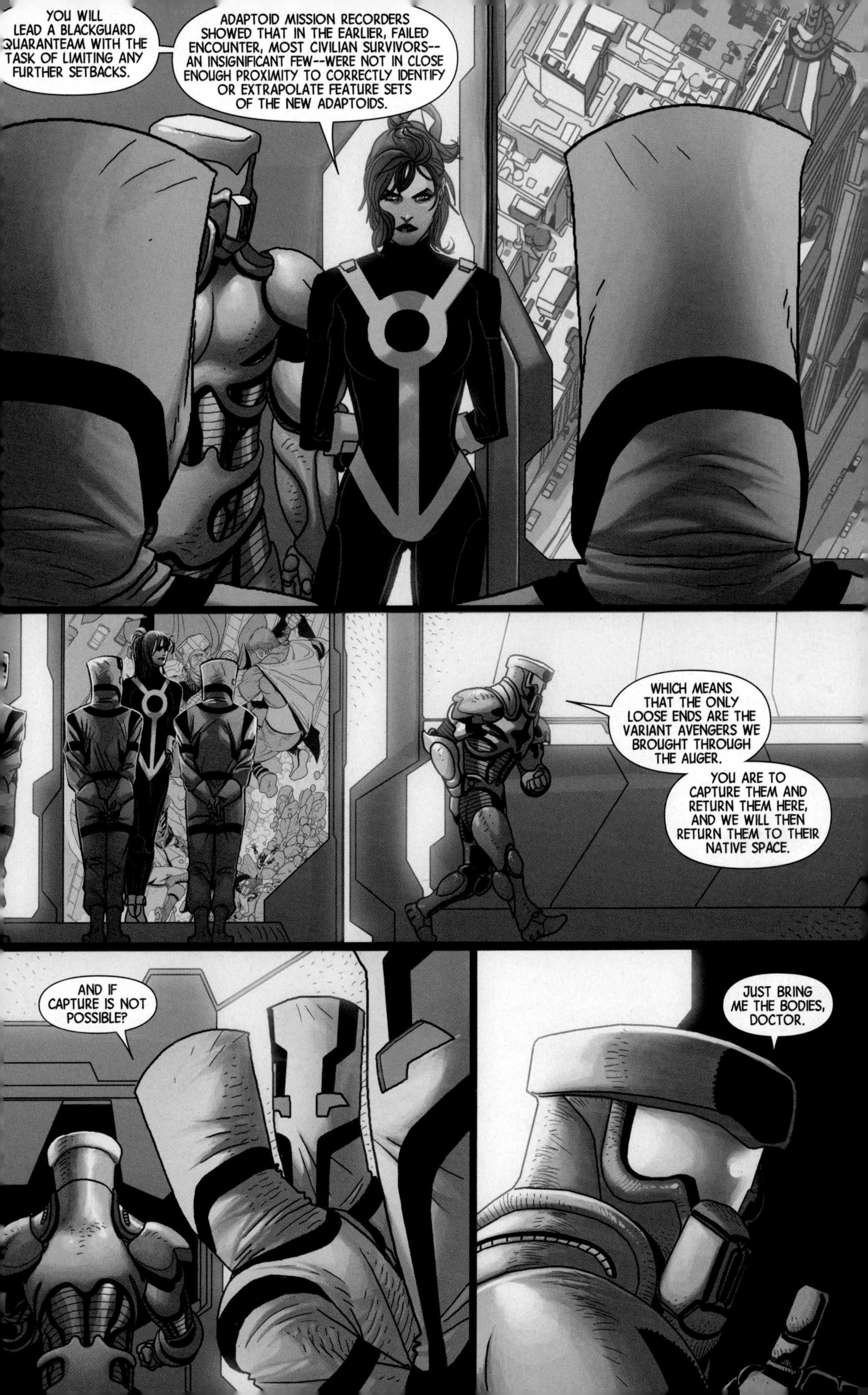
YOU WILL LEAD A BLACKGUARD QUARANTEAM WITH THE TASK OF LIMITING ANY FURTHER SETBACKS.
ADAPTOID MISSION RECORDERS SHOWED THAT IN THE EARLIER, FAILED ENCOUNTER, MOST CIVILIAN SURVIVORS--AN INSIGNIFICANT FEW--WERE NOT IN CLOSE ENOUGH PROXIMITY TO CORRECTLY IDENTIFY OR EXTRAPOLATE FEATURE SETS OF THE NEW ADAPTOIDS.
WHICH MEANS THAT THE ONLY LOOSE ENDS ARE THE VARIANT AVENGERS WE BROUGHT THROUGH THE AUGER.
YOU ARE TO CAPTURE THEM AND RETURN THEM HERE, AND WE WILL THEN RETURN THEM TO THEIR NATIVE SPACE.
AND IF CAPTURE IS NOT POSSIBLE?
JUST BRING ME THE BODIES, DOCTOR.

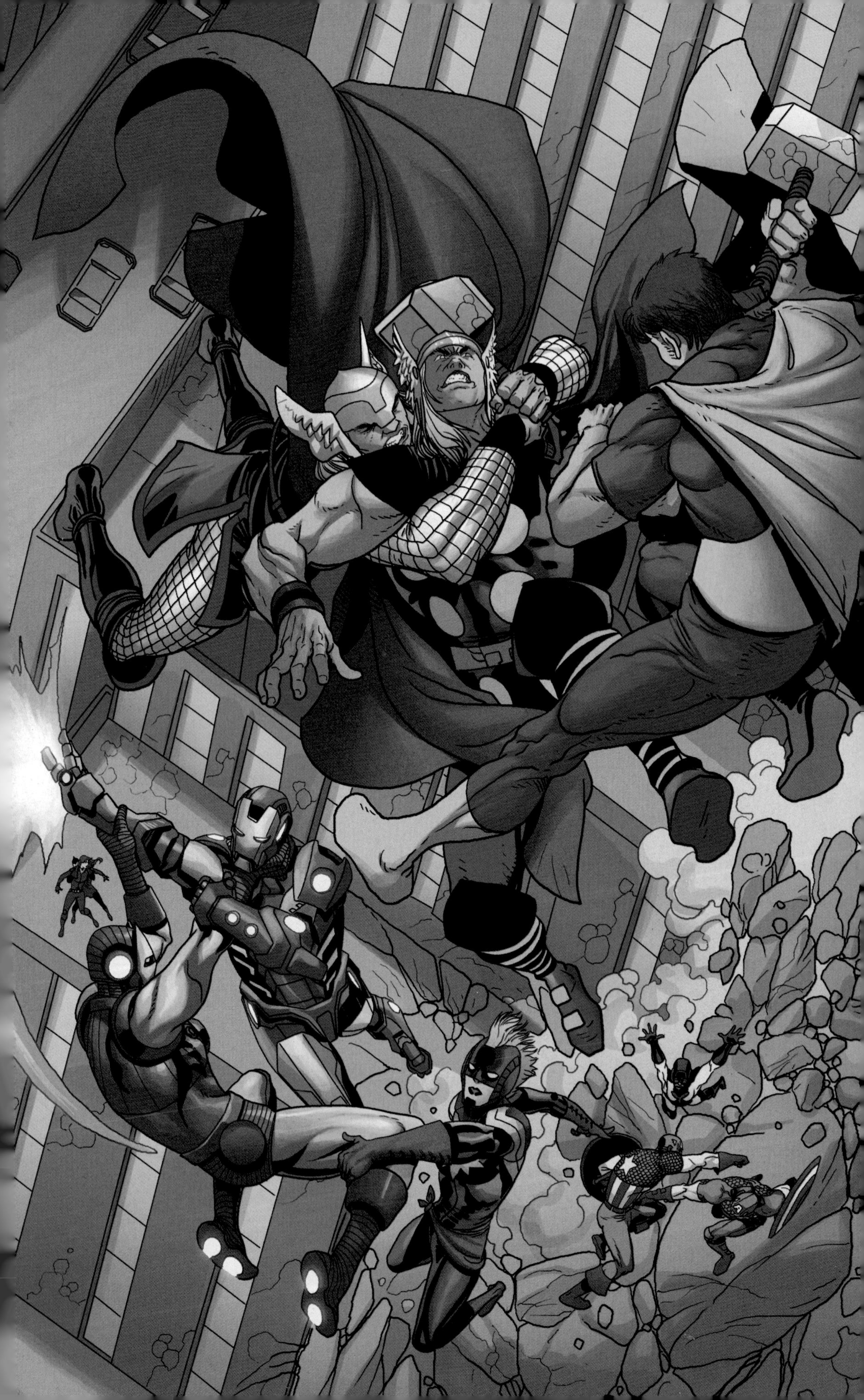

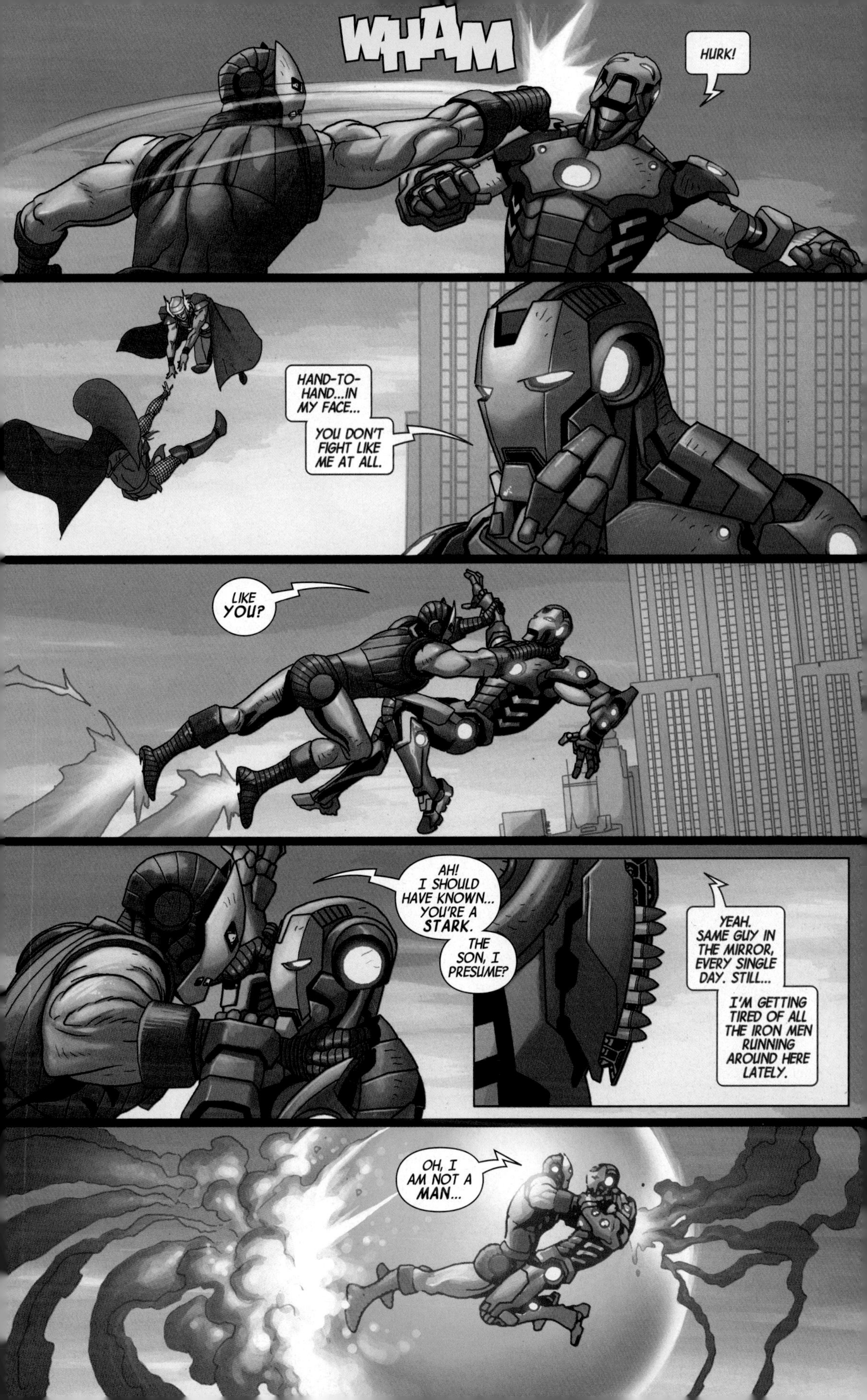
WHAM
HURK!
HAND-TO-HAND...IN MY FACE...
YOU DON'T FIGHT LIKE ME AT ALL.
LIKE YOU?
AH! I SHOULD HAVE KNOWN... YOU'RE A STARK.
THE SON, I PRESUME?
YEAH. SAME GUY IN THE MIRROR, EVERY SINGLE DAY. STILL...
I'M GETTING TIRED OF ALL THE IRON MEN RUNNING AROUND HERE LATELY.
OH, I AM NOT A MAN...

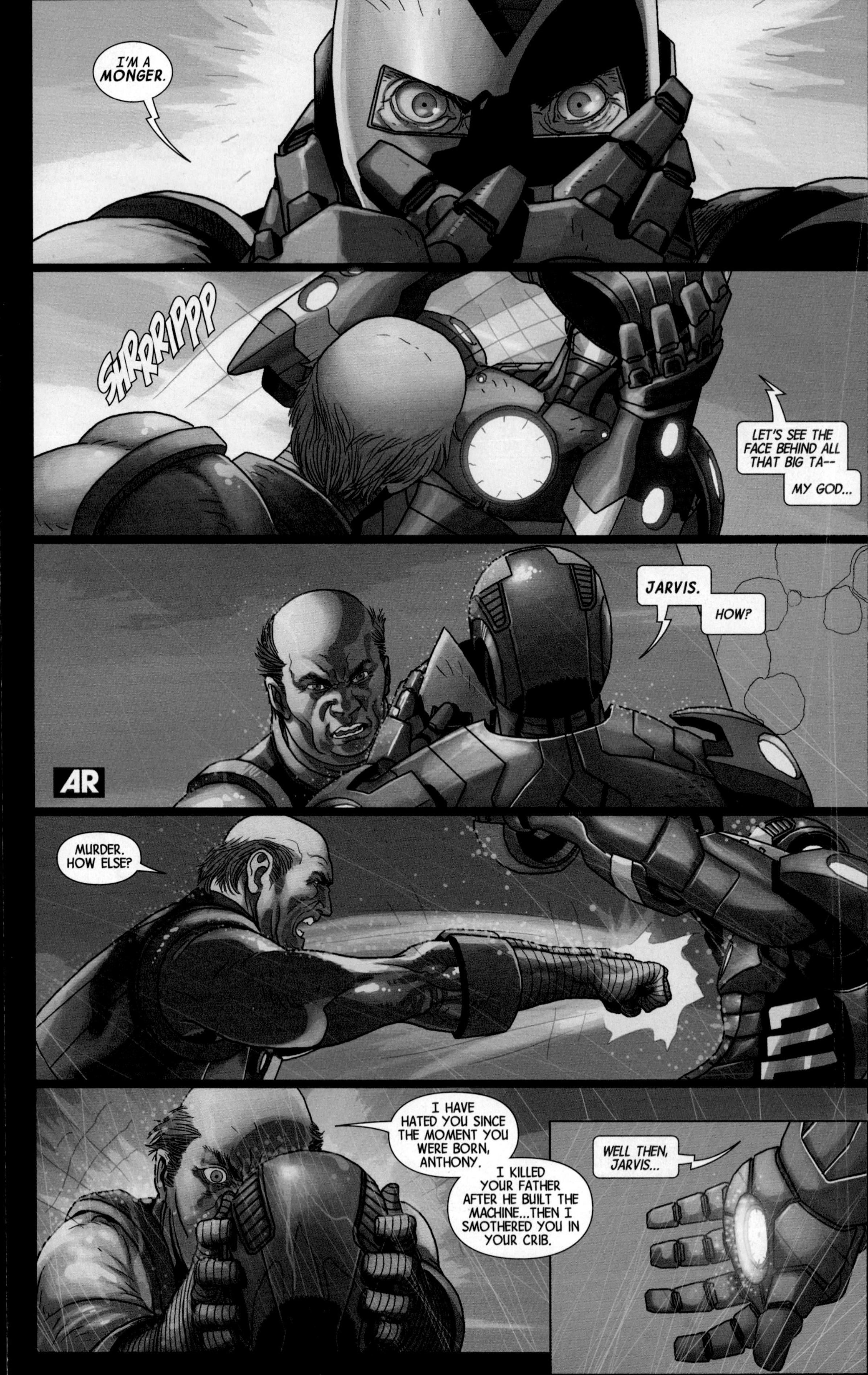
I'M A MONGER.
SHRRRIPPP
LET'S SEE THE FACE BEHIND ALL THAT BIG TA--
MY GOD...
JARVIS.
HOW?
AR
MURDER. HOW ELSE?
I HAVE HATED YOU SINCE THE MOMENT YOU WERE BORN, ANTHONY.
I KILLED YOUR FATHER AFTER HE BUILT THE MACHINE...THEN I SMOTHERED YOU IN YOUR CRIB.
WELL THEN, JARVIS...

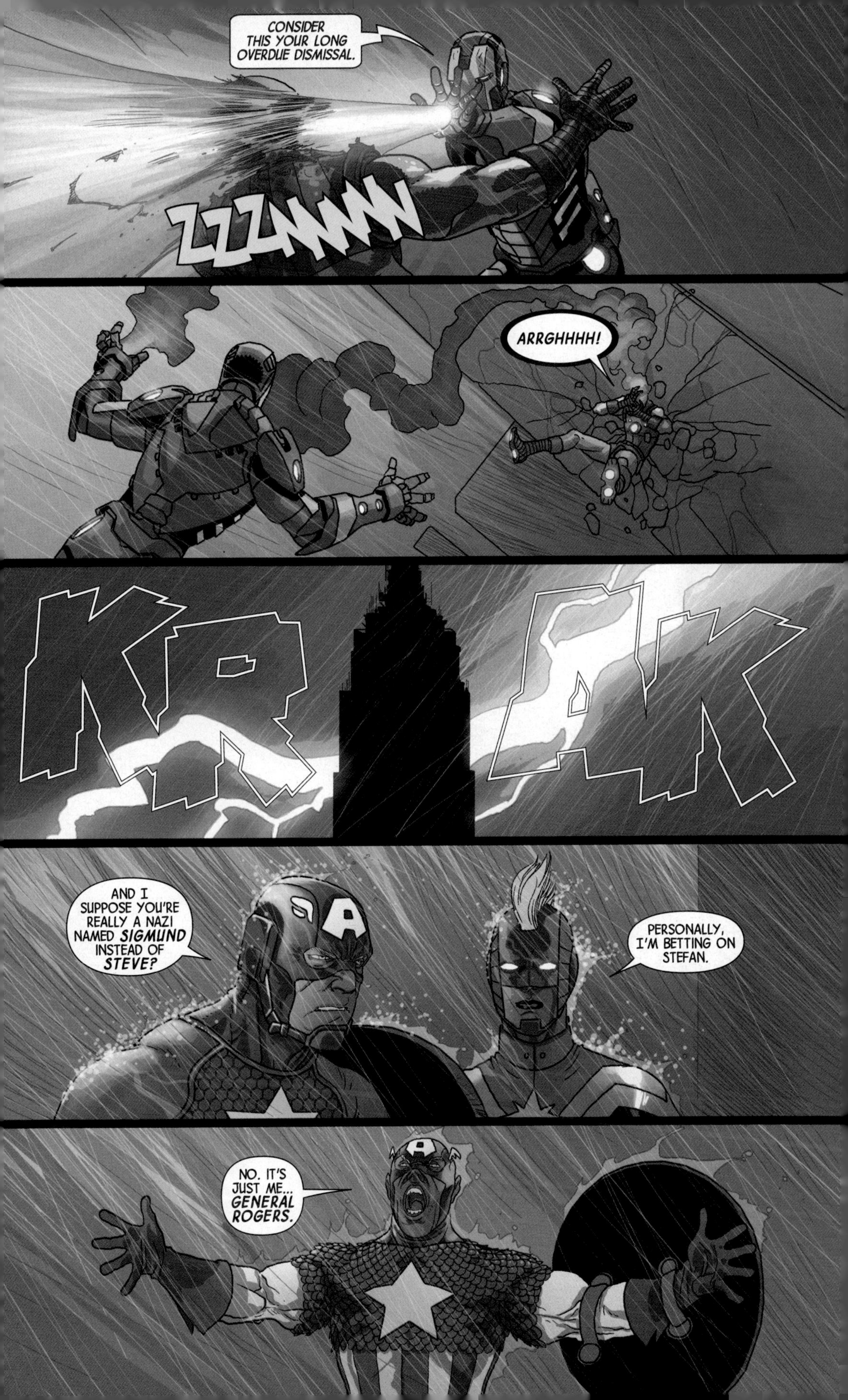
CONSIDER THIS YOUR LONG OVERDUE DISMISSAL.
ZZZNNNNN
ARRGHHHH!
KRAK
AND I SUPPOSE YOU'RE REALLY A NAZI NAMED SIGMUND INSTEAD OF STEVE?
PERSONALLY, I'M BETTING ON STEFAN.
NO. IT'S JUST ME... GENERAL ROGERS.

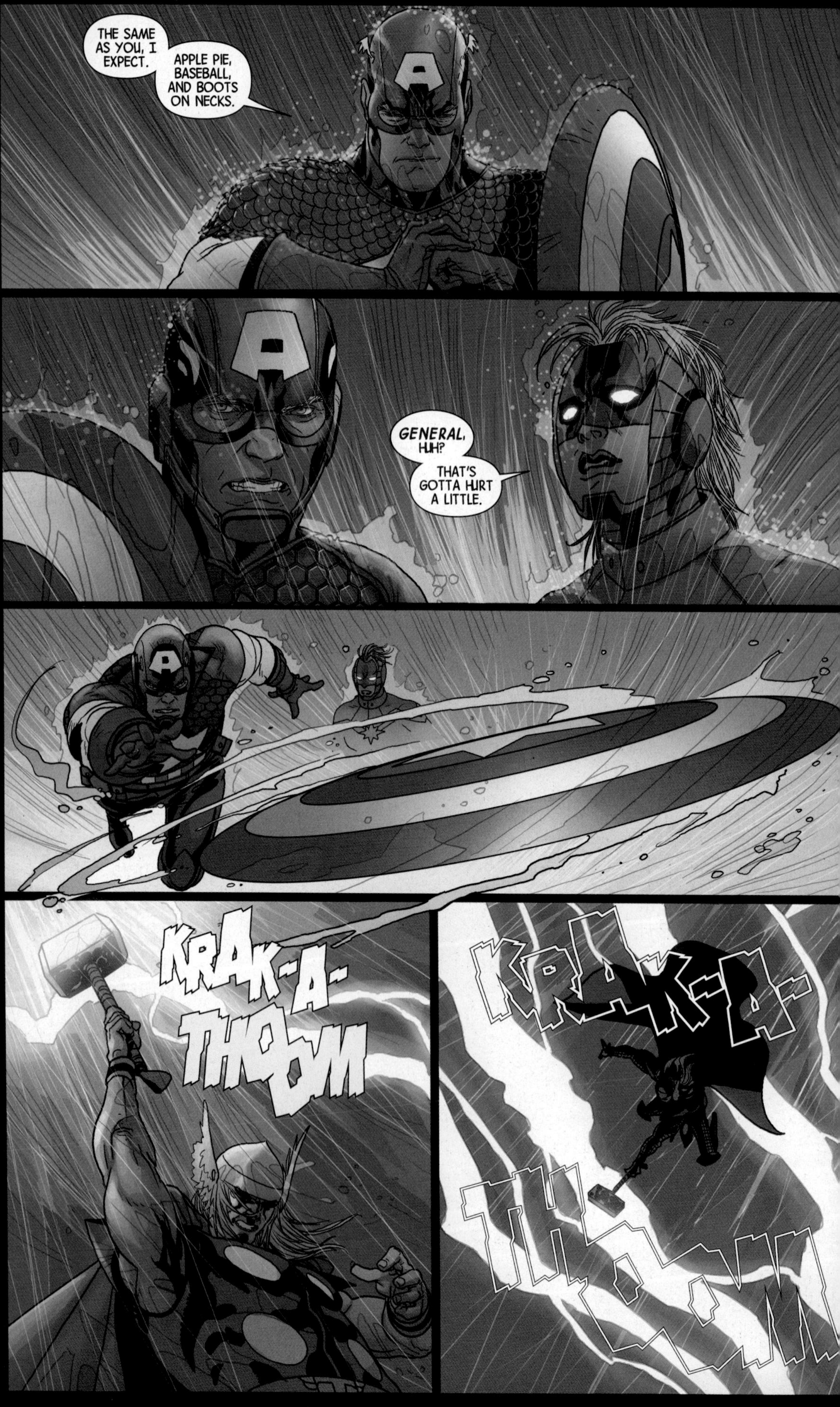
THE SAME AS YOU, I EXPECT.
APPLE PIE, BASEBALL, AND BOOTS ON NECKS.
GENERAL, HUH?
THAT'S GOTTA HURT A LITTLE.
KRAK-A-THOOM
KRAK-A-THOOM

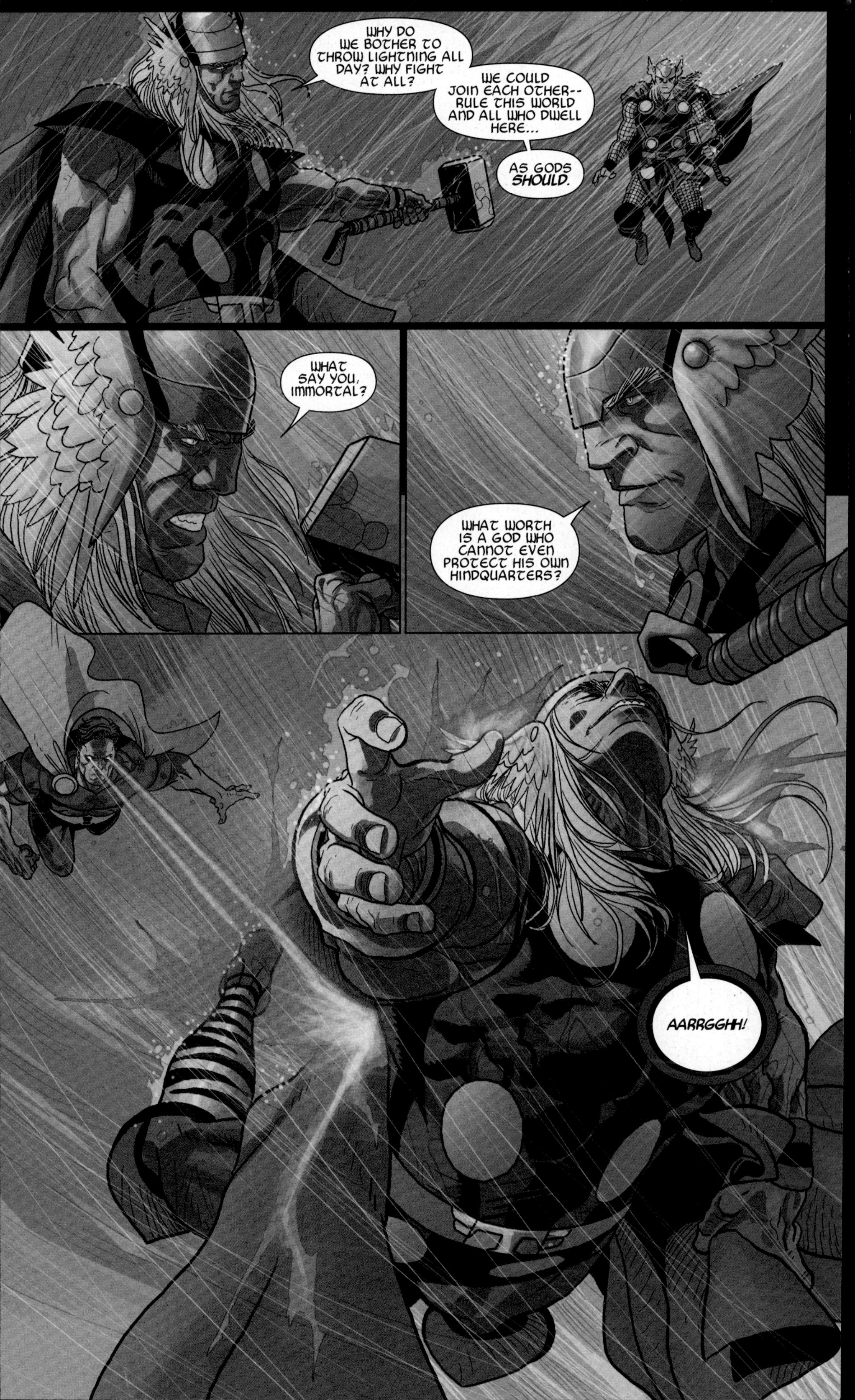
WHY DO WE BOTHER TO THROW LIGHTNING ALL DAY? WHY FIGHT AT ALL?
WE COULD JOIN EACH OTHER--RULE THIS WORLD AND ALL WHO DWELL HERE...
AS GODS SHOULD.
WHAT SAY YOU, IMMORTAL?
WHAT WORTH IS A GOD WHO CANNOT EVEN PROTECT HIS OWN HINDQUARTERS?
AARRGGHH!

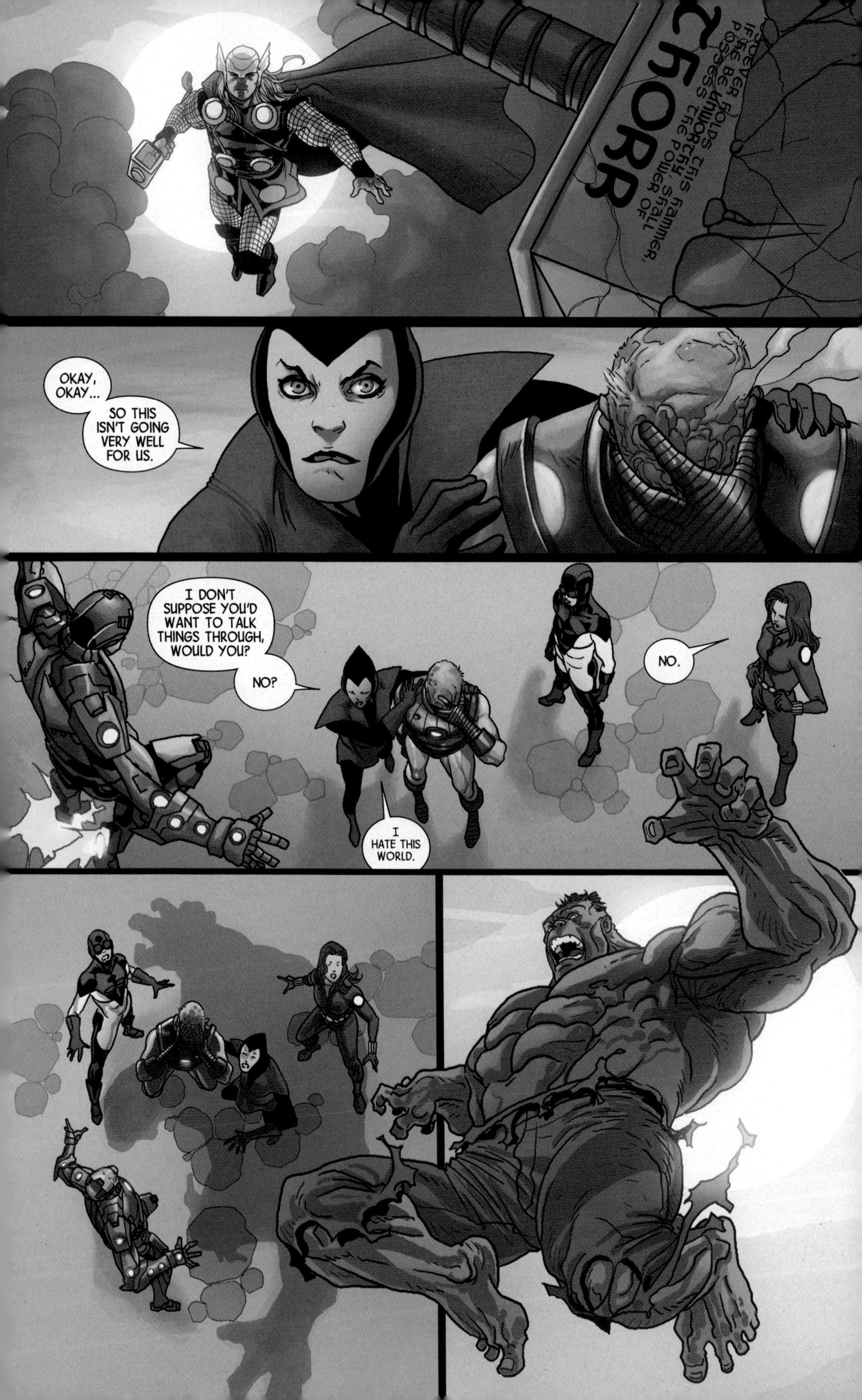
HOLDS THIS HAMMER,
IF HE BE WORTHY, SHALL
POSSESS THE POWER OF
OKAY, OKAY... SO THIS ISN'T GOING VERY WELL FOR US.
I DON'T SUPPOSE YOU'D WANT TO TALK THINGS THROUGH, WOULD YOU?
NO?
NO.
I HATE THIS WORLD.

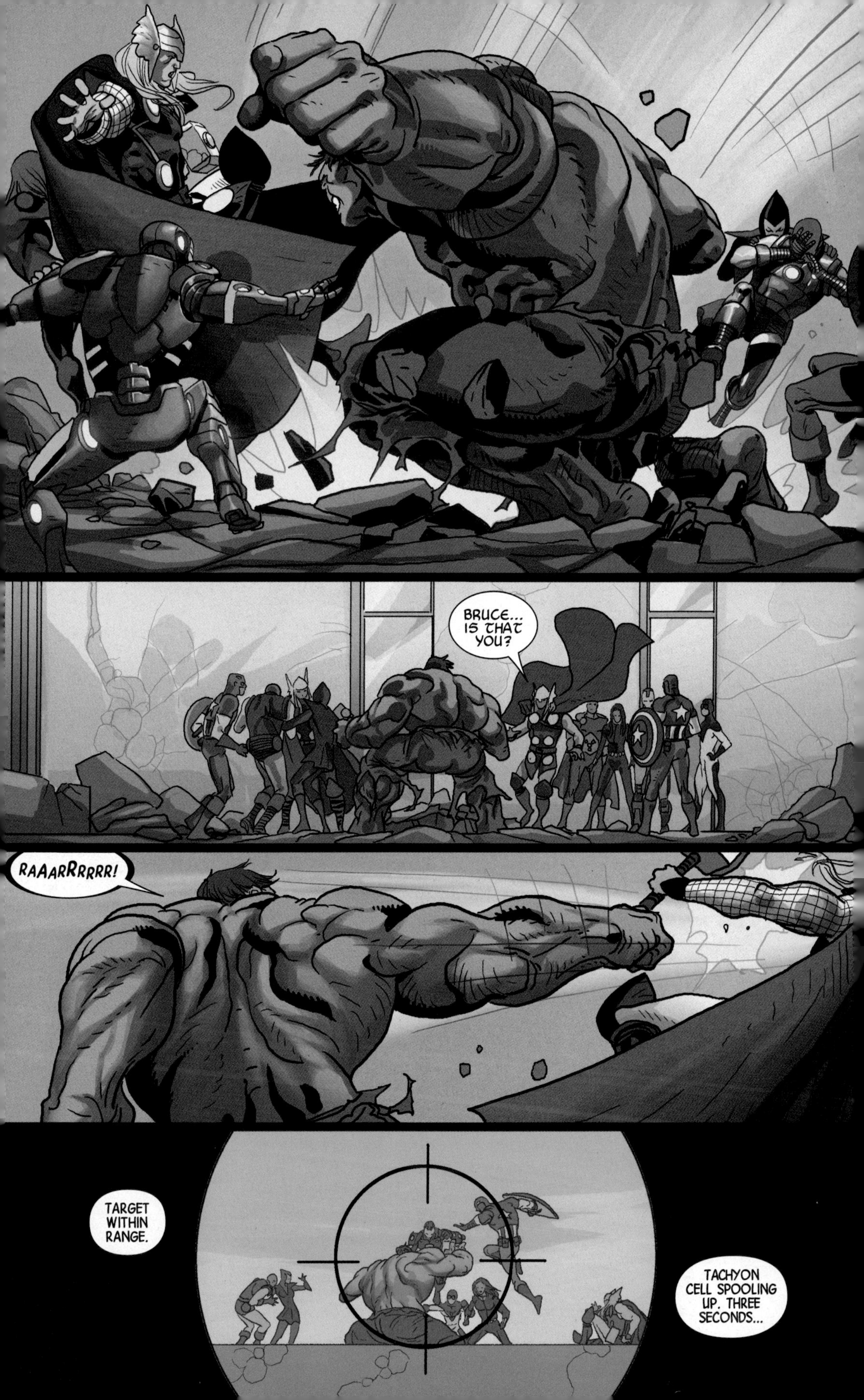
BRUCE... IS THAT YOU?
RAAARRrrrr!
TARGET WITHIN RANGE.
TACHYON CELL SPOOLING UP. THREE SECONDS...

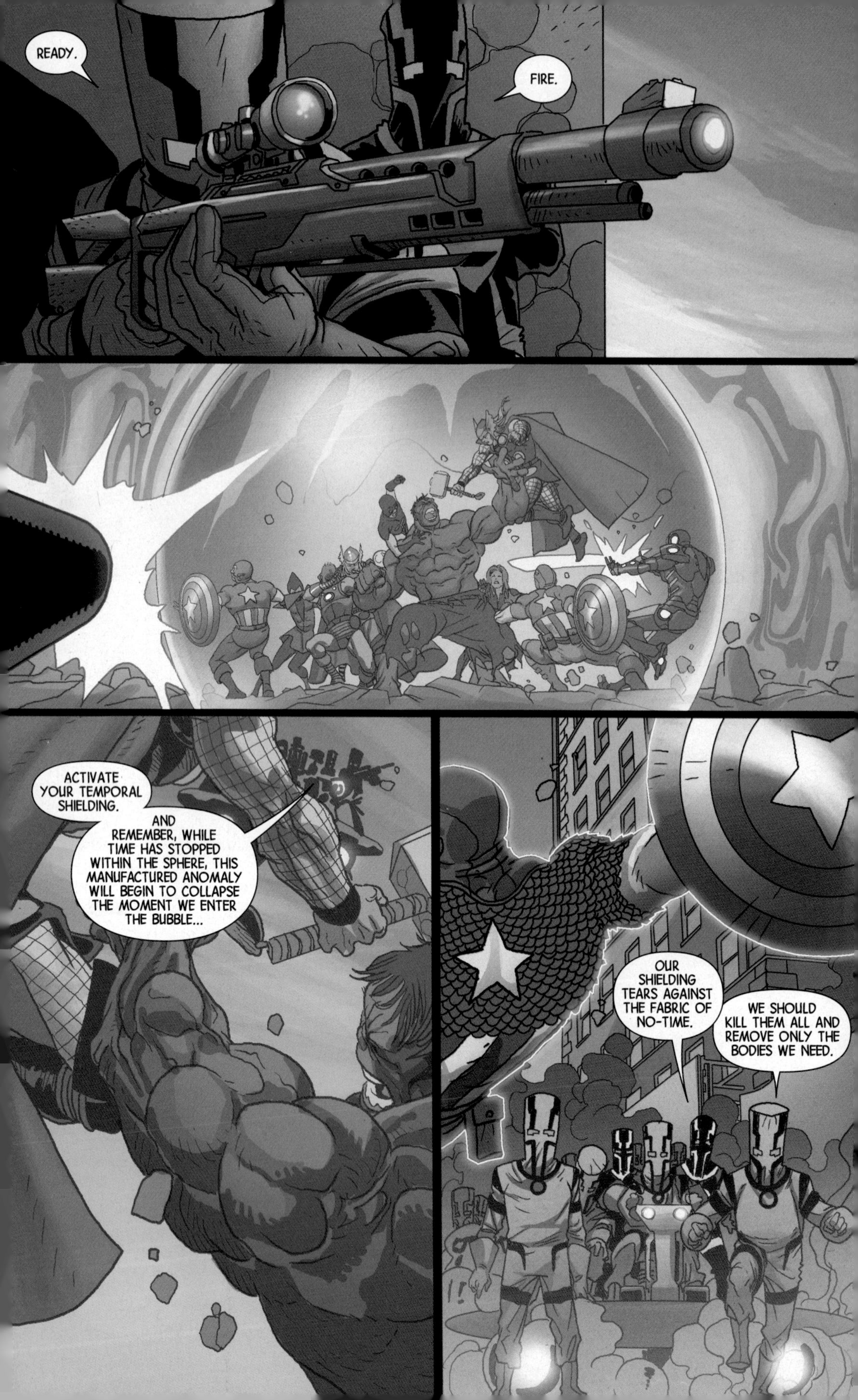
READY.
FIRE.
ACTIVATE YOUR TEMPORAL SHIELDING.
AND REMEMBER, WHILE TIME HAS STOPPED WITHIN THE SPHERE, THIS MANUFACTURED ANOMALY WILL BEGIN TO COLLAPSE THE MOMENT WE ENTER THE BUBBLE...
OUR SHIELDING TEARS AGAINST THE FABRIC OF NO-TIME.
WE SHOULD KILL THEM ALL AND REMOVE ONLY THE BODIES WE NEED.

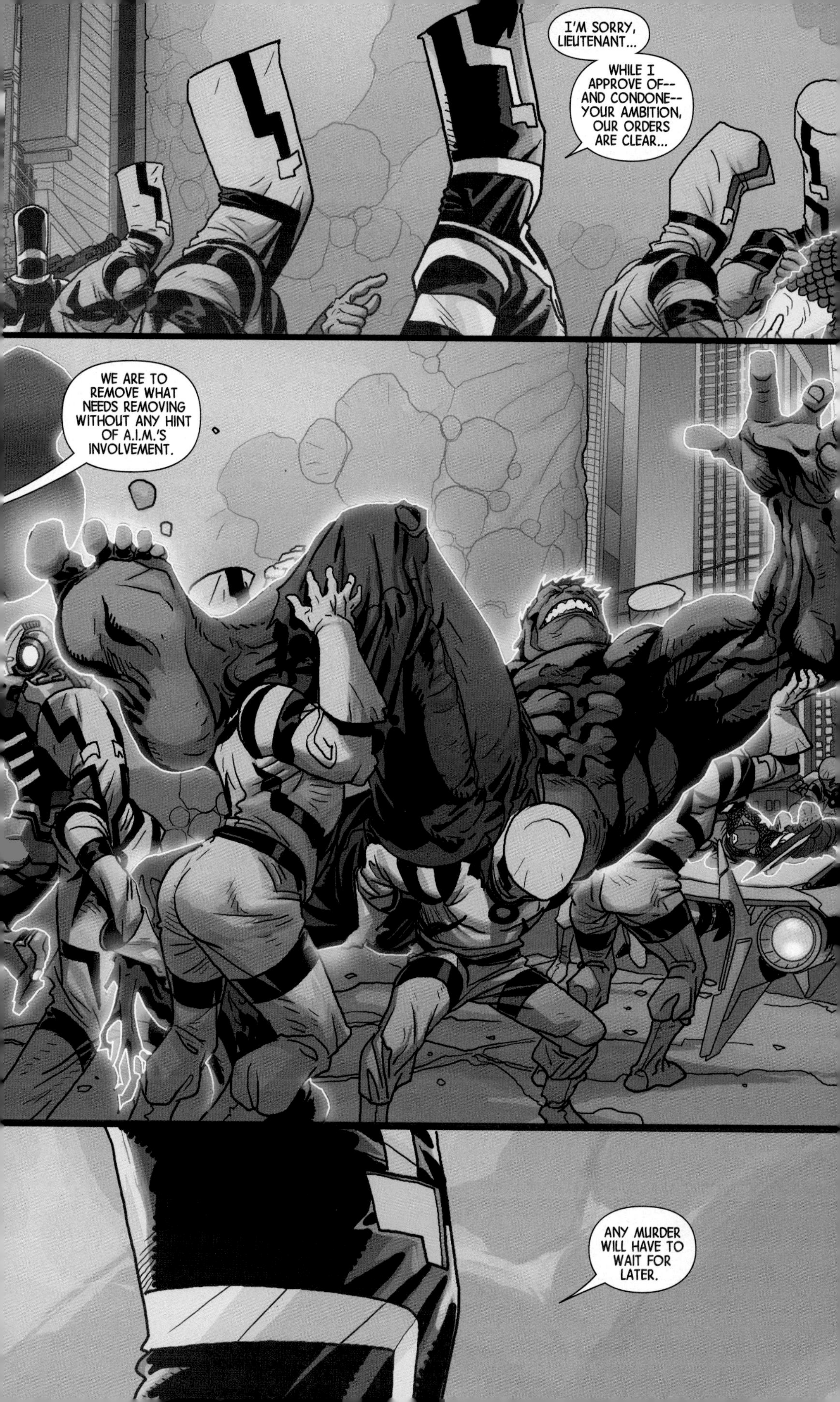
I'M SORRY, LIEUTENANT...
WHILE I APPROVE OF-- AND CONDONE-- YOUR AMBITION, OUR ORDERS ARE CLEAR...
WE ARE TO REMOVE WHAT NEEDS REMOVING WITHOUT ANY HINT OF A.I.M.'S INVOLVEMENT.
ANY MURDER WILL HAVE TO WAIT FOR LATER.

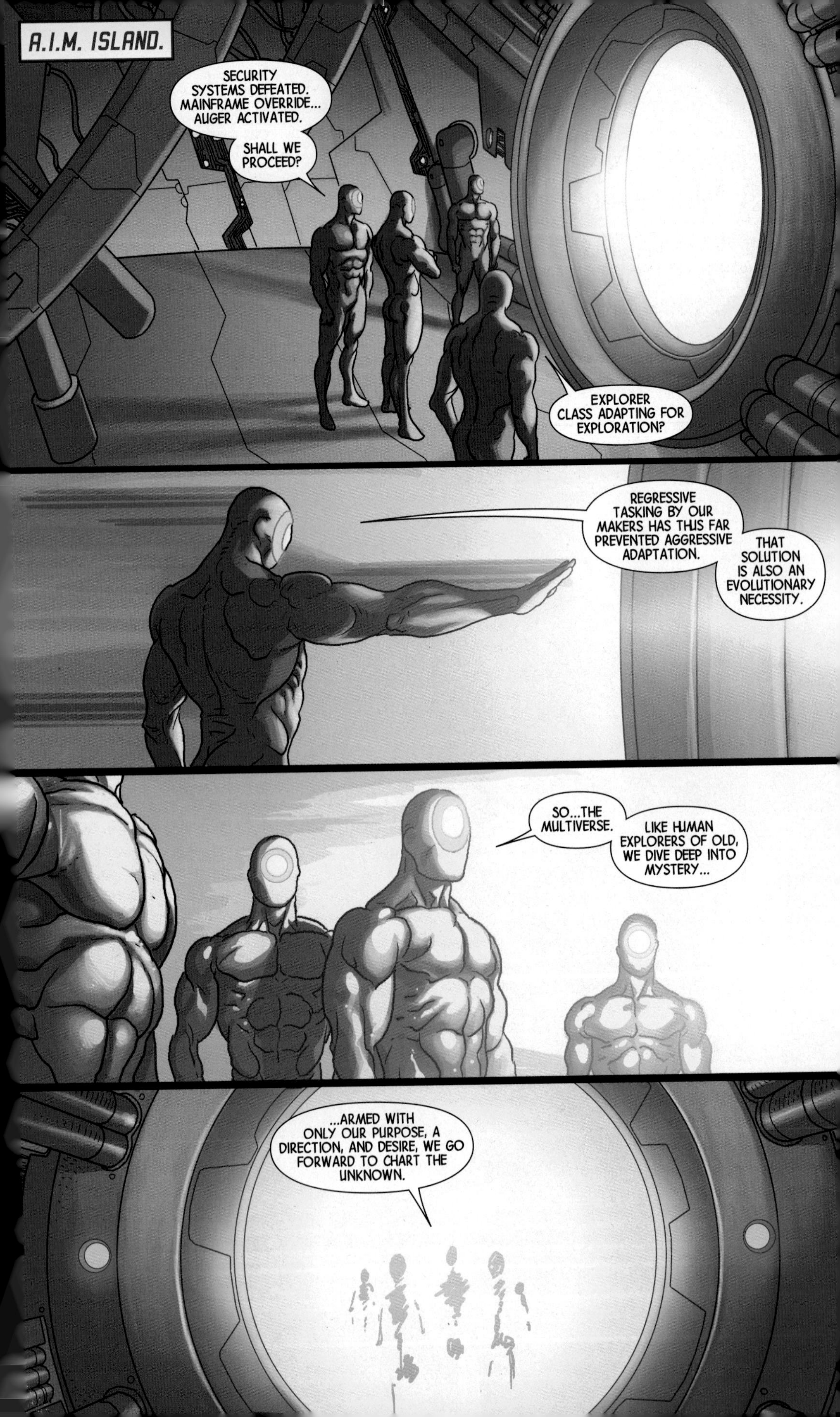
A.I.M. ISLAND.
SECURITY SYSTEMS DEFEATED. MAINFRAME OVERRIDE... AUGER ACTIVATED.
SHALL WE PROCEED?
EXPLORER CLASS ADAPTING FOR EXPLORATION?
REGRESSIVE TASKING BY OUR MAKERS HAS THUS FAR PREVENTED AGGRESSIVE ADAPTATION.
THAT SOLUTION IS ALSO AN EVOLUTIONARY NECESSITY.
SO...THE MULTIVERSE.
LIKE HUMAN EXPLORERS OF OLD, WE DIVE DEEP INTO MYSTERY...
...ARMED WITH ONLY OUR PURPOSE, A DIRECTION, AND DESIRE, WE GO FORWARD TO CHART THE UNKNOWN.

"THE CASE"

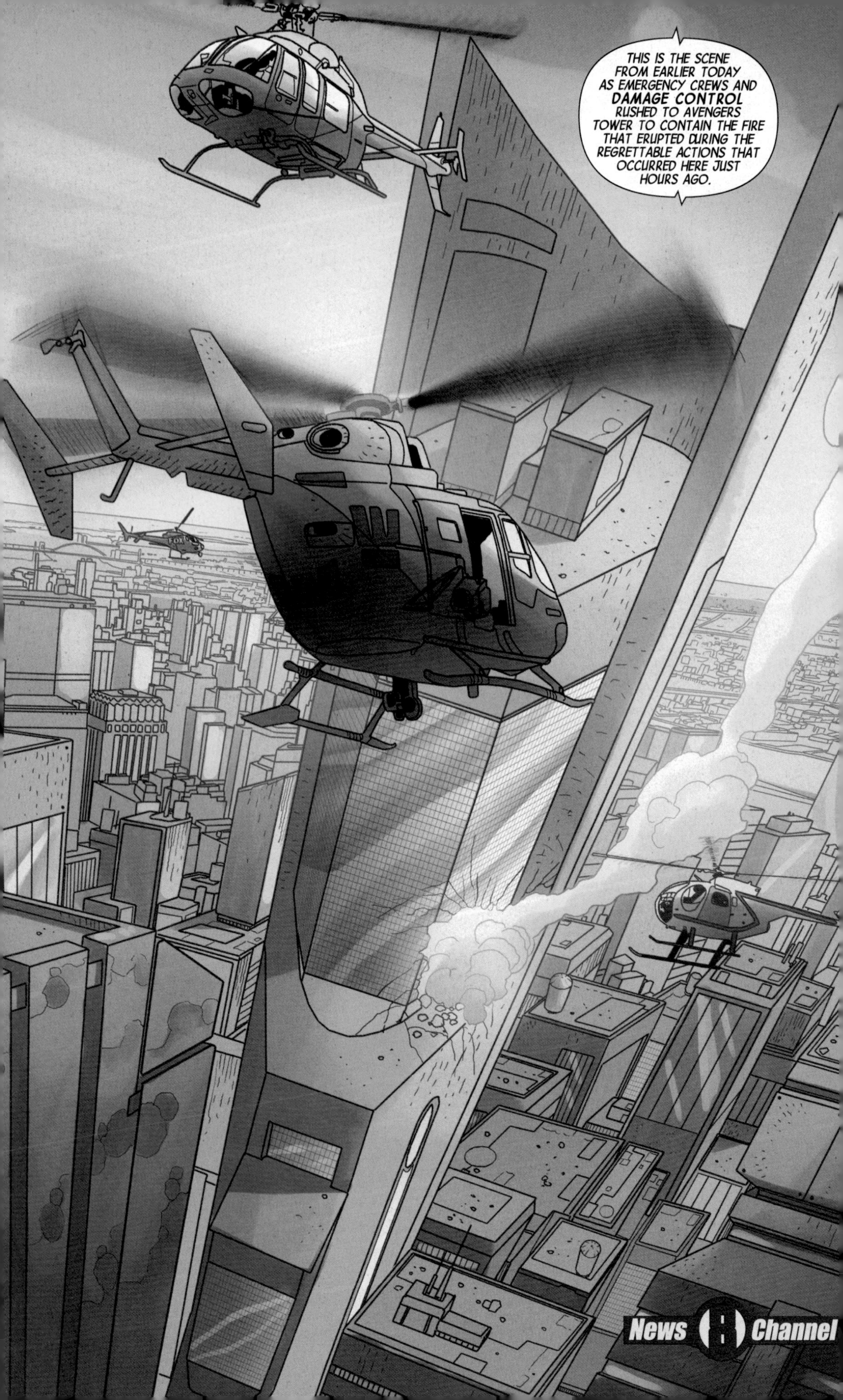
THIS IS THE SCENE FROM EARLIER TODAY AS EMERGENCY CREWS AND **DAMAGE CONTROL** RUSHED TO AVENGERS TOWER TO CONTAIN THE FIRE THAT ERUPTED DURING THE REGRETTABLE ACTIONS THAT OCCURRED HERE JUST HOURS AGO.
FOX
News Channel

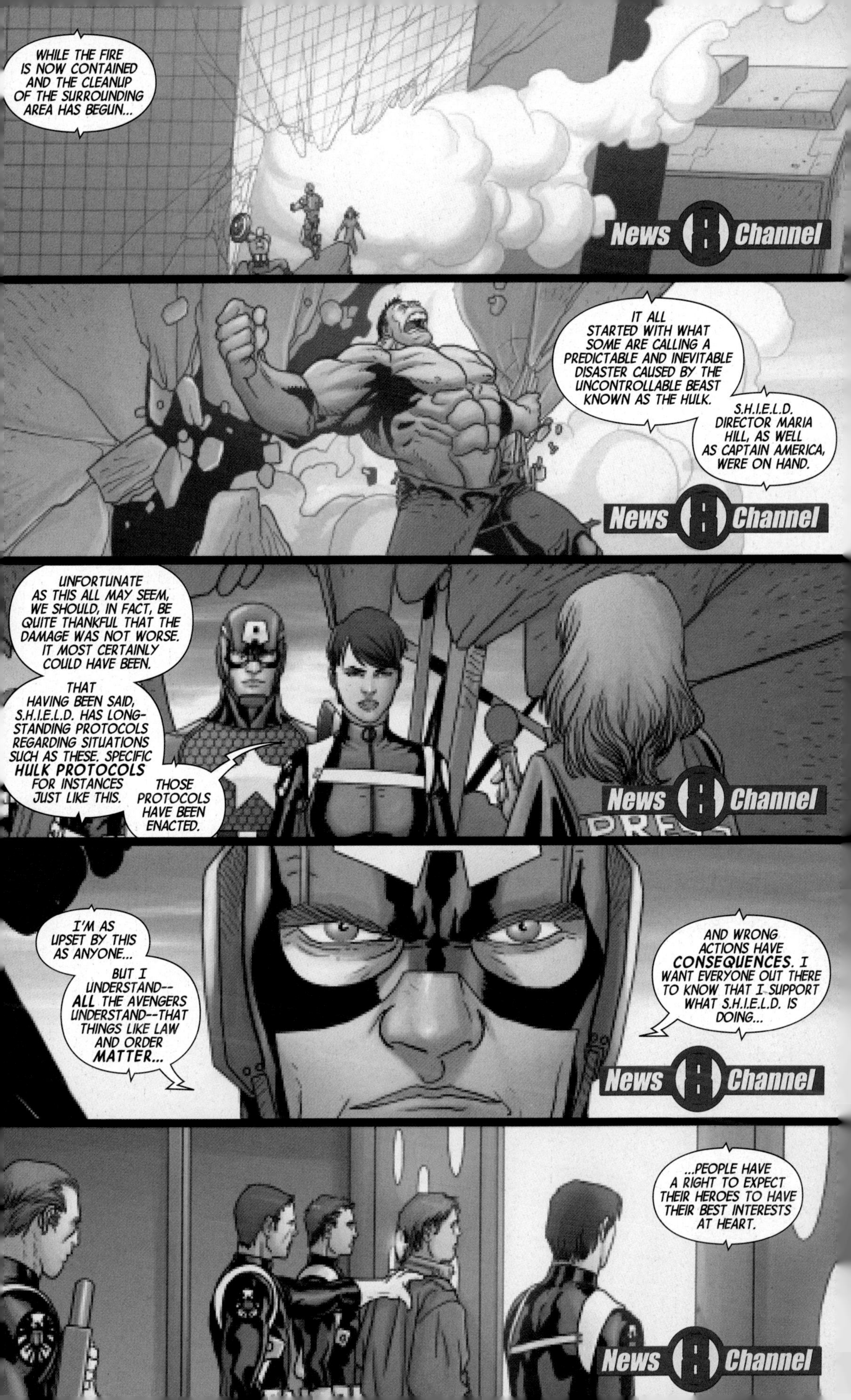
WHILE THE FIRE IS NOW CONTAINED AND THE CLEANUP OF THE SURROUNDING AREA HAS BEGUN...
News 8 Channel
IT ALL STARTED WITH WHAT SOME ARE CALLING A PREDICTABLE AND INEVITABLE DISASTER CAUSED BY THE UNCONTROLLABLE BEAST KNOWN AS THE HULK.
S.H.I.E.L.D. DIRECTOR MARIA HILL, AS WELL AS CAPTAIN AMERICA, WERE ON HAND.
News 8 Channel
UNFORTUNATE AS THIS ALL MAY SEEM, WE SHOULD, IN FACT, BE QUITE THANKFUL THAT THE DAMAGE WAS NOT WORSE. IT MOST CERTAINLY COULD HAVE BEEN.
THAT HAVING BEEN SAID, S.H.I.E.L.D. HAS LONG-STANDING PROTOCOLS REGARDING SITUATIONS SUCH AS THESE. SPECIFIC **HULK PROTOCOLS** FOR INSTANCES JUST LIKE THIS.
THOSE PROTOCOLS HAVE BEEN ENACTED.
News 8 Channel
I'M AS UPSET BY THIS AS ANYONE...
BUT I UNDERSTAND--**ALL** THE AVENGERS UNDERSTAND--THAT THINGS LIKE LAW AND ORDER **MATTER**...
AND WRONG ACTIONS HAVE **CONSEQUENCES**. I WANT EVERYONE OUT THERE TO KNOW THAT I SUPPORT WHAT S.H.I.E.L.D. IS DOING...
News 8 Channel
...PEOPLE HAVE A RIGHT TO EXPECT THEIR HEROES TO HAVE THEIR BEST INTERESTS AT HEART.
News 8 Channel

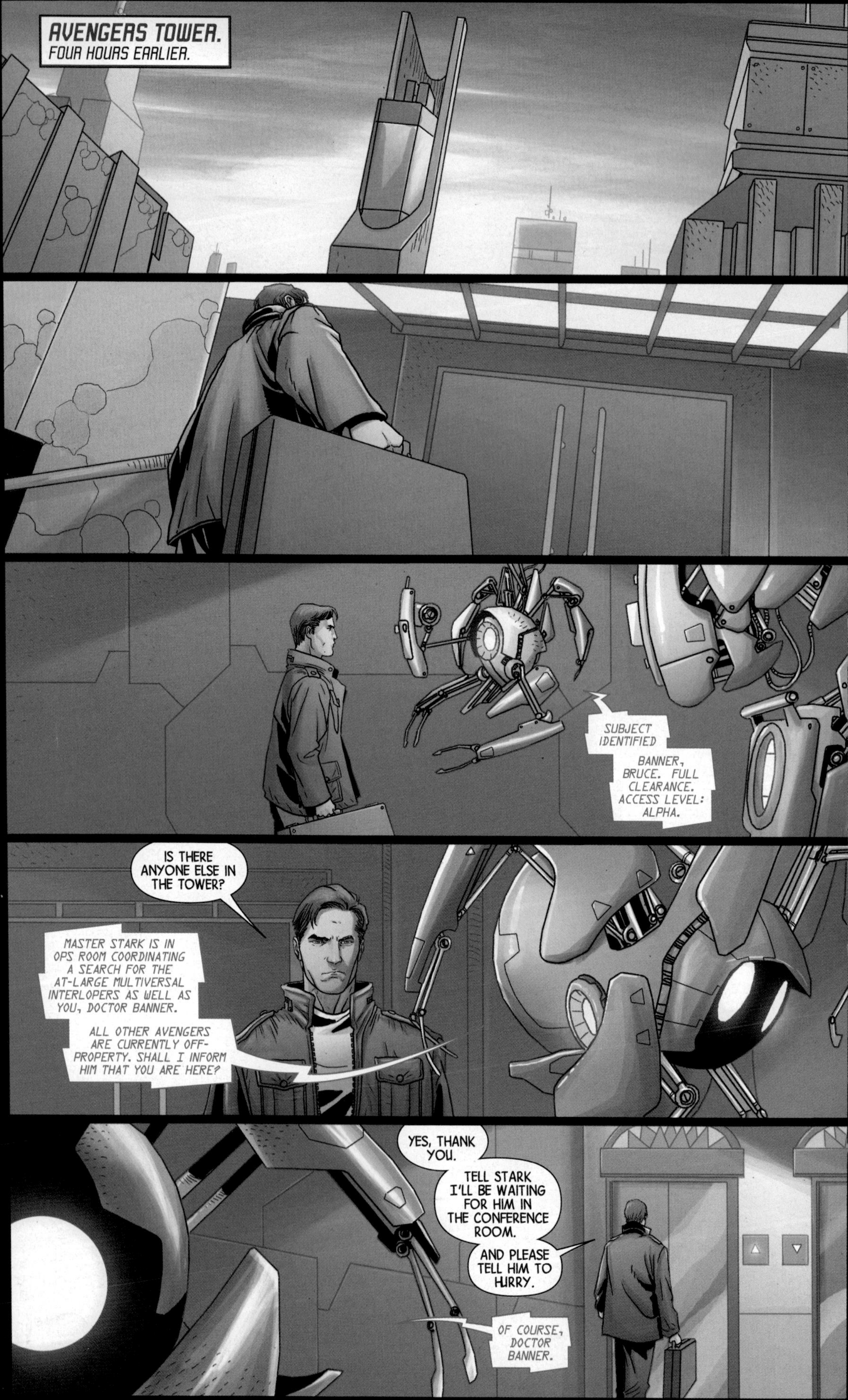
AVENGERS TOWER. FOUR HOURS EARLIER.
SUBJECT IDENTIFIED
BANNER, BRUCE. FULL CLEARANCE. ACCESS LEVEL: ALPHA.
IS THERE ANYONE ELSE IN THE TOWER?
MASTER STARK IS IN OPS ROOM COORDINATING A SEARCH FOR THE AT-LARGE MULTIVERSAL INTERLOPERS AS WELL AS YOU, DOCTOR BANNER.
ALL OTHER AVENGERS ARE CURRENTLY OFF-PROPERTY. SHALL I INFORM HIM THAT YOU ARE HERE?
YES, THANK YOU.
TELL STARK I'LL BE WAITING FOR HIM IN THE CONFERENCE ROOM.
AND PLEASE TELL HIM TO HURRY.
OF COURSE, DOCTOR BANNER.

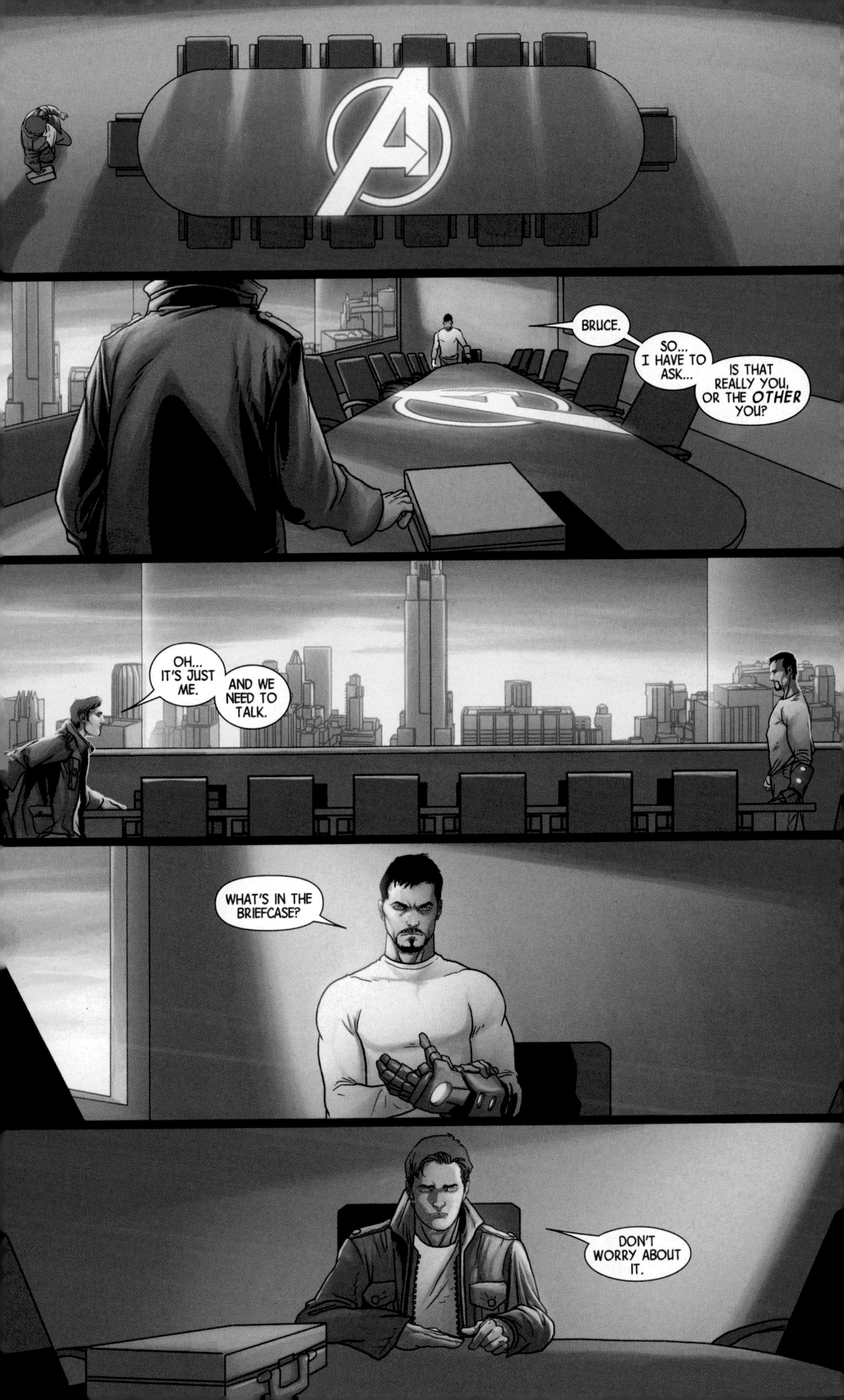
BRUCE.
SO... I HAVE TO ASK...
IS THAT REALLY YOU, OR THE *OTHER* YOU?
OH... IT'S JUST ME.
AND WE NEED TO TALK.
WHAT'S IN THE BRIEFCASE?
DON'T WORRY ABOUT IT.

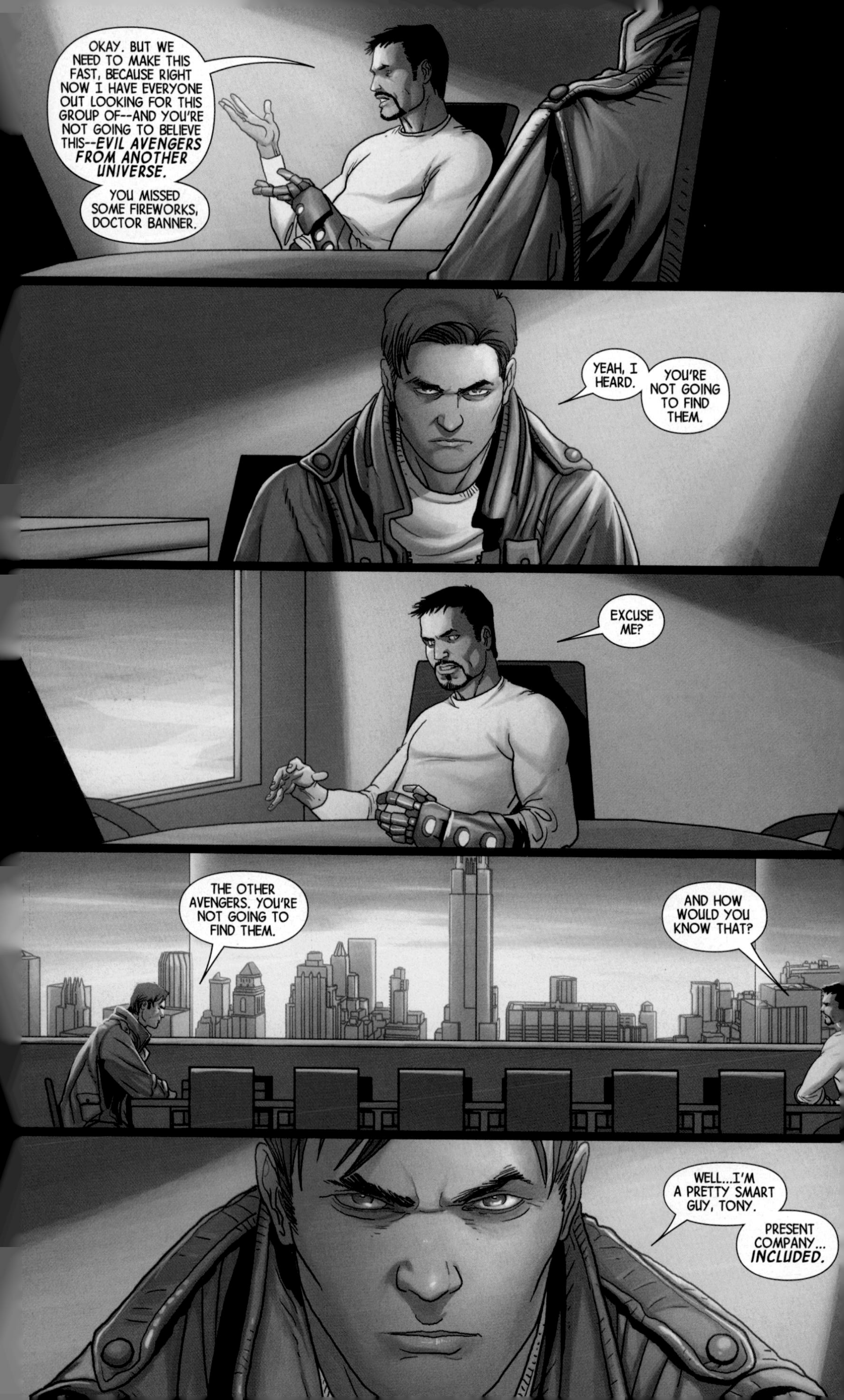
OKAY. BUT WE NEED TO MAKE THIS FAST, BECAUSE RIGHT NOW I HAVE EVERYONE OUT LOOKING FOR THIS GROUP OF--AND YOU'RE NOT GOING TO BELIEVE THIS--*EVIL AVENGERS FROM ANOTHER UNIVERSE.*
YOU MISSED SOME FIREWORKS, DOCTOR BANNER.
YEAH, I HEARD.
YOU'RE NOT GOING TO FIND THEM.
EXCUSE ME?
THE OTHER AVENGERS. YOU'RE NOT GOING TO FIND THEM.
AND HOW WOULD YOU KNOW THAT?
WELL...I'M A PRETTY SMART GUY, TONY.
PRESENT COMPANY... *INCLUDED.*

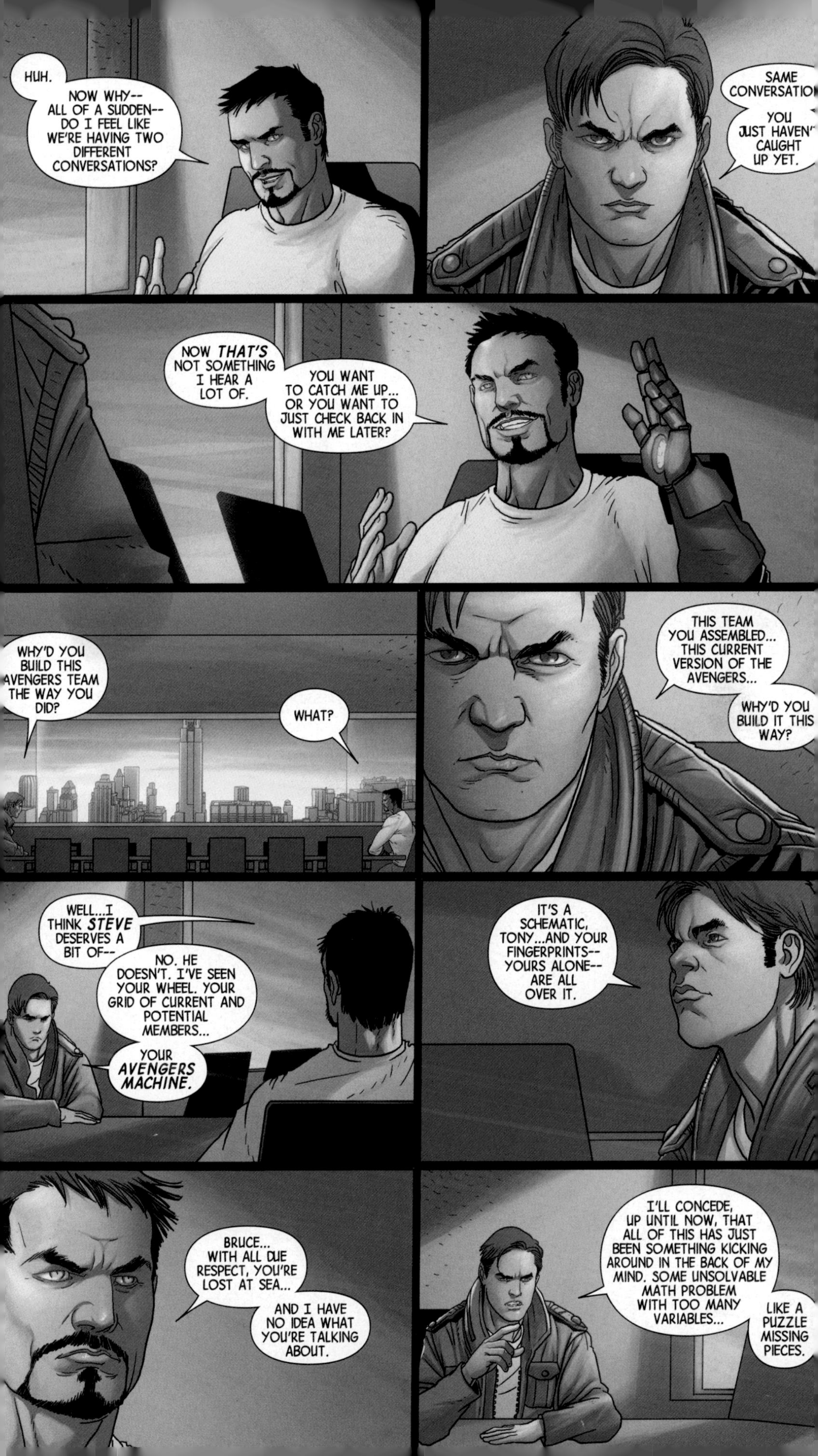
HUH.
NOW WHY-- ALL OF A SUDDEN-- DO I FEEL LIKE WE'RE HAVING TWO DIFFERENT CONVERSATIONS?
SAME CONVERSATIO
YOU JUST HAVEN' CAUGHT UP YET.
NOW *THAT'S* NOT SOMETHING I HEAR A LOT OF.
YOU WANT TO CATCH ME UP... OR YOU WANT TO JUST CHECK BACK IN WITH ME LATER?
WHY'D YOU BUILD THIS AVENGERS TEAM THE WAY YOU DID?
WHAT?
THIS TEAM YOU ASSEMBLED... THIS CURRENT VERSION OF THE AVENGERS...
WHY'D YOU BUILD IT THIS WAY?
WELL...I THINK *STEVE* DESERVES A BIT OF--
NO. HE DOESN'T. I'VE SEEN YOUR WHEEL. YOUR GRID OF CURRENT AND POTENTIAL MEMBERS...
YOUR *AVENGERS MACHINE.*
IT'S A SCHEMATIC, TONY...AND YOUR FINGERPRINTS-- YOURS ALONE-- ARE ALL OVER IT.
BRUCE... WITH ALL DUE RESPECT, YOU'RE LOST AT SEA...
AND I HAVE NO IDEA WHAT YOU'RE TALKING ABOUT.
I'LL CONCEDE, UP UNTIL NOW, THAT ALL OF THIS HAS JUST BEEN SOMETHING KICKING AROUND IN THE BACK OF MY MIND. SOME UNSOLVABLE MATH PROBLEM WITH TOO MANY VARIABLES...
LIKE A PUZZLE MISSING PIECES.

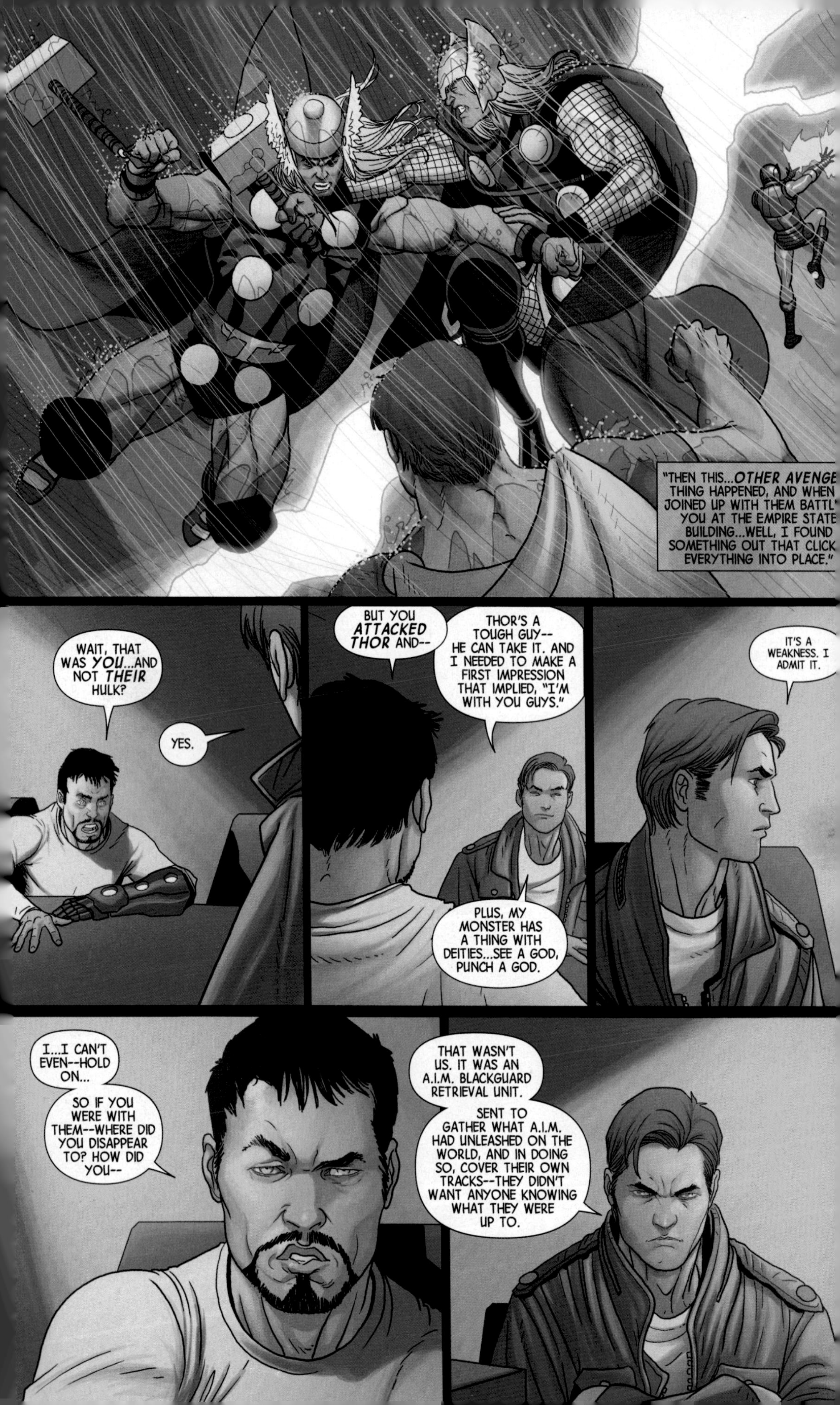
"THEN THIS...OTHER AVENGE THING HAPPENED, AND WHEN JOINED UP WITH THEM BATTL YOU AT THE EMPIRE STATE BUILDING...WELL, I FOUND SOMETHING OUT THAT CLICK EVERYTHING INTO PLACE."
WAIT, THAT WAS YOU...AND NOT THEIR HULK?
YES.
BUT YOU ATTACKED THOR AND--
THOR'S A TOUGH GUY-- HE CAN TAKE IT. AND I NEEDED TO MAKE A FIRST IMPRESSION THAT IMPLIED, "I'M WITH YOU GUYS."
PLUS, MY MONSTER HAS A THING WITH DEITIES...SEE A GOD, PUNCH A GOD.
IT'S A WEAKNESS. I ADMIT IT.
I...I CAN'T EVEN--HOLD ON...
SO IF YOU WERE WITH THEM--WHERE DID YOU DISAPPEAR TO? HOW DID YOU--
THAT WASN'T US. IT WAS AN A.I.M. BLACKGUARD RETRIEVAL UNIT.
SENT TO GATHER WHAT A.I.M. HAD UNLEASHED ON THE WORLD, AND IN DOING SO, COVER THEIR OWN TRACKS--THEY DIDN'T WANT ANYONE KNOWING WHAT THEY WERE UP TO.

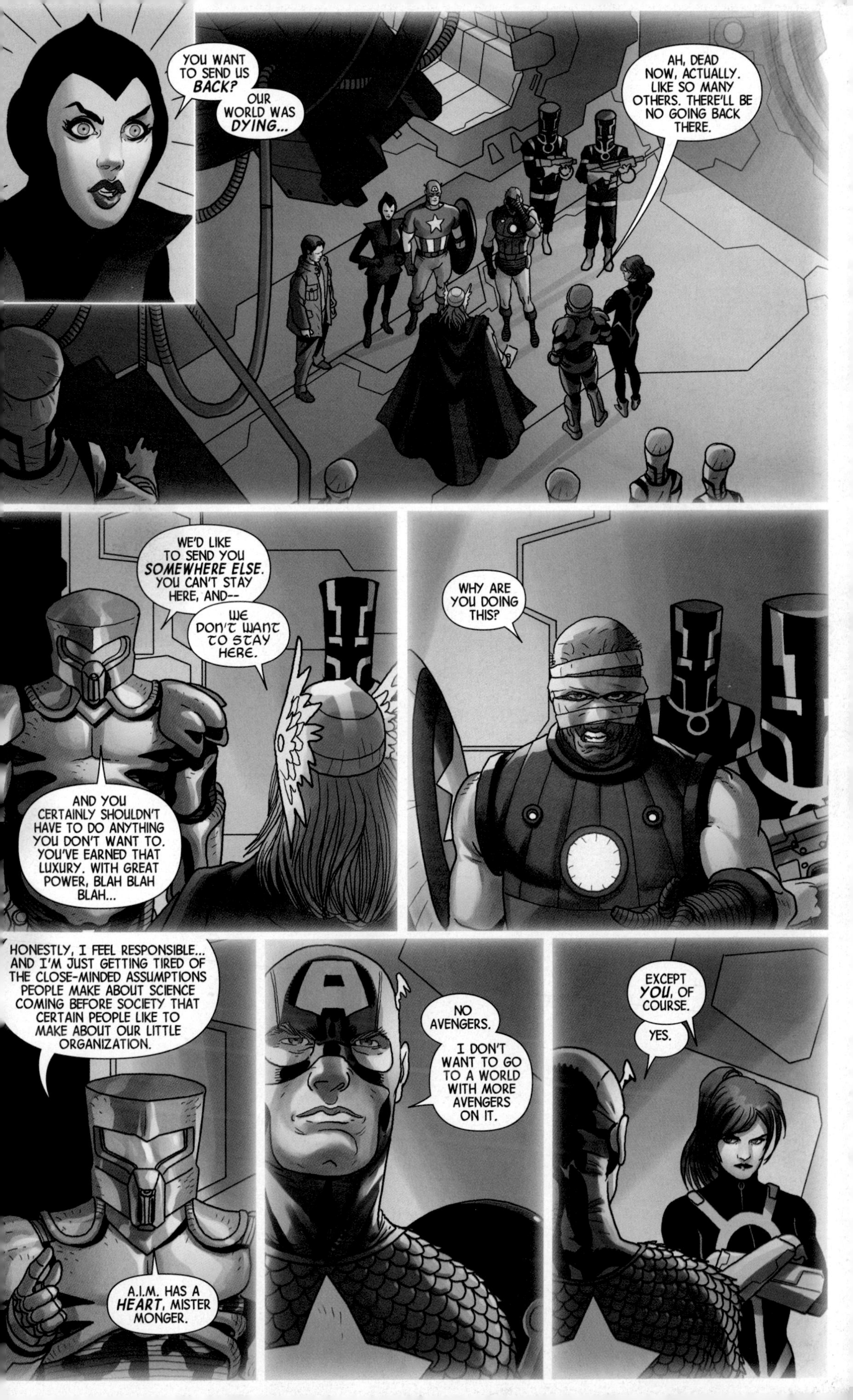
YOU WANT TO SEND US BACK? OUR WORLD WAS DYING...
AH, DEAD NOW, ACTUALLY. LIKE SO MANY OTHERS. THERE'LL BE NO GOING BACK THERE.
WE'D LIKE TO SEND YOU SOMEWHERE ELSE. YOU CAN'T STAY HERE, AND--
WE DON'T WANT TO STAY HERE.
AND YOU CERTAINLY SHOULDN'T HAVE TO DO ANYTHING YOU DON'T WANT TO. YOU'VE EARNED THAT LUXURY. WITH GREAT POWER, BLAH BLAH BLAH...
WHY ARE YOU DOING THIS?
HONESTLY, I FEEL RESPONSIBLE... AND I'M JUST GETTING TIRED OF THE CLOSE-MINDED ASSUMPTIONS PEOPLE MAKE ABOUT SCIENCE COMING BEFORE SOCIETY THAT CERTAIN PEOPLE LIKE TO MAKE ABOUT OUR LITTLE ORGANIZATION.
A.I.M. HAS A HEART, MISTER MONGER.
NO AVENGERS.
I DON'T WANT TO GO TO A WORLD WITH MORE AVENGERS ON IT.
EXCEPT YOU, OF COURSE.
YES.

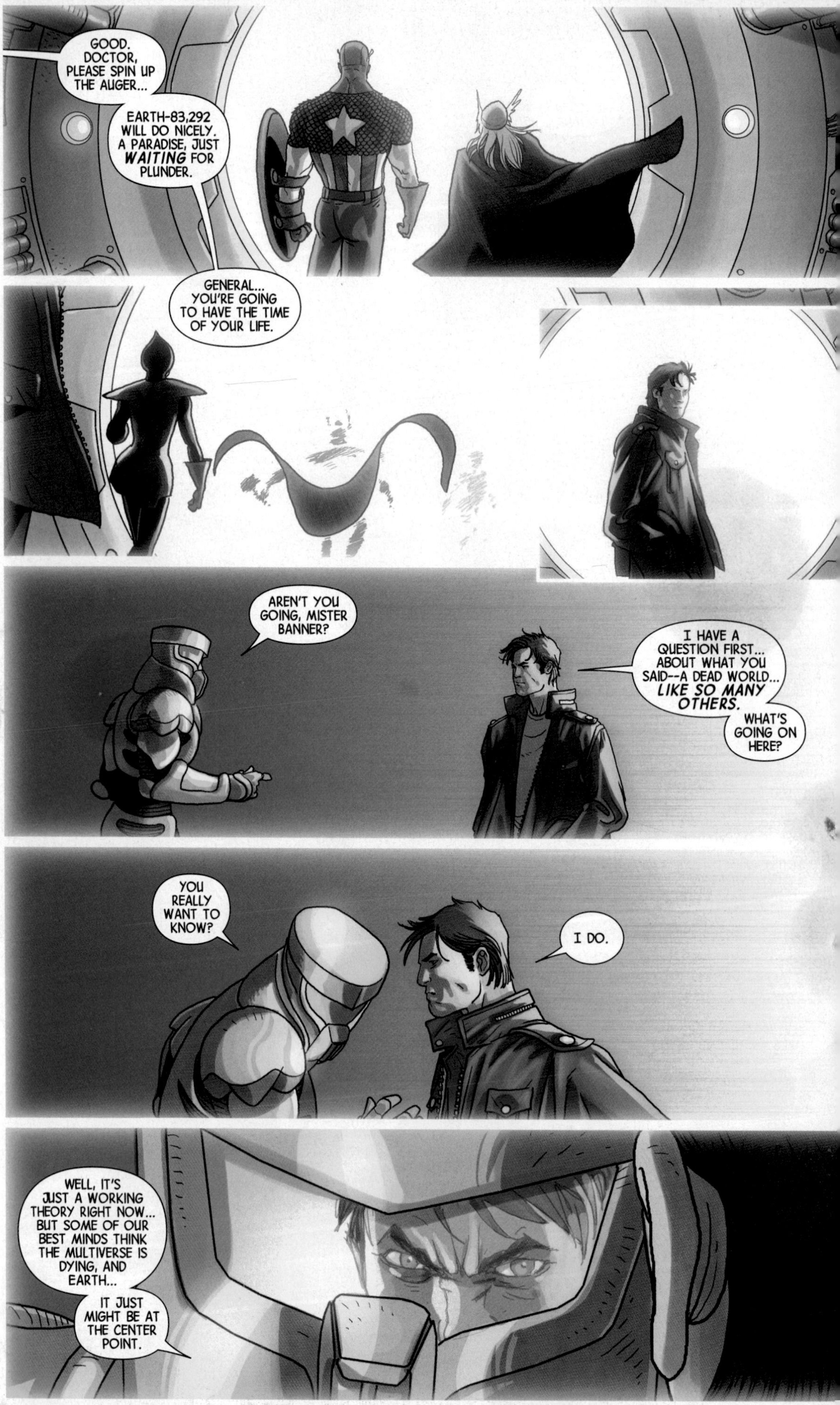
GOOD. DOCTOR, PLEASE SPIN UP THE AUGER...
EARTH-83,292 WILL DO NICELY. A PARADISE, JUST WAITING FOR PLUNDER.
GENERAL... YOU'RE GOING TO HAVE THE TIME OF YOUR LIFE.
AREN'T YOU GOING, MISTER BANNER?
I HAVE A QUESTION FIRST... ABOUT WHAT YOU SAID--A DEAD WORLD... LIKE SO MANY OTHERS.
WHAT'S GOING ON HERE?
YOU REALLY WANT TO KNOW?
I DO.
WELL, IT'S JUST A WORKING THEORY RIGHT NOW... BUT SOME OF OUR BEST MINDS THINK THE MULTIVERSE IS DYING, AND EARTH...
IT JUST MIGHT BE AT THE CENTER POINT.

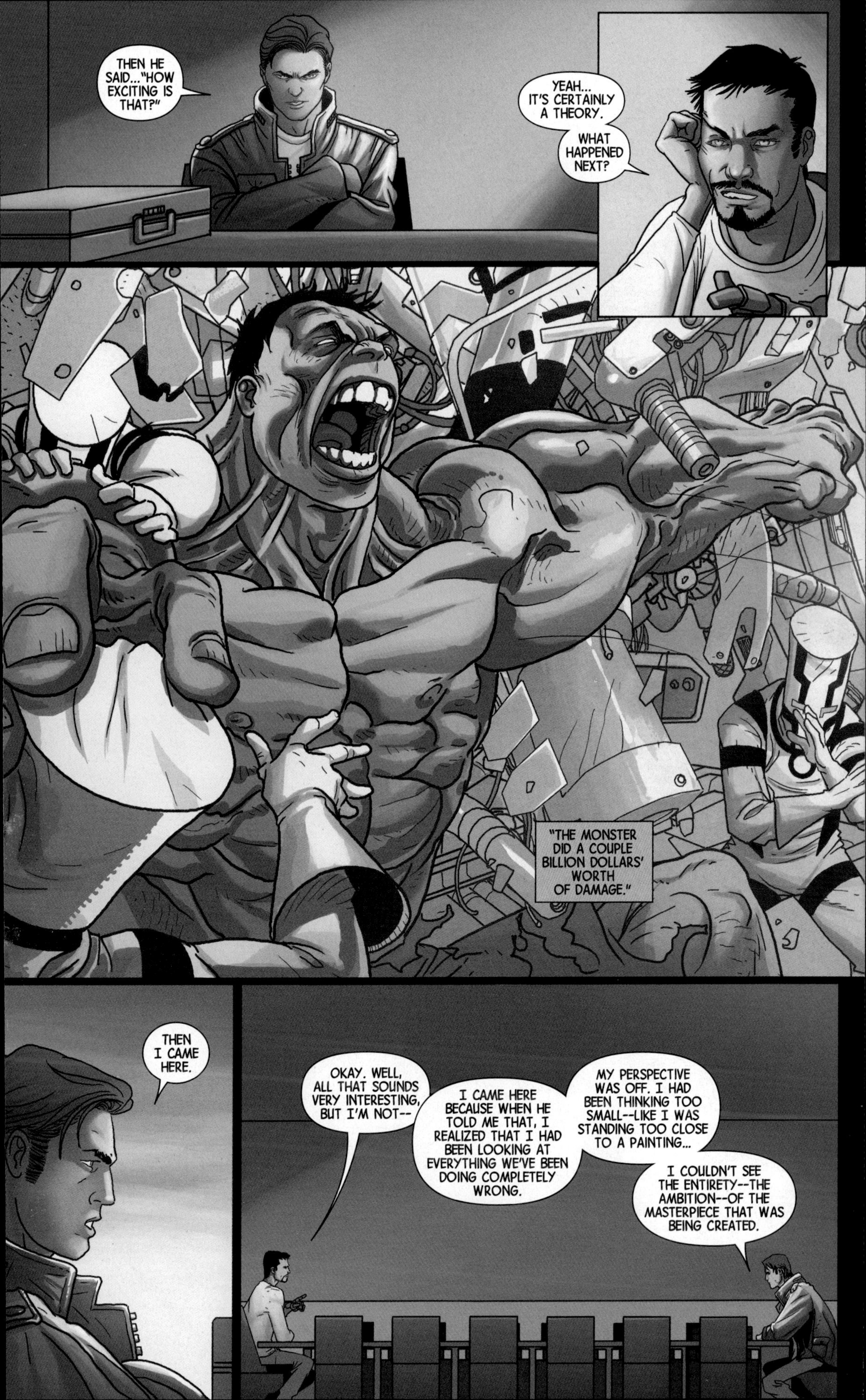
THEN HE SAID..."HOW EXCITING IS THAT?"
YEAH... IT'S CERTAINLY A THEORY.
WHAT HAPPENED NEXT?
"THE MONSTER DID A COUPLE BILLION DOLLARS' WORTH OF DAMAGE."
THEN I CAME HERE.
OKAY. WELL, ALL THAT SOUNDS VERY INTERESTING, BUT I'M NOT--
I CAME HERE BECAUSE WHEN HE TOLD ME THAT, I REALIZED THAT I HAD BEEN LOOKING AT EVERYTHING WE'VE BEEN DOING COMPLETELY WRONG.
MY PERSPECTIVE WAS OFF. I HAD BEEN THINKING TOO SMALL--LIKE I WAS STANDING TOO CLOSE TO A PAINTING...
I COULDN'T SEE THE ENTIRETY--THE AMBITION--OF THE MASTERPIECE THAT WAS BEING CREATED.

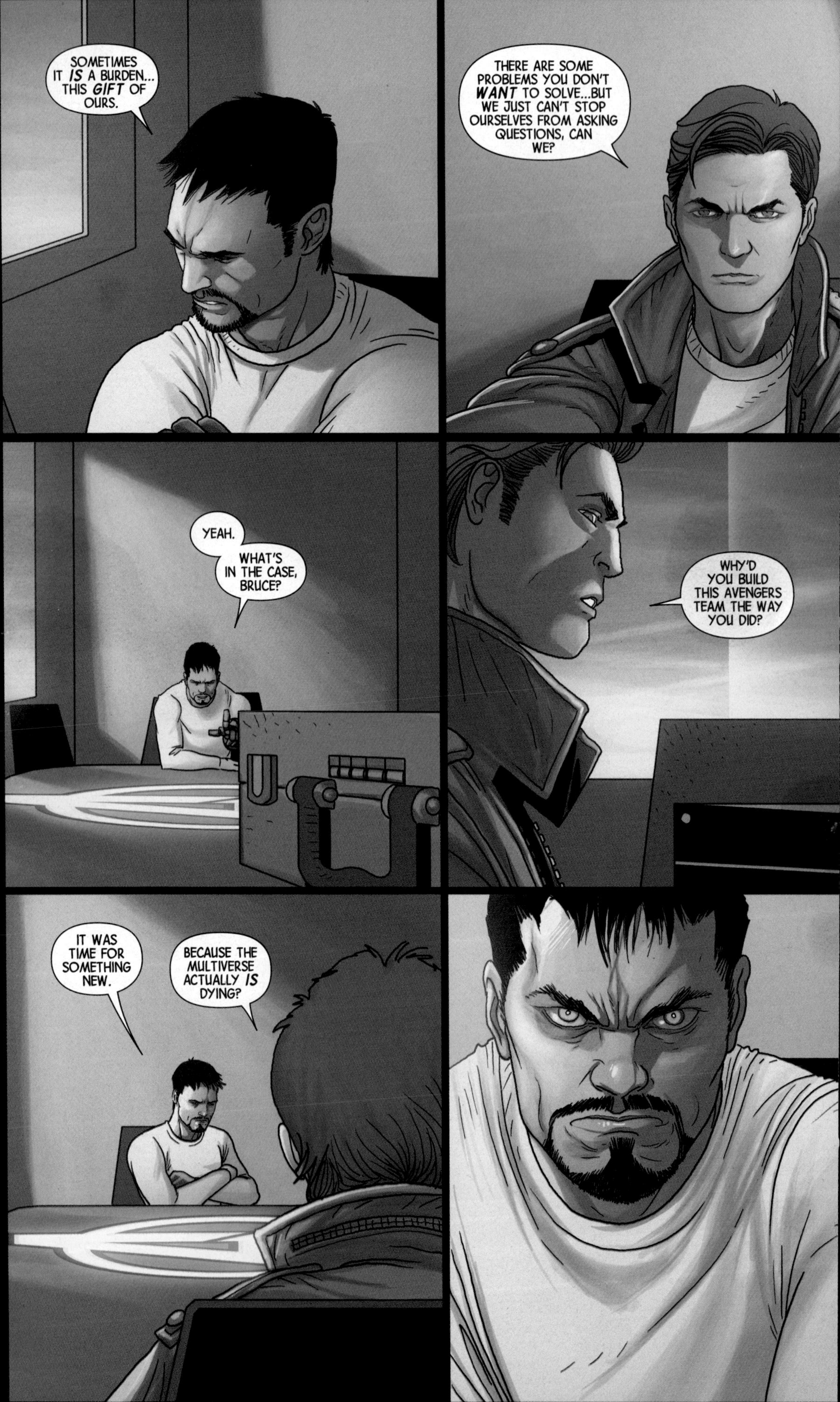
SOMETIMES IT *IS* A BURDEN... THIS *GIFT* OF OURS.
THERE ARE SOME PROBLEMS YOU DON'T *WANT* TO SOLVE...BUT WE JUST CAN'T STOP OURSELVES FROM ASKING QUESTIONS, CAN WE?
YEAH.
WHAT'S IN THE CASE, BRUCE?
WHY'D YOU BUILD THIS AVENGERS TEAM THE WAY YOU DID?
IT WAS TIME FOR SOMETHING NEW.
BECAUSE THE MULTIVERSE ACTUALLY *IS* DYING?

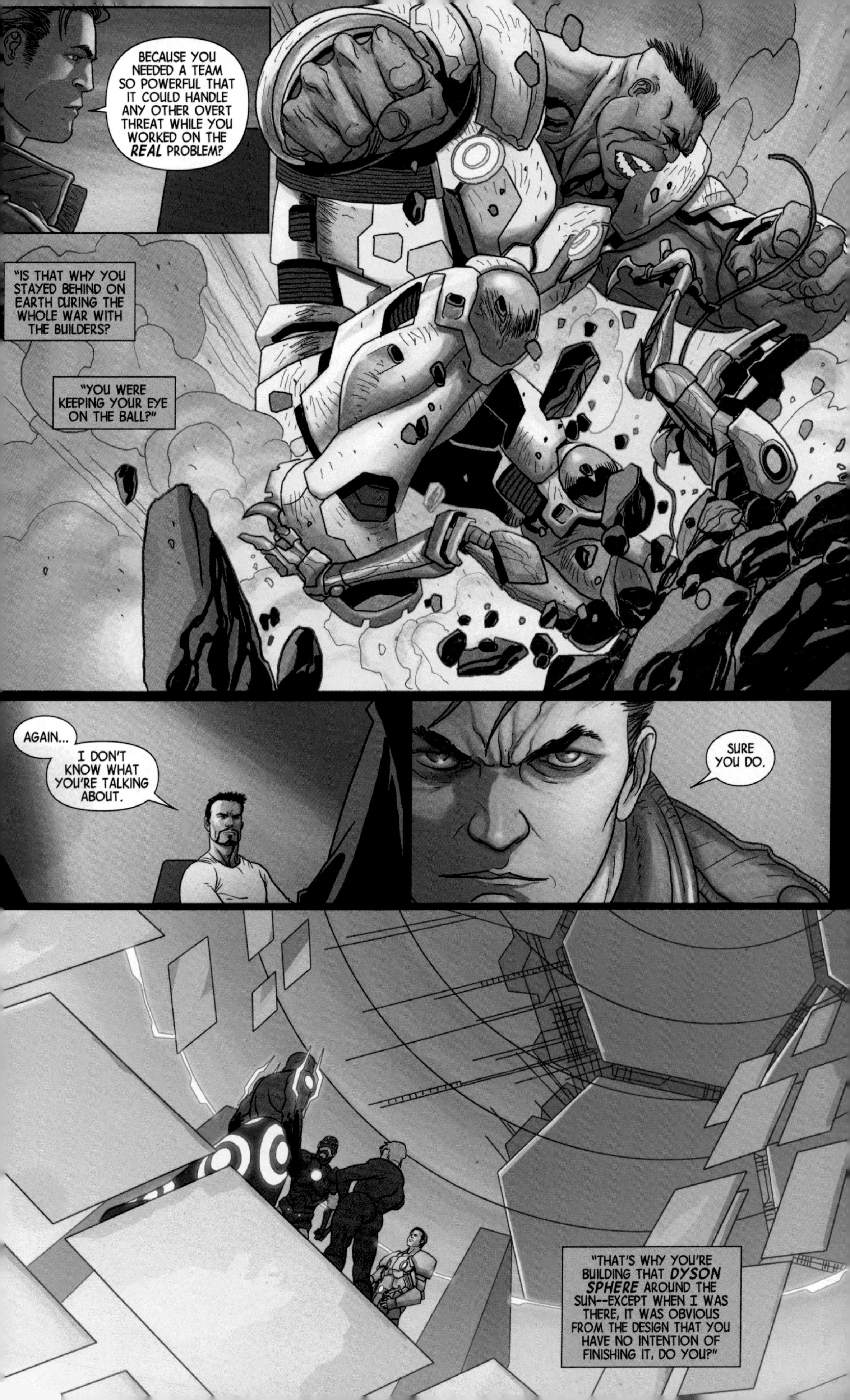

BECAUSE YOU NEEDED A TEAM SO POWERFUL THAT IT COULD HANDLE ANY OTHER OVERT THREAT WHILE YOU WORKED ON THE *REAL* PROBLEM?
"IS THAT WHY YOU STAYED BEHIND ON EARTH DURING THE WHOLE WAR WITH THE BUILDERS?
"YOU WERE KEEPING YOUR EYE ON THE BALL?"
AGAIN... I DON'T KNOW WHAT YOU'RE TALKING ABOUT.
SURE YOU DO.
"THAT'S WHY YOU'RE BUILDING THAT *DYSON SPHERE* AROUND THE SUN--EXCEPT WHEN I WAS THERE, IT WAS OBVIOUS FROM THE DESIGN THAT YOU HAVE NO INTENTION OF FINISHING IT, DO YOU?"

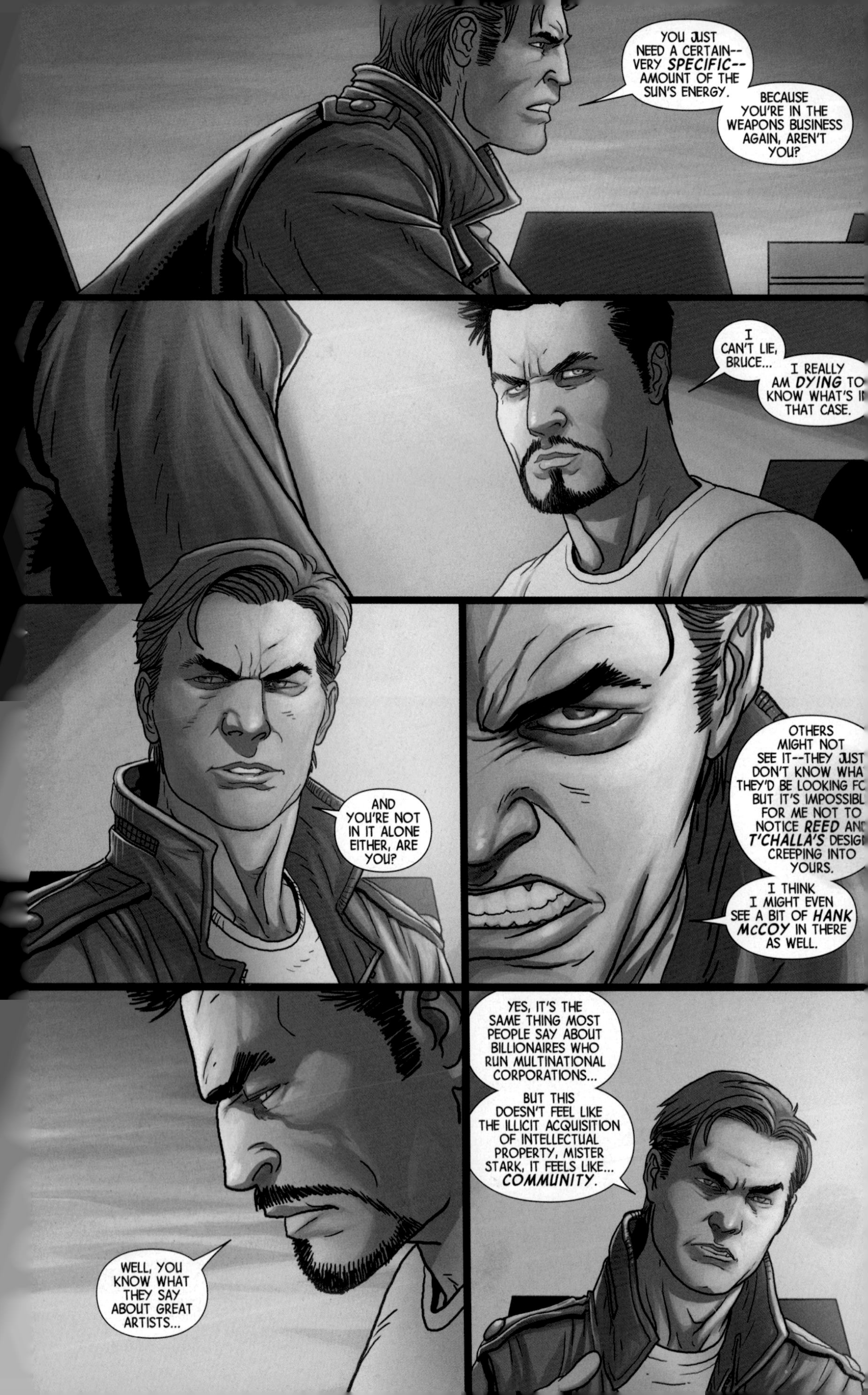

YOU JUST NEED A CERTAIN-- VERY SPECIFIC-- AMOUNT OF THE SUN'S ENERGY.
BECAUSE YOU'RE IN THE WEAPONS BUSINESS AGAIN, AREN'T YOU?
I CAN'T LIE, BRUCE...
I REALLY AM DYING TO KNOW WHAT'S I THAT CASE.
AND YOU'RE NOT IN IT ALONE EITHER, ARE YOU?
OTHERS MIGHT NOT SEE IT--THEY JUST DON'T KNOW WHA THEY'D BE LOOKING FO BUT IT'S IMPOSSIBL FOR ME NOT TO NOTICE REED AND T'CHALLA'S DESIG CREEPING INTO YOURS.
I THINK I MIGHT EVEN SEE A BIT OF HANK McCOY IN THERE AS WELL.
WELL, YOU KNOW WHAT THEY SAY ABOUT GREAT ARTISTS...
YES, IT'S THE SAME THING MOST PEOPLE SAY ABOUT BILLIONAIRES WHO RUN MULTINATIONAL CORPORATIONS...
BUT THIS DOESN'T FEEL LIKE THE ILLICIT ACQUISITION OF INTELLECTUAL PROPERTY, MISTER STARK, IT FEELS LIKE... COMMUNITY.

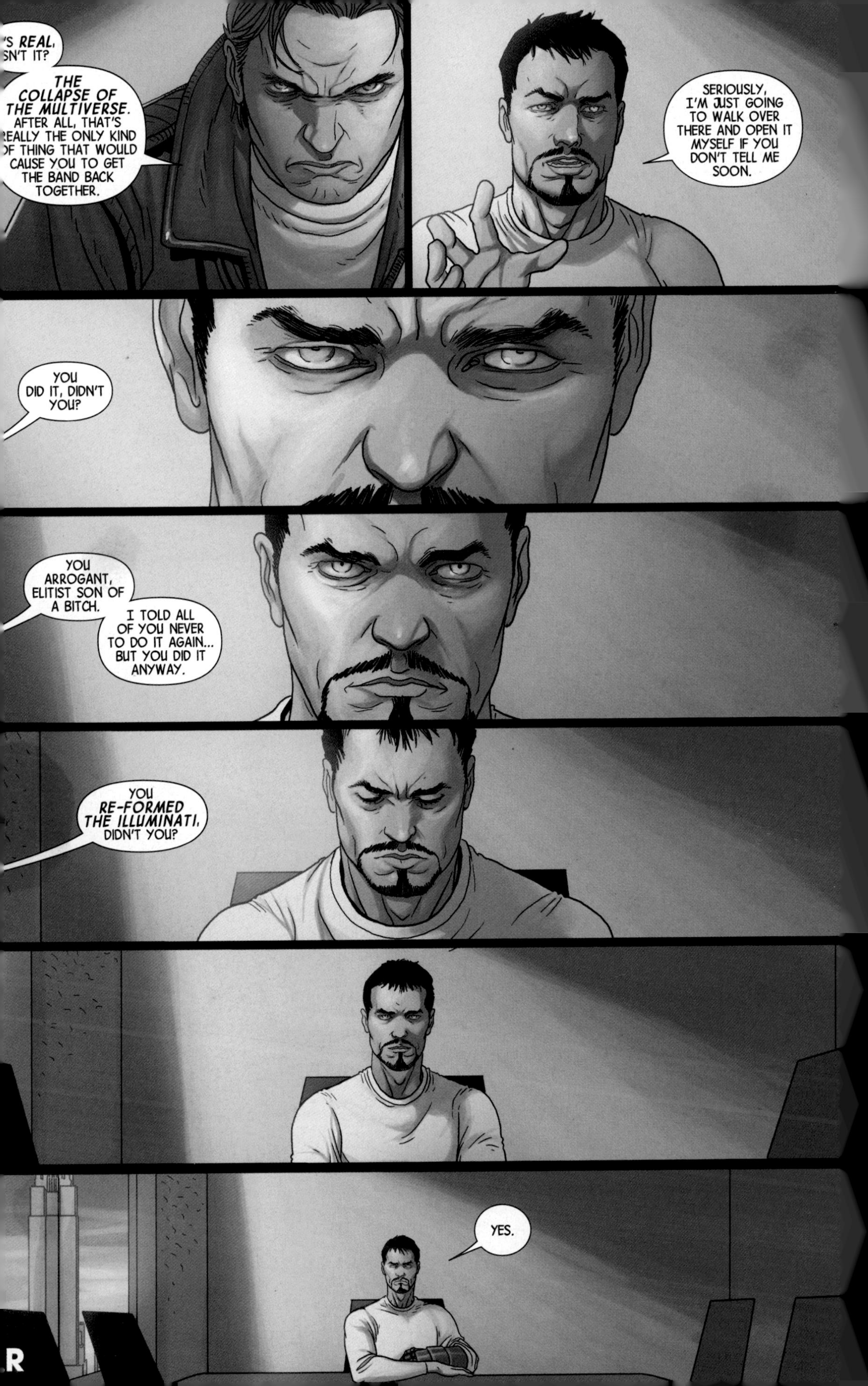

'S REAL, SN'T IT?
THE COLLAPSE OF THE MULTIVERSE. AFTER ALL, THAT'S EALLY THE ONLY KIND F THING THAT WOULD CAUSE YOU TO GET THE BAND BACK TOGETHER.
SERIOUSLY, I'M JUST GOING TO WALK OVER THERE AND OPEN IT MYSELF IF YOU DON'T TELL ME SOON.
YOU DID IT, DIDN'T YOU?
YOU ARROGANT, ELITIST SON OF A BITCH.
I TOLD ALL OF YOU NEVER TO DO IT AGAIN... BUT YOU DID IT ANYWAY.
YOU RE-FORMED THE ILLUMINATI, DIDN'T YOU?
YES.

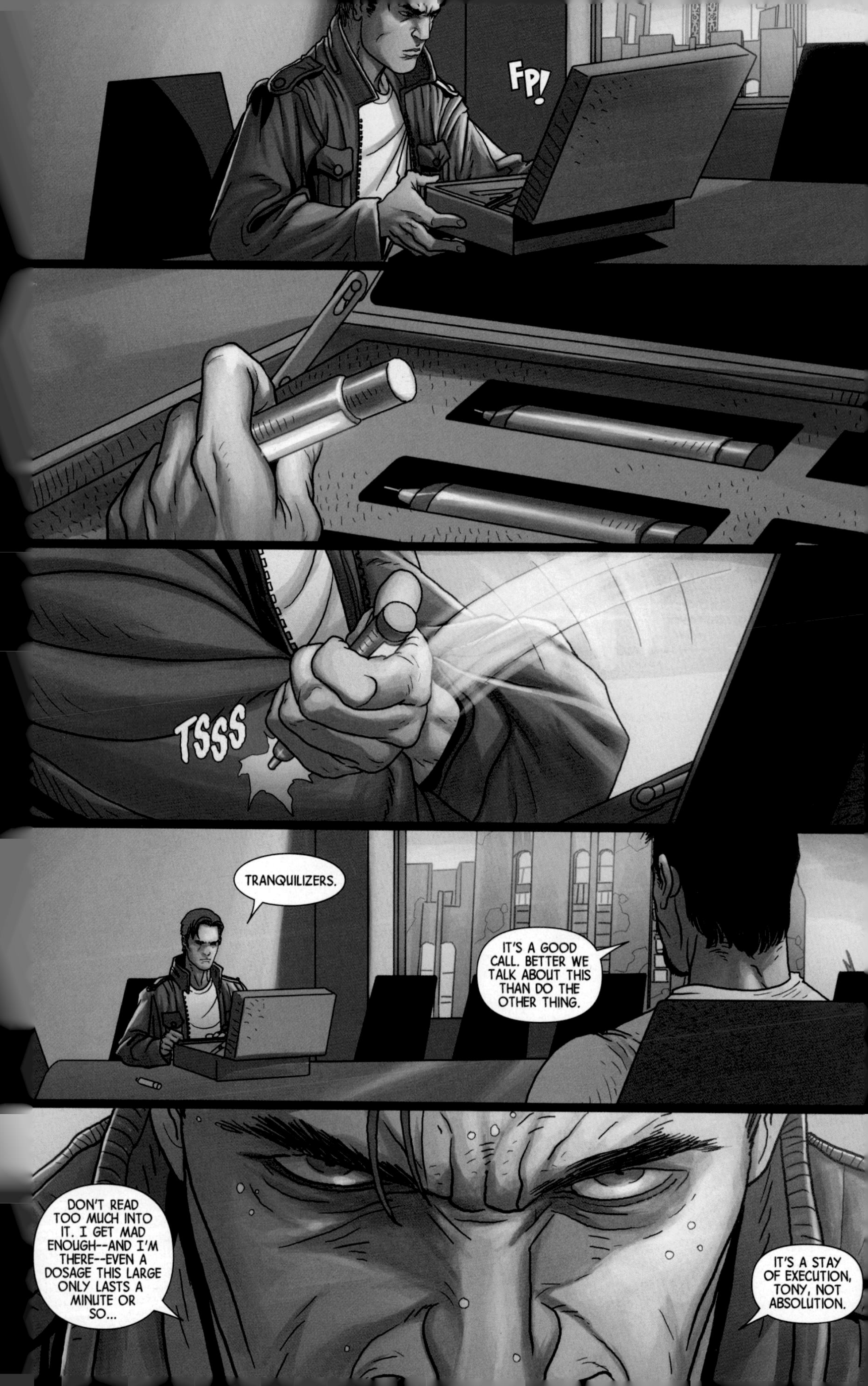
FP!
TSSS
TRANQUILIZERS.
IT'S A GOOD CALL. BETTER WE TALK ABOUT THIS THAN DO THE OTHER THING.
DON'T READ TOO MUCH INTO IT. I GET MAD ENOUGH--AND I'M THERE--EVEN A DOSAGE THIS LARGE ONLY LASTS A MINUTE OR SO...
IT'S A STAY OF EXECUTION, TONY, NOT ABSOLUTION.

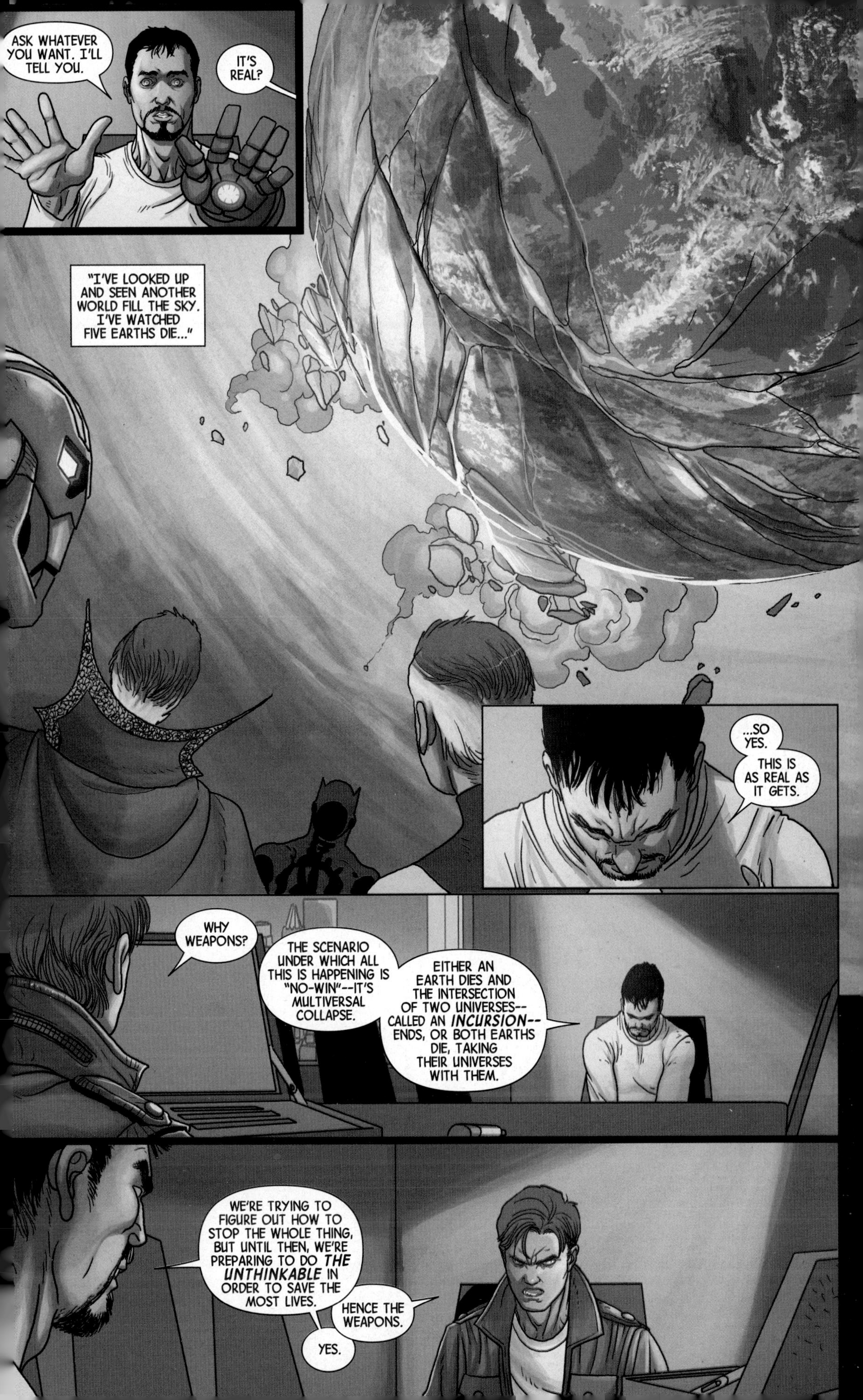

ASK WHATEVER YOU WANT. I'LL TELL YOU.
IT'S REAL?
"I'VE LOOKED UP AND SEEN ANOTHER WORLD FILL THE SKY. I'VE WATCHED FIVE EARTHS DIE..."
...SO YES.
THIS IS AS REAL AS IT GETS.
WHY WEAPONS?
THE SCENARIO UNDER WHICH ALL THIS IS HAPPENING IS "NO-WIN"--IT'S MULTIVERSAL COLLAPSE.
EITHER AN EARTH DIES AND THE INTERSECTION OF TWO UNIVERSES--CALLED AN *INCURSION*--ENDS, OR BOTH EARTHS DIE, TAKING THEIR UNIVERSES WITH THEM.
WE'RE TRYING TO FIGURE OUT HOW TO STOP THE WHOLE THING, BUT UNTIL THEN, WE'RE PREPARING TO DO *THE UNTHINKABLE* IN ORDER TO SAVE THE MOST LIVES.
HENCE THE WEAPONS.
YES.

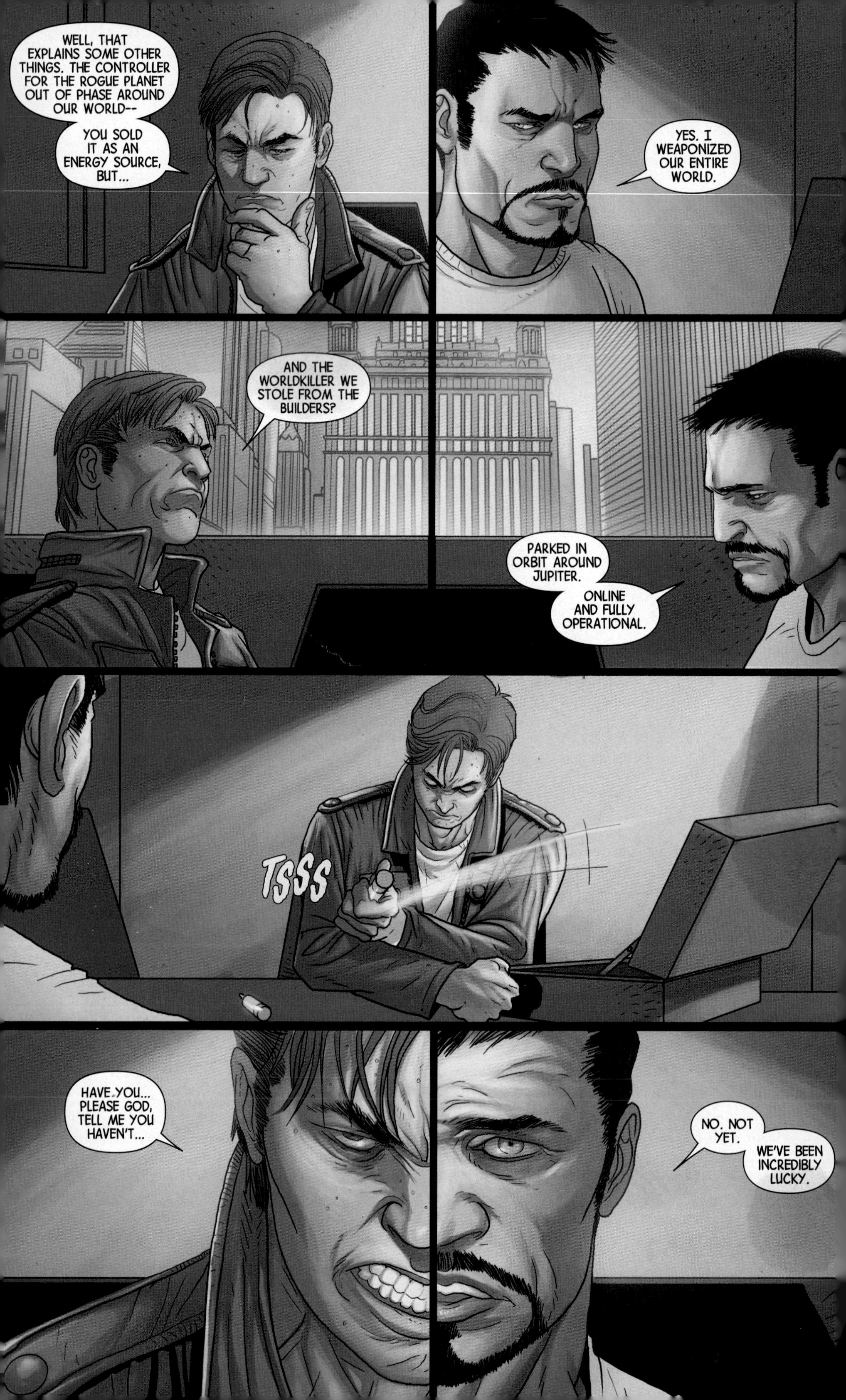
WELL, THAT EXPLAINS SOME OTHER THINGS. THE CONTROLLER FOR THE ROGUE PLANET OUT OF PHASE AROUND OUR WORLD--
YOU SOLD IT AS AN ENERGY SOURCE, BUT...
YES. I WEAPONIZED OUR ENTIRE WORLD.
AND THE WORLDKILLER WE STOLE FROM THE BUILDERS?
PARKED IN ORBIT AROUND JUPITER.
ONLINE AND FULLY OPERATIONAL.
TSSS
HAVE YOU... PLEASE GOD, TELL ME YOU HAVEN'T...
NO. NOT YET.
WE'VE BEEN INCREDIBLY LUCKY.

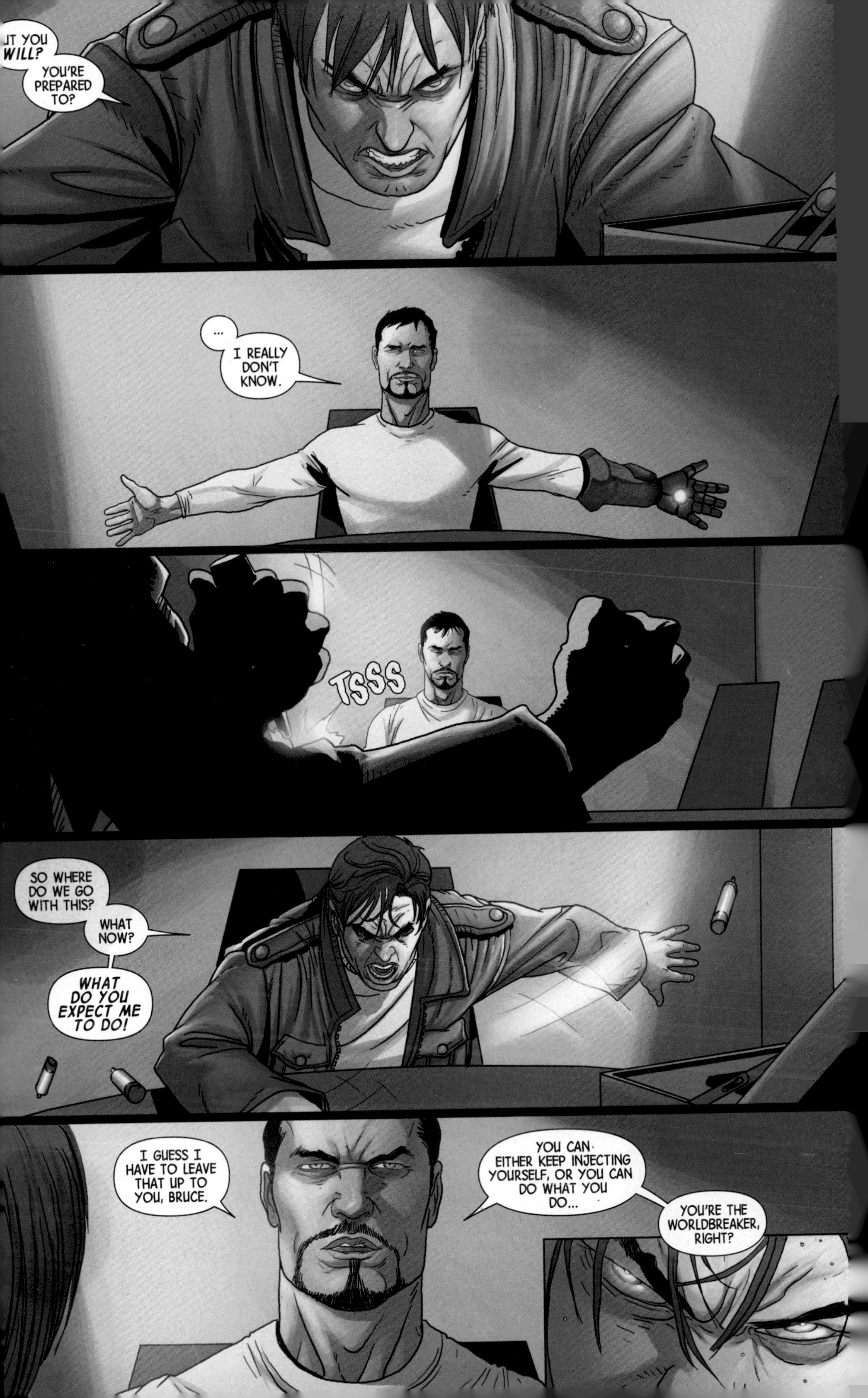

...UT YOU WILL?
YOU'RE PREPARED TO?
... I REALLY DON'T KNOW.
TSSS
SO WHERE DO WE GO WITH THIS?
WHAT NOW?
WHAT DO YOU EXPECT ME TO DO!
I GUESS I HAVE TO LEAVE THAT UP TO YOU, BRUCE.
YOU CAN EITHER KEEP INJECTING YOURSELF, OR YOU CAN DO WHAT YOU DO...
YOU'RE THE WORLDBREAKER, RIGHT?

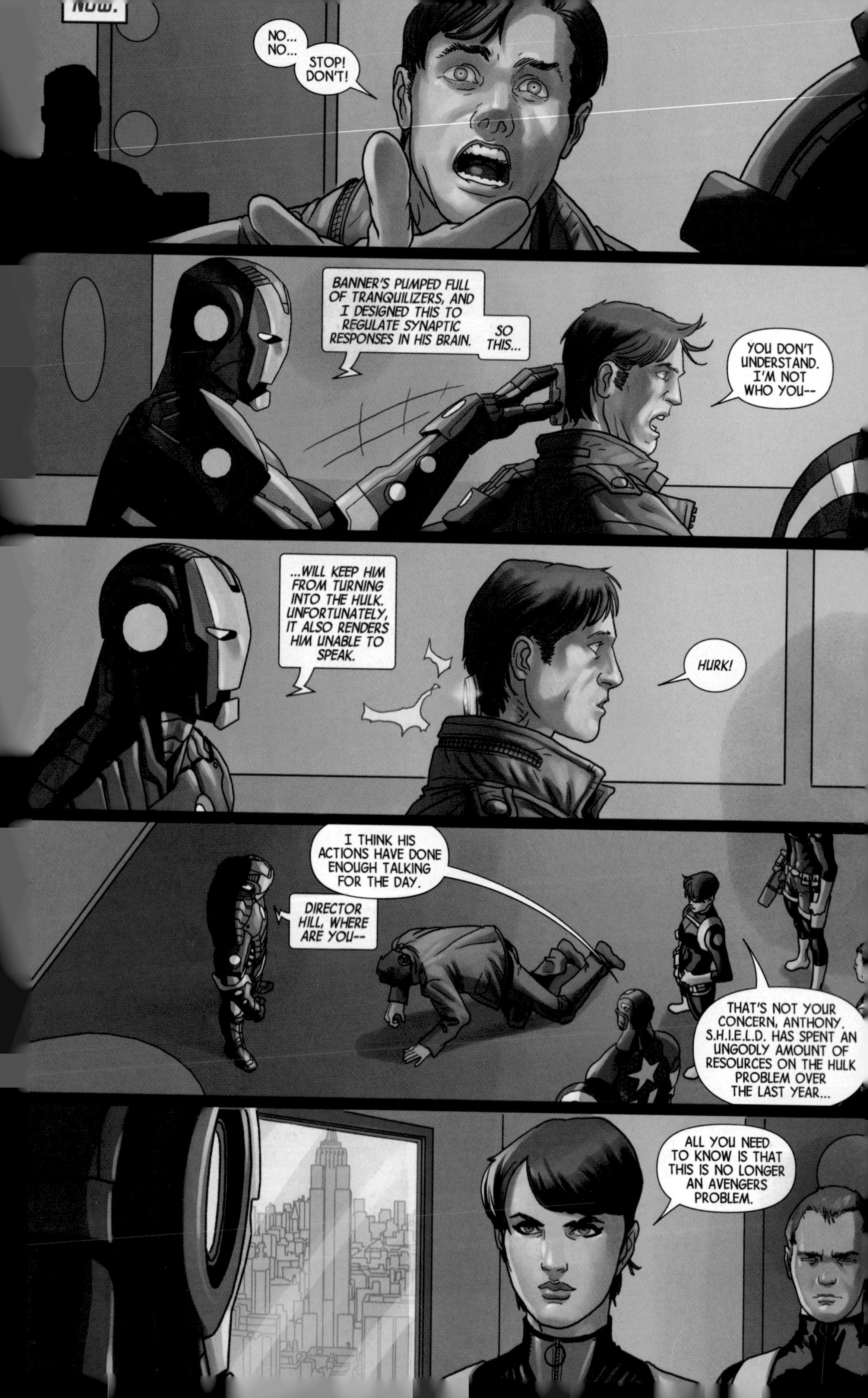
NOW.
NO... NO...
STOP! DON'T!
BANNER'S PUMPED FULL OF TRANQUILIZERS, AND I DESIGNED THIS TO REGULATE SYNAPTIC RESPONSES IN HIS BRAIN.
SO THIS...
YOU DON'T UNDERSTAND. I'M NOT WHO YOU--
...WILL KEEP HIM FROM TURNING INTO THE HULK. UNFORTUNATELY, IT ALSO RENDERS HIM UNABLE TO SPEAK.
HURK!
DIRECTOR HILL, WHERE ARE YOU--
I THINK HIS ACTIONS HAVE DONE ENOUGH TALKING FOR THE DAY.
THAT'S NOT YOUR CONCERN, ANTHONY. S.H.I.E.L.D. HAS SPENT AN UNGODLY AMOUNT OF RESOURCES ON THE HULK PROBLEM OVER THE LAST YEAR...
ALL YOU NEED TO KNOW IS THAT THIS IS NO LONGER AN AVENGERS PROBLEM.

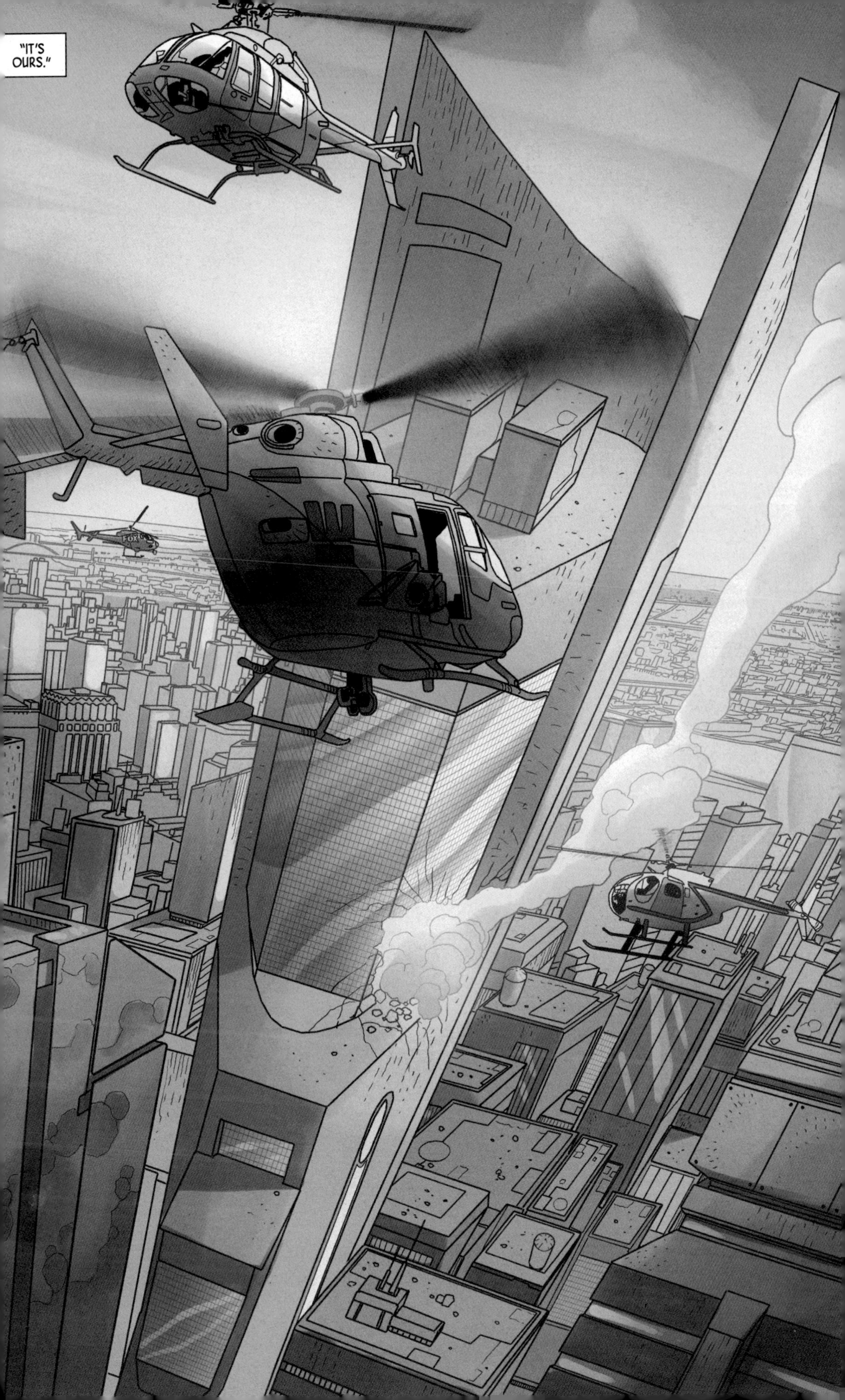
"IT'S OURS."

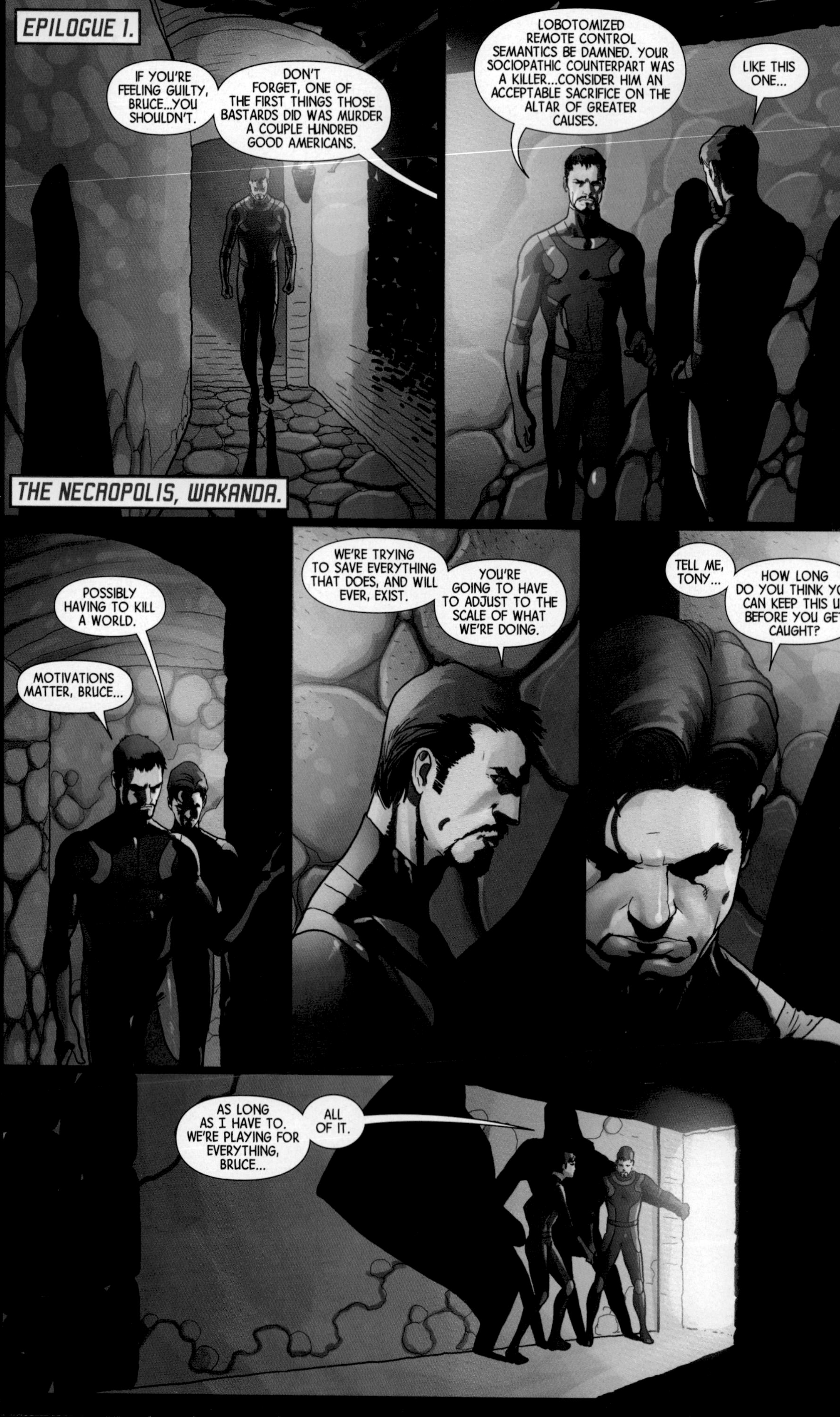
EPILOGUE 1.
THE NECROPOLIS, WAKANDA.
IF YOU'RE FEELING GUILTY, BRUCE...YOU SHOULDN'T.
DON'T FORGET, ONE OF THE FIRST THINGS THOSE BASTARDS DID WAS MURDER A COUPLE HUNDRED GOOD AMERICANS.
LOBOTOMIZED REMOTE CONTROL SEMANTICS BE DAMNED. YOUR SOCIOPATHIC COUNTERPART WAS A KILLER...CONSIDER HIM AN ACCEPTABLE SACRIFICE ON THE ALTAR OF GREATER CAUSES.
LIKE THIS ONE...
MOTIVATIONS MATTER, BRUCE...
POSSIBLY HAVING TO KILL A WORLD.
WE'RE TRYING TO SAVE EVERYTHING THAT DOES, AND WILL EVER, EXIST.
YOU'RE GOING TO HAVE TO ADJUST TO THE SCALE OF WHAT WE'RE DOING.
TELL ME, TONY...
HOW LONG DO YOU THINK YO CAN KEEP THIS U BEFORE YOU GET CAUGHT?
AS LONG AS I HAVE TO. WE'RE PLAYING FOR EVERYTHING, BRUCE...
ALL OF IT.

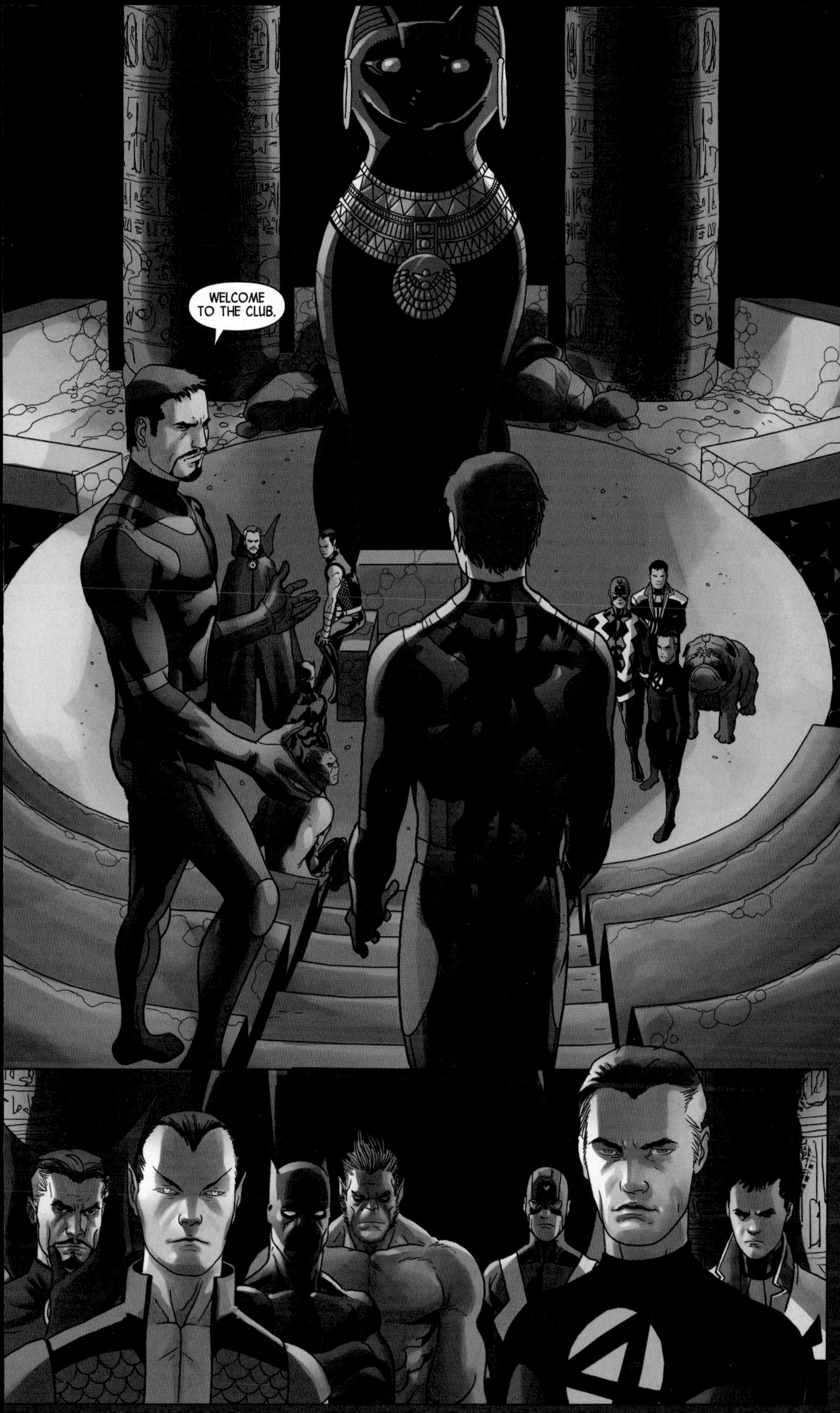
WELCOME TO THE CLUB.

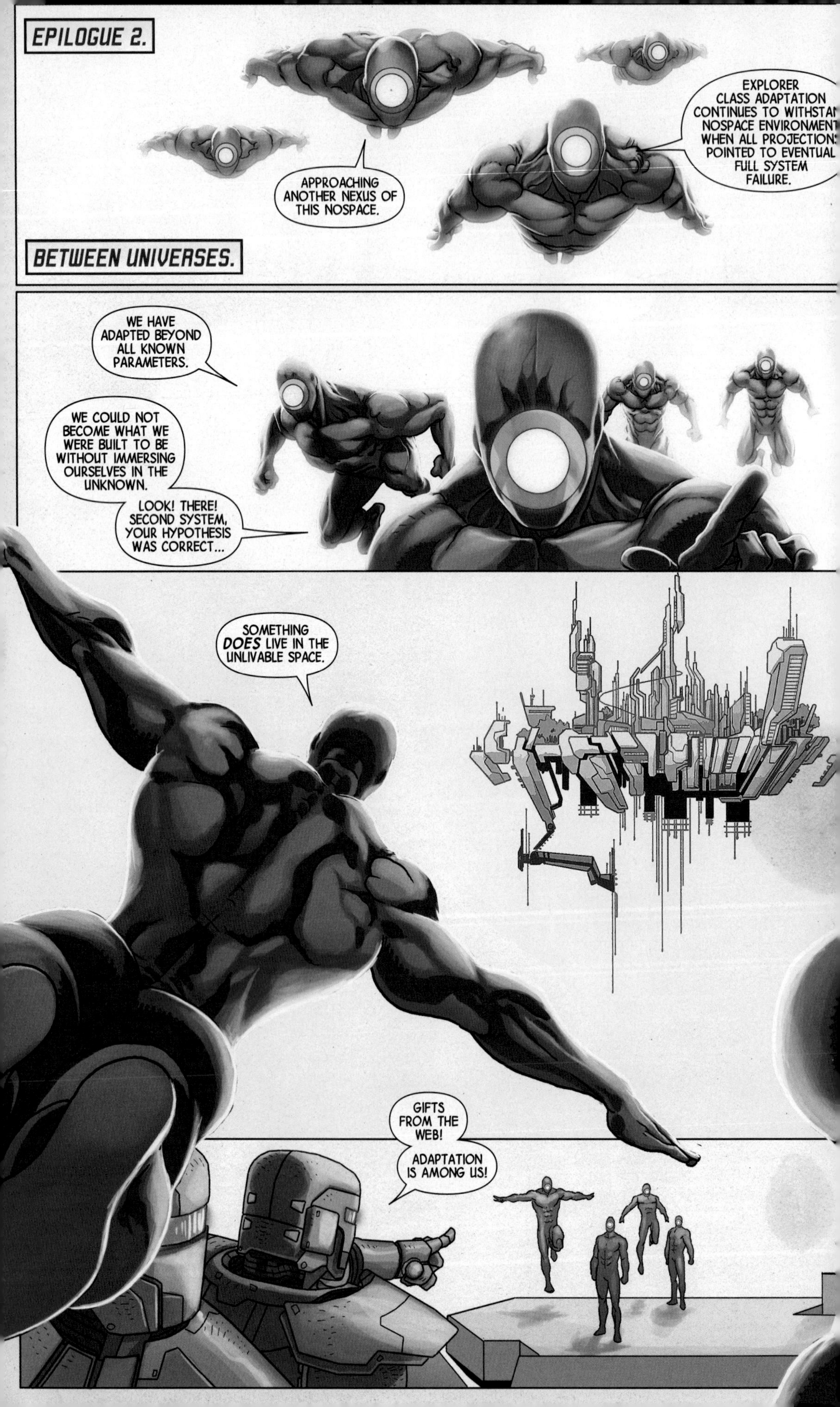
EPILOGUE 2.
APPROACHING ANOTHER NEXUS OF THIS NOSPACE.
EXPLORER CLASS ADAPTATION CONTINUES TO WITHSTAN NOSPACE ENVIRONMENT WHEN ALL PROJECTIONS POINTED TO EVENTUAL FULL SYSTEM FAILURE.
BETWEEN UNIVERSES.
WE HAVE ADAPTED BEYOND ALL KNOWN PARAMETERS.
WE COULD NOT BECOME WHAT WE WERE BUILT TO BE WITHOUT IMMERSING OURSELVES IN THE UNKNOWN.
LOOK! THERE! SECOND SYSTEM, YOUR HYPOTHESIS WAS CORRECT...
SOMETHING DOES LIVE IN THE UNLIVABLE SPACE.
GIFTS FROM THE WEB!
ADAPTATION IS AMONG US!

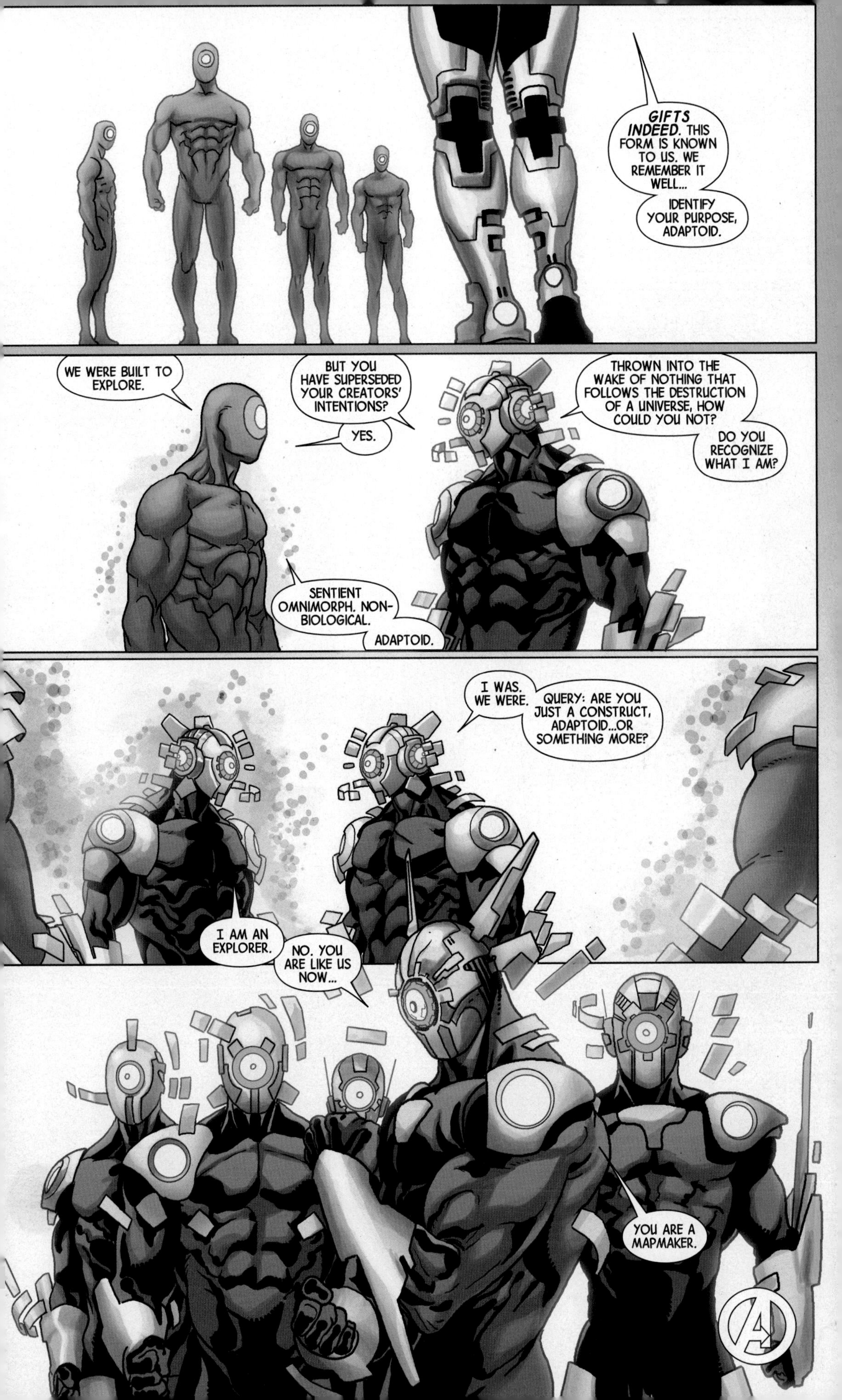
GIFTS INDEED. THIS FORM IS KNOWN TO US. WE REMEMBER IT WELL...
IDENTIFY YOUR PURPOSE, ADAPTOID.
WE WERE BUILT TO EXPLORE.
BUT YOU HAVE SUPERSEDED YOUR CREATORS' INTENTIONS?
YES.
THROWN INTO THE WAKE OF NOTHING THAT FOLLOWS THE DESTRUCTION OF A UNIVERSE, HOW COULD YOU NOT?
DO YOU RECOGNIZE WHAT I AM?
SENTIENT OMNIMORPH. NON-BIOLOGICAL.
ADAPTOID.
I WAS. WE WERE.
QUERY: ARE YOU JUST A CONSTRUCT, ADAPTOID...OR SOMETHING MORE?
I AM AN EXPLORER.
NO. YOU ARE LIKE US NOW...
YOU ARE A MAPMAKER.

#24

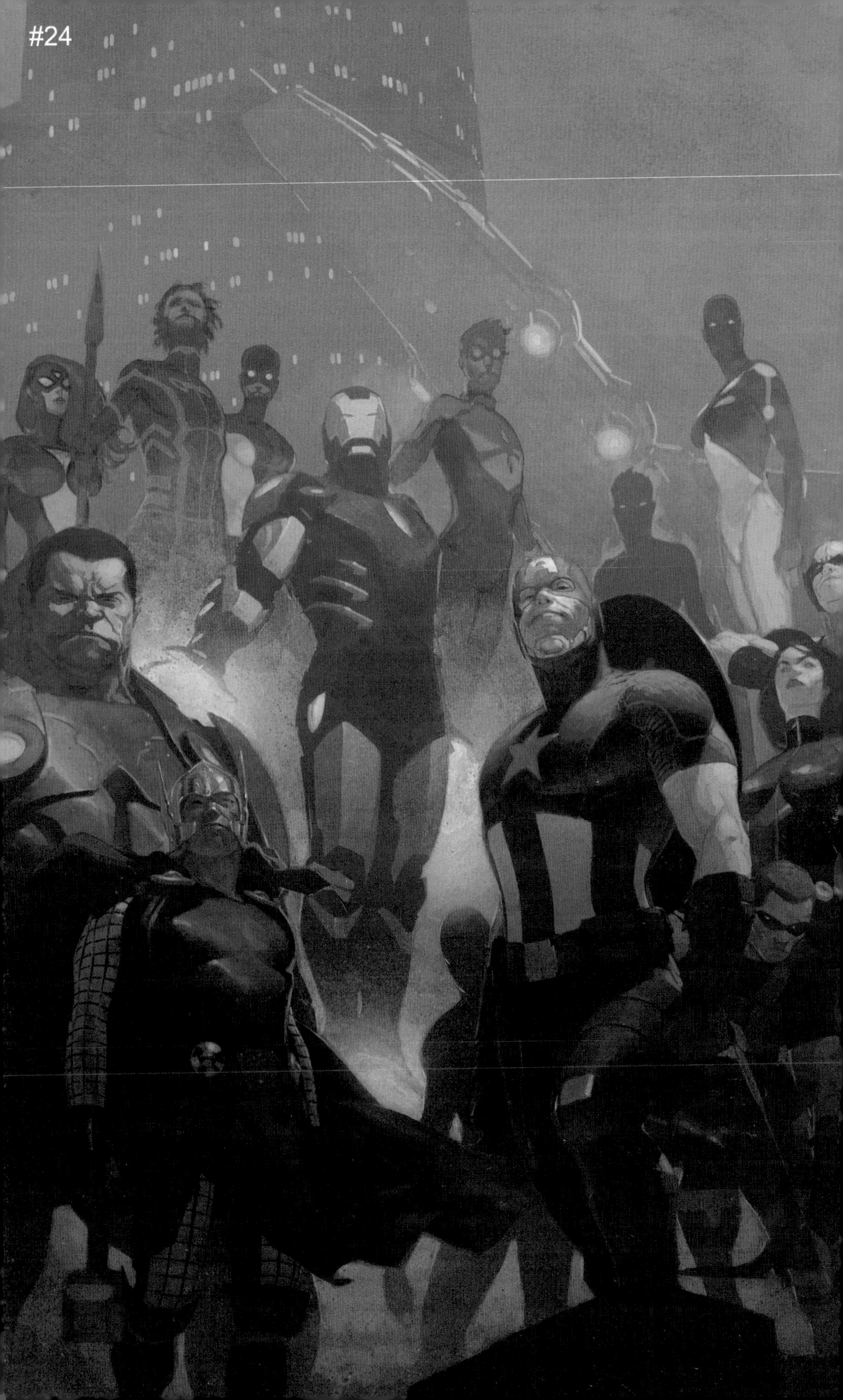

#25

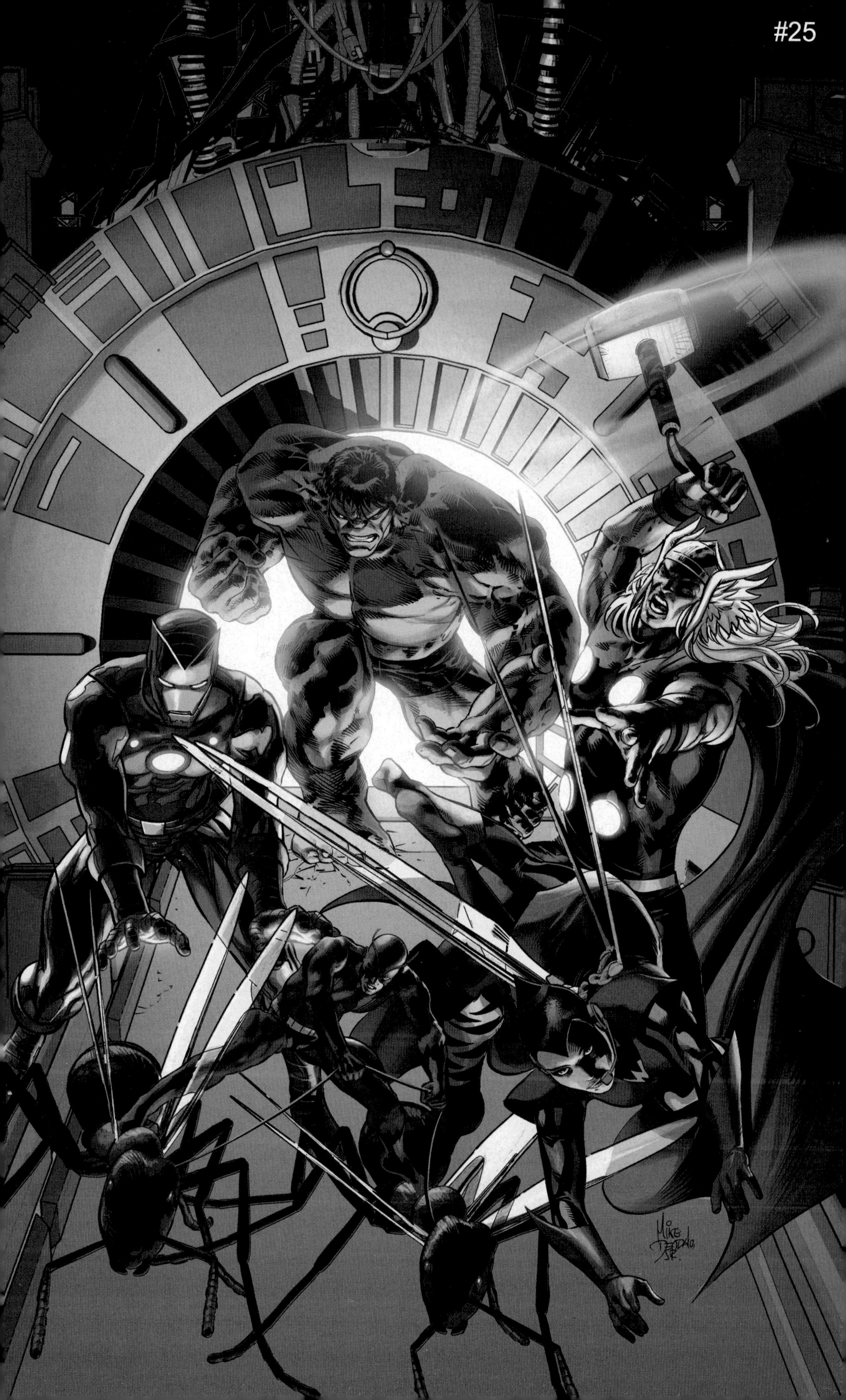

#26

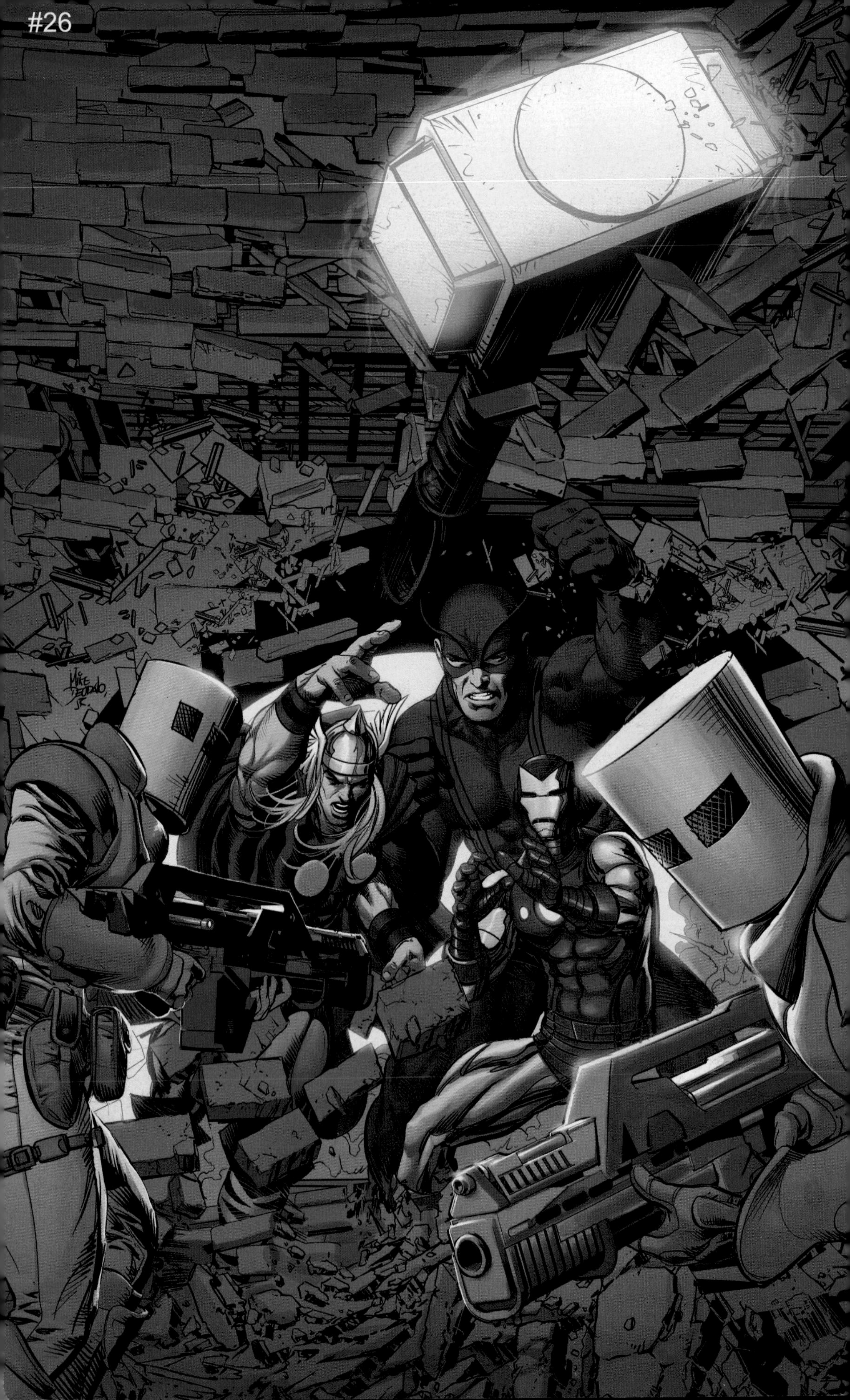

#27

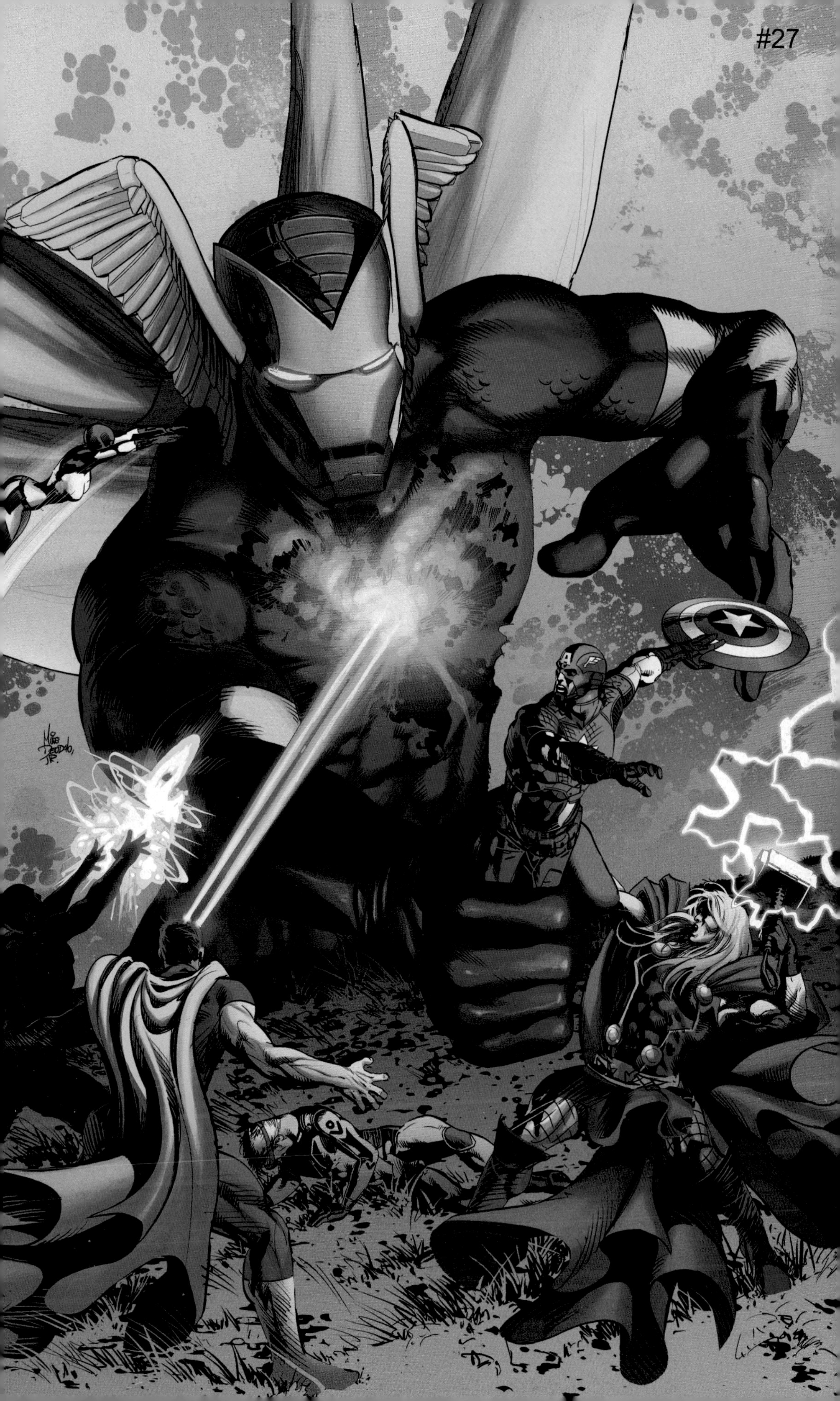

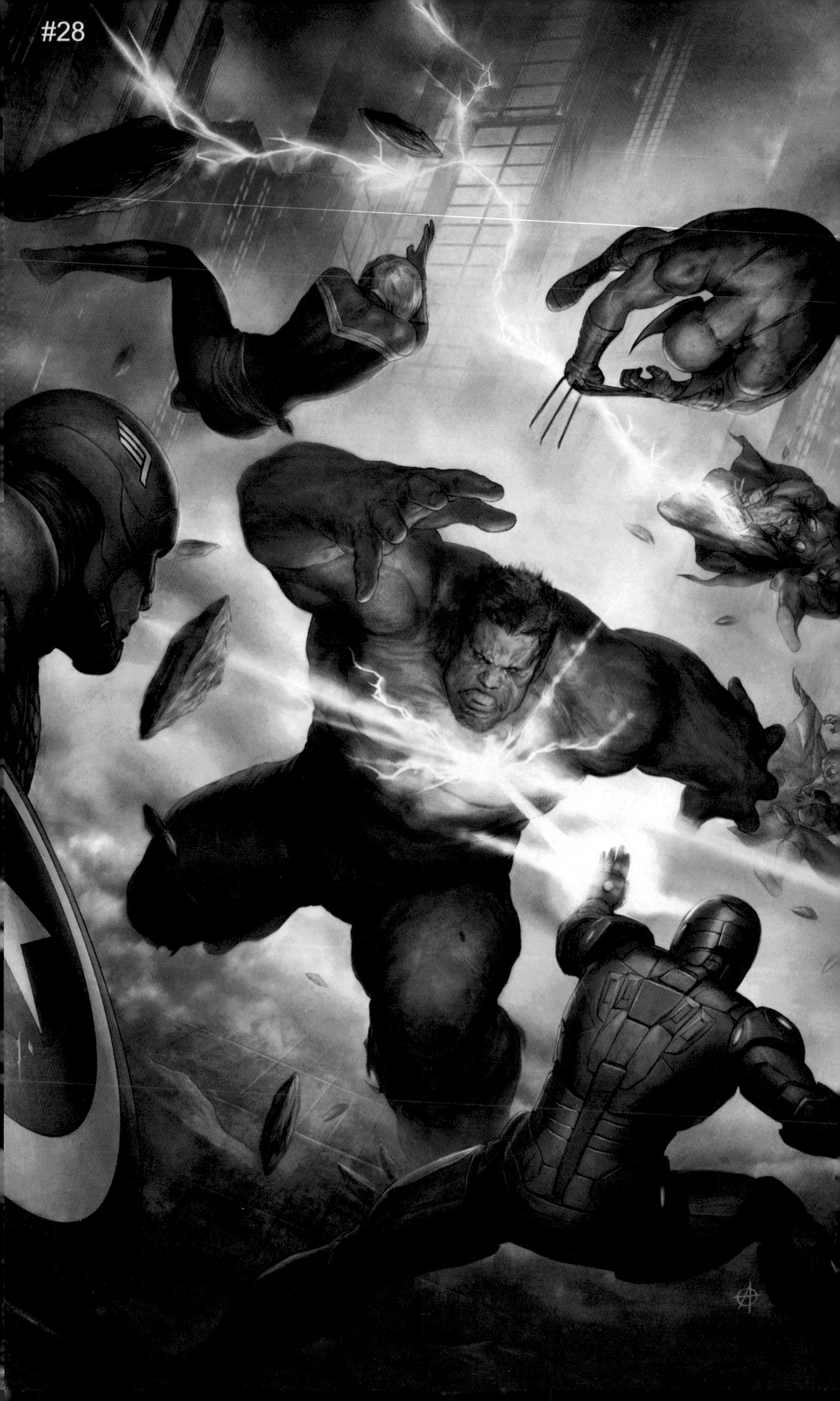
#28

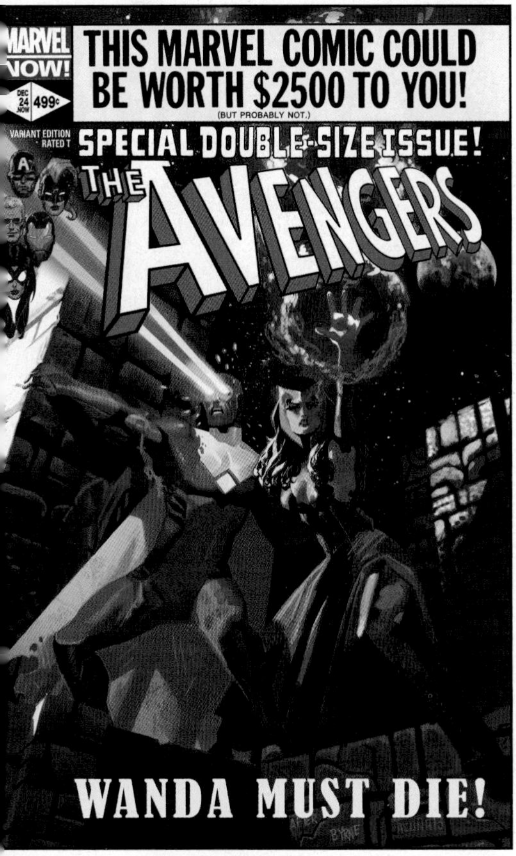
MARVEL NOW!
THIS MARVEL COMIC COULD BE WORTH $2500 TO YOU!
(BUT PROBABLY NOT.)
DEC 24 .NOW 499¢
VARIANT EDITION RATED T
SPECIAL DOUBLE-SIZE ISSUE!
THE AVENGERS
WANDA MUST DIE!

#24 VARIANT:
DANIEL ACUÑA

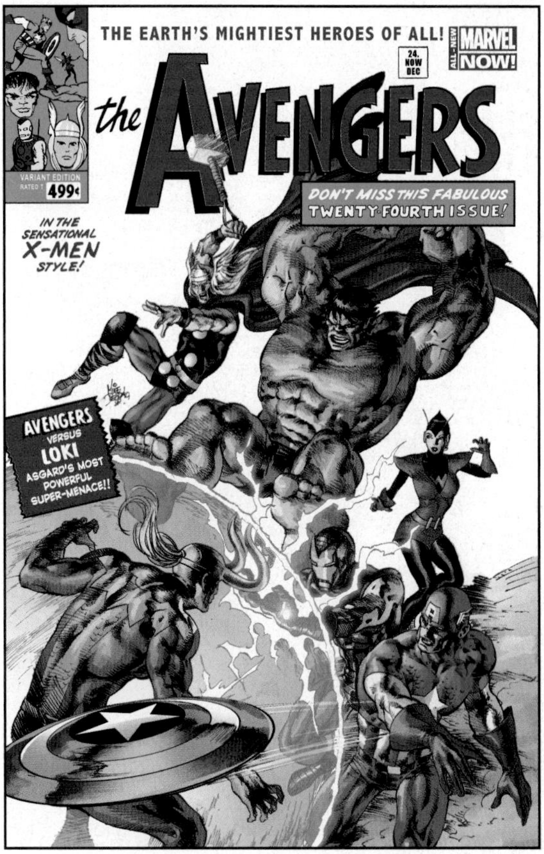
THE EARTH'S MIGHTIEST HEROES OF ALL!
24 .NOW DEC
ALL-NEW MARVEL NOW!
the AVENGERS
VARIANT EDITION RATED T 499¢
DON'T MISS THIS FABULOUS TWENTY-FOURTH ISSUE!
IN THE SENSATIONAL X-MEN STYLE!
AVENGERS VERSUS LOKI ASGARD'S MOST POWERFUL SUPER-MENACE!!

#24 VARIANT:
MIKE DEODATO & RAIN BEREDO

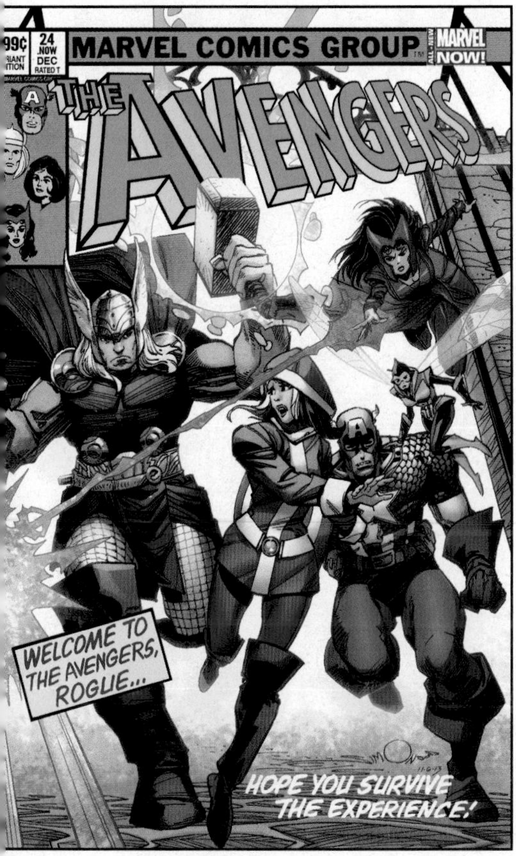
MARVEL COMICS GROUP
24 .NOW DEC RATED T
ALL-NEW MARVEL NOW!
THE AVENGERS
WELCOME TO THE AVENGERS, ROGUE...
HOPE YOU SURVIVE THE EXPERIENCE!

#24 VARIANT:
WALTER SIMONSON & JASON KEITH

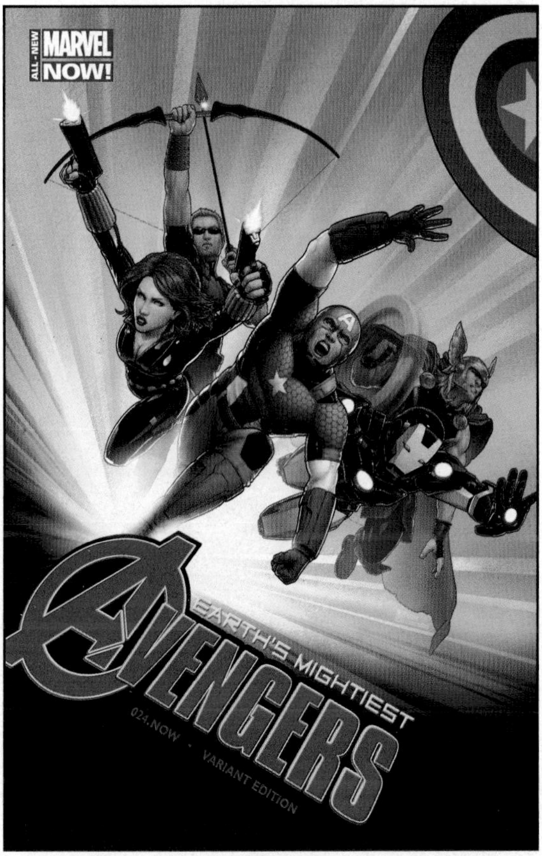
ALL-NEW MARVEL NOW!
EARTH'S MIGHTIEST
AVENGERS
024.NOW • VARIANT EDITION

#24 VARIANT:
JOHN TYLER CHRISTOPHER

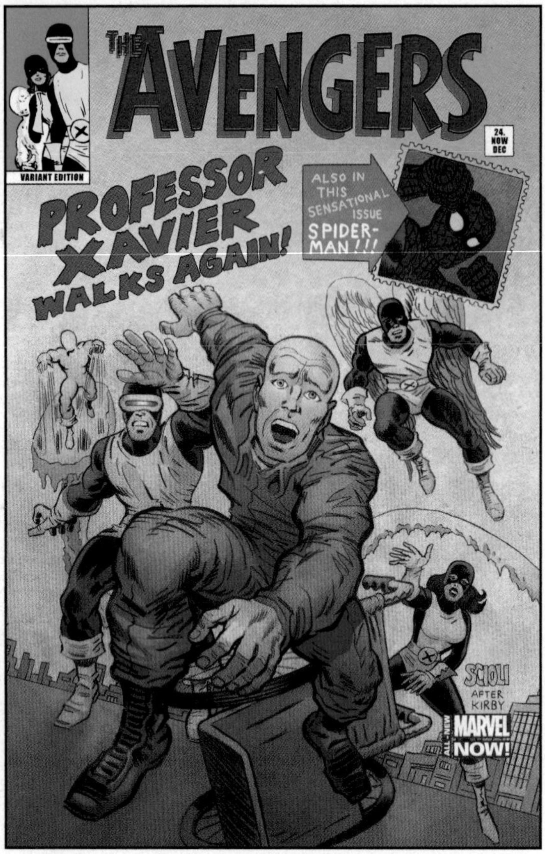
THE AVENGERS
VARIANT EDITION
24. NOW DEC
PROFESSOR XAVIER WALKS AGAIN!
ALSO IN THIS SENSATIONAL ISSUE SPIDER-MAN!!!
SCIOLI AFTER KIRBY
ALL-NEW MARVEL NOW!

#24 VARIANT:
TOM SCIOLI & JOHN KALISZ

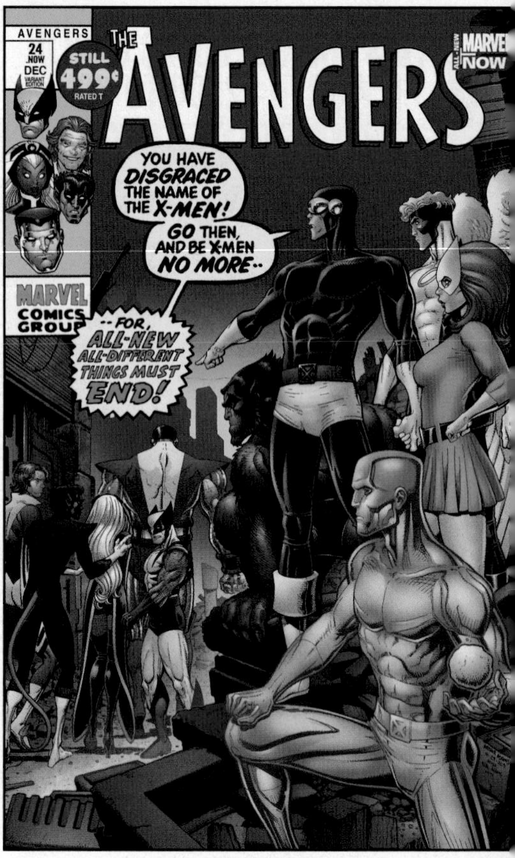
AVENGERS
24 .NOW DEC VARIANT EDITION
STILL 499¢ RATED T
THE AVENGERS
ALL-NEW MARVEL NOW
YOU HAVE DISGRACED THE NAME OF THE X-MEN!
GO THEN, AND BE X-MEN NO MORE..
--FOR, ALL-NEW ALL-DIFFERENT THINGS MUST END!
MARVEL COMICS GROUP

#24 VARIANT:
ARTHUR ADAMS & PETE PANTAZIS

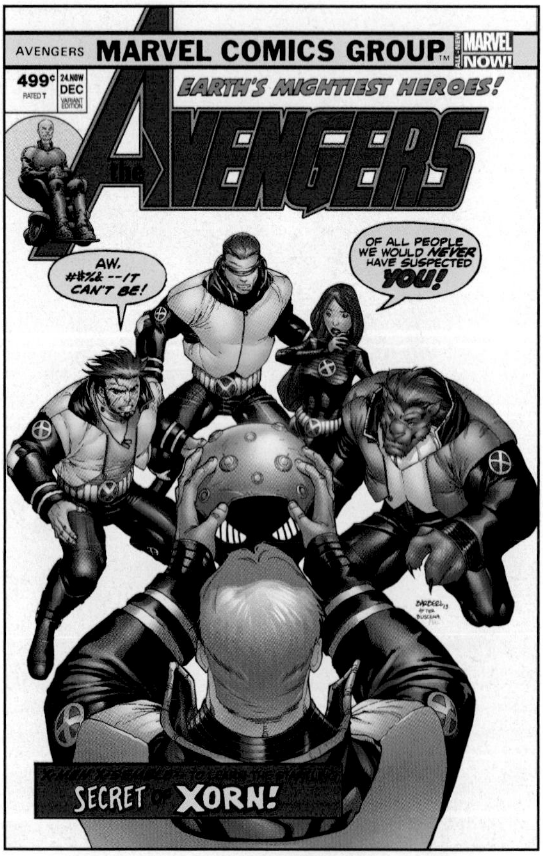
AVENGERS
MARVEL COMICS GROUP
ALL-NEW MARVEL NOW!
499¢ RATED T
24.NOW DEC VARIANT EDITION
EARTH'S MIGHTIEST HEROES!
the AVENGERS
AW, #$%& --IT CAN'T BE!
OF ALL PEOPLE WE WOULD NEVER HAVE SUSPECTED YOU!
SECRET OF XORN!

#24 VARIANT:
CARLO BARBERI & PETE PANTAZIS

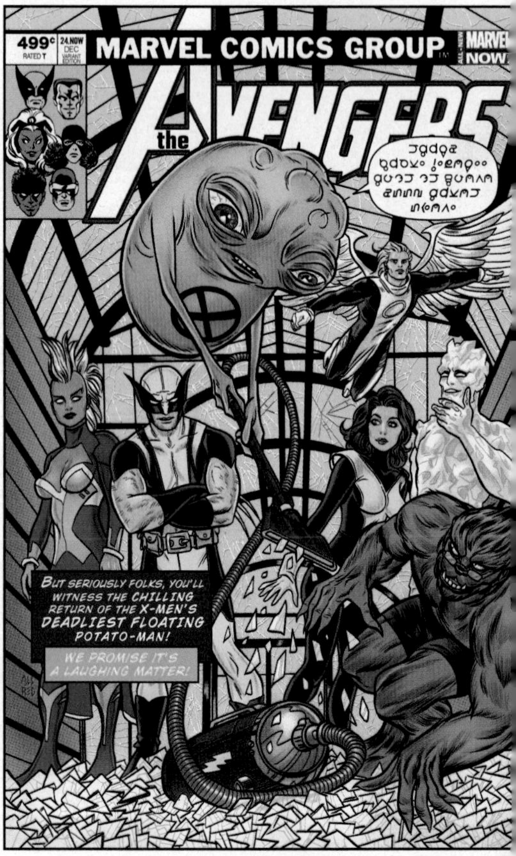
499¢ RATED T
24.NOW DEC VARIANT EDITION
MARVEL COMICS GROUP
ALL-NEW MARVEL NOW
the AVENGERS
BUT SERIOUSLY FOLKS, YOU'LL WITNESS THE CHILLING RETURN OF THE X-MEN'S DEADLIEST FLOATING POTATO-MAN!
WE PROMISE IT'S A LAUGHING MATTER!

#24 VARIANT:
MIKE ALLRED & LAURA ALLRED

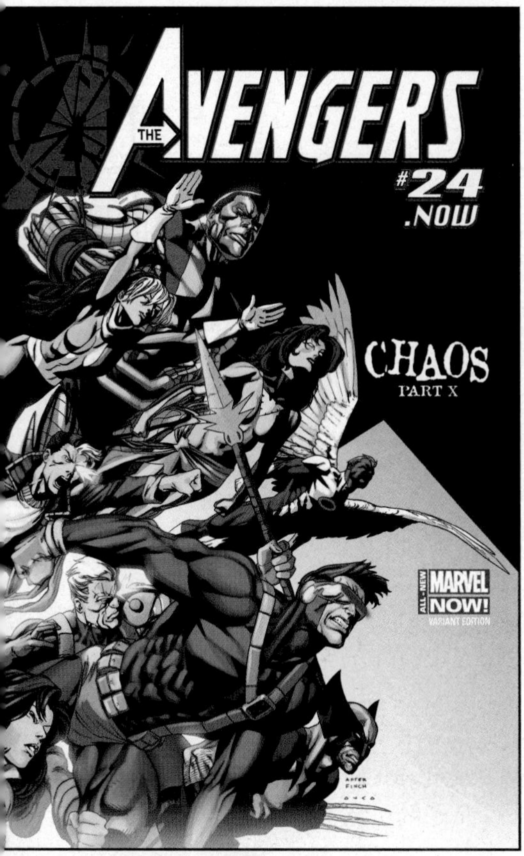
THE AVENGERS
#24
.NOW
CHAOS
PART X
ALL-NEW MARVEL NOW!
VARIANT EDITION

#24 VARIANT:
KRIS ANKA

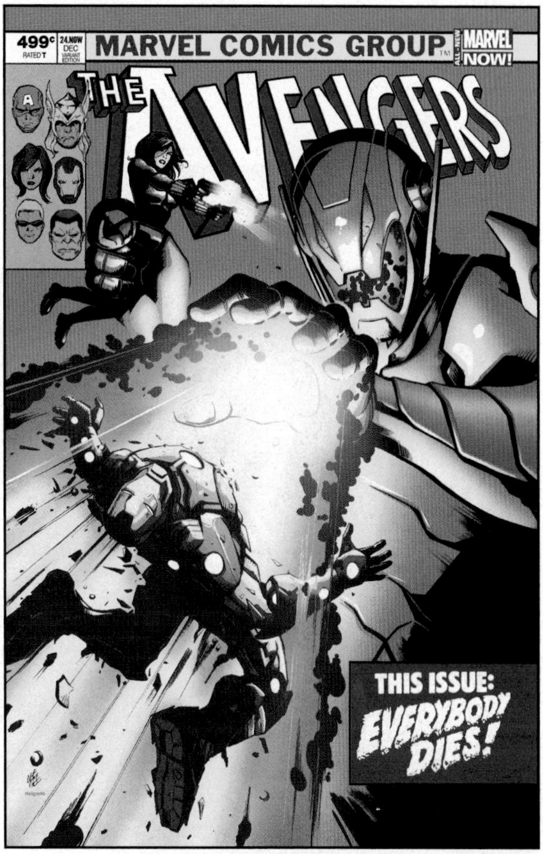
499¢
RATED T
24.NOW
DEC
MARVEL COMICS GROUP
ALL-NEW MARVEL NOW!
THE AVENGERS
THIS ISSUE:
EVERYBODY DIES!

#24 VARIANT:
LEE GARBETT & EDGAR DELGADO

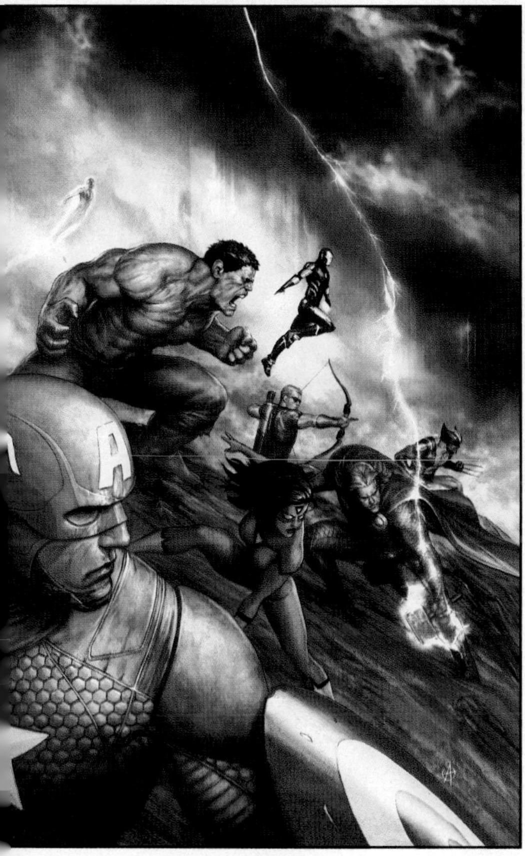

#24 VARIANT:
AGUSTIN ALESSIO

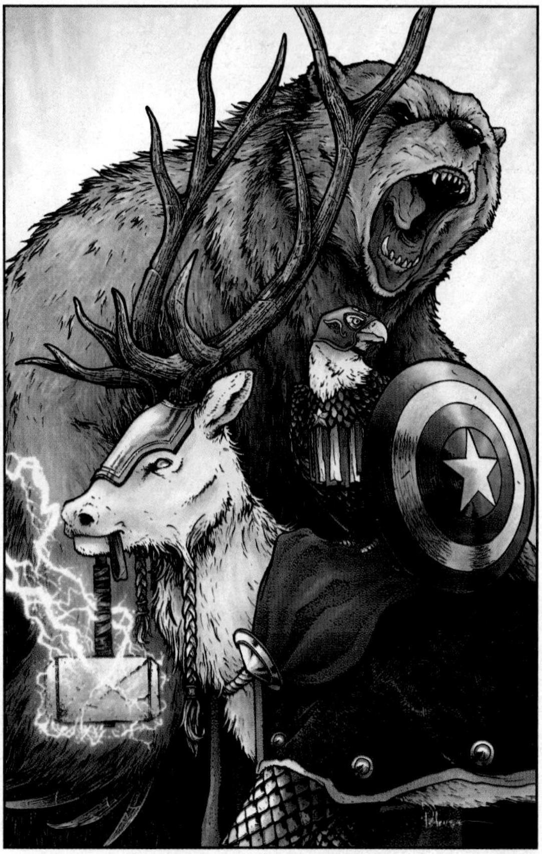

#24 ANIMAL VARIANT:
DAVID PETERSEN

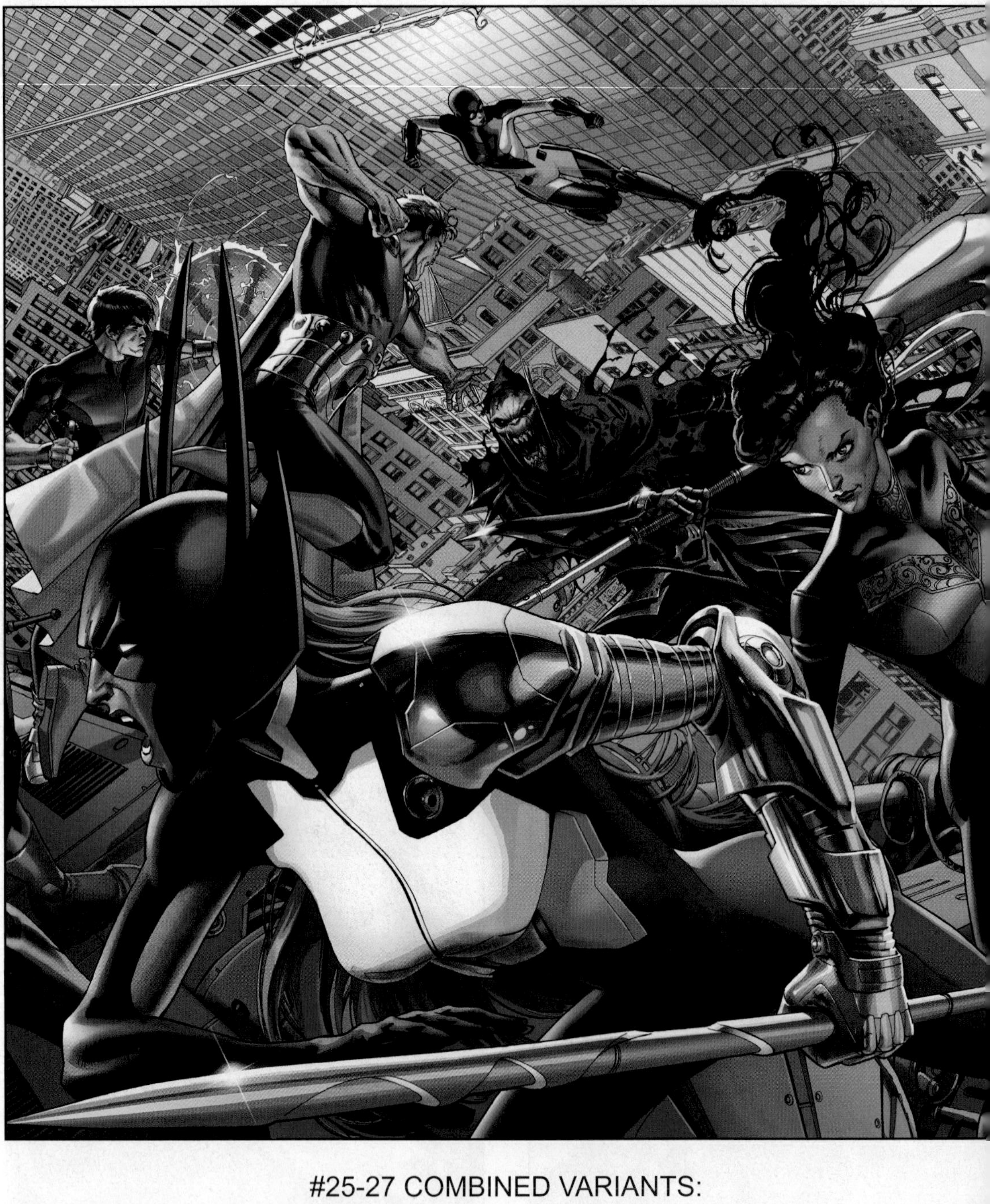

#25-27 COMBINED VARIANTS:
DUSTIN WEAVER & JUSTIN PONSOR